Workbook

Joan Saslow ■ Allen Ascher

with Julie C. Rouse

PEARSON
Longman

Summit: English for Today's World   1
Workbook

Pearson Education, 10 Bank Street, White Plains, NY 10606

Staff credits: The people who made up the *Summit 1* Workbook team—representing
editorial, production, design, manufacturing, and multimedia—are Rhea Banker, Dave Dickey,
Pamela Fishman, Ann France, Aliza Greenblatt, Mike Kemper, Sasha Kintzler, and Jessica Miller-Smith.

Text composition: Word & Image Design Studio, Inc.

Text font: 10 / 12 Frutiger

Cover photograph: "Apex," by Rhea Banker. Copyright © 2006 by Rhea Banker.

Illustration credits: Steve Attoe: pages 4, 82. Leanne Franson: pages 24, 84. Brian Hughes: page 17. Stephen Hutchings:
page 55 (top). Suzanne Mogensen: page 3. Steve Schulman: page 33. Neil Stewart/NSV: pages 52, 55 (bottom), 92.

Photo credits: p. 6 AP/Wide World Photos; p. 14 ImageSource/age fotostock; p. 15 Schlager Roland/epa/Corbis; p. 22
BananaStock/age fotostock; p. 27 (left) Gerry Ellis/Getty Images, (middle) Patrick Robert/ Sygma/Corbis, (right)
EPA/UNICEF/Shehzad Nooran /Landov; p. 31 (left to right) John Springer Collection/Corbis, Muntz/Getty Images,
ImageSource/age fotostock, Jacques Alexandre/age fotostock, Kupka/age fotostock, Angela Wyant/Getty Images, Hulton
Archive/Getty Images, SuperStock, Inc./SuperStock; p. 35 (top) Mauro Fermariello/Photo Researchers, Inc., (bottom) Nicolas
Russell/Getty Images; p. 36 Araldo de Luca/Corbis; p. 44 Photo by Global Volunteers/www.globalvolunteers.org; p. 45
photolibrary/ PictureQuest; p. 53 Park Street/PhotoEdit, Inc.; p. 61 (1) Frank Siteman/PhotoEdit, Inc., (2) Hemera/age fotostock, (3)
Dave & Les Jacobs/age fotostock, (4) Plush Studios/age fotostock; p. 62 Fujifotos/The Image Works; p. 72 Bruce Forster/Getty
Images; p. 76 ThinkStock LLC/Index Stock Imagery; p. 78 Digital Vision/age fotostock; p. 84 (1) ImageSource/age fotostock, (2)
ImageSource/age fotostock, (3) Con Tanasiuk/age fotostock, (4) Marcus Mok/Getty Images; p. 85 Keystone/Getty Images; p. 88
Bernardo De Niz/Reuters/Corbis; p. 93 (top left) Sanna Lindberg/age fotostock, (top right) Matthieu Spohn/age fotostock, (bottom
left) Digital Vision/age fotostock, (bottom right) BananaStock/age fotostock.

Text credits: Page 40: "Top Ten Most Annoying Personal Behaviors" reprinted with permission by Donna Dilley, Biz Manners
Columnist, Blue Ridge Business Journal, Roanoke, VA 24011. Page 55: "The Stag with Beautiful Antlers," from *Little Book of Fables*.
Copyright © 2004 by Ediciones Ekaré, Venezuela. English translation copyright © 2004 by Susan Ouriou. First published in English
by Groundwood Books, Ltd. in 2004. Reprinted by permission of the publisher.

ISBN 0-13-110629-5

Printed in the United States of America

10 11 12 13 14 15 V012 15 14 13 12 11 10

CONTENTS

UNIT 1   New Perspectives **1**

UNIT 2   Musical Moods **10**

UNIT 3   Money Matters **21**

UNIT 4   Looking Good **31**

UNIT 5   Community **39**

UNIT 6   Animals **50**

UNIT 7   Advertising and Consumers **60**

UNIT 8   Family Trends **70**

UNIT 9   History's Mysteries **82**

UNIT 10 Your Free Time **91**

New Perspectives

PREVIEW

1 Read the article and take the quiz.

Do You Have What It Takes to Work Abroad?

TRAVEL

Are you bored with your day-to-day life? Sick of the daily grind? If you've had enough of your dull, daily routine, then working in another country may be the life-changing experience you need.

Can you imagine yourself living and working in some far-away location? Maybe you picture yourself working as a computer programmer in Beijing and practicing *tai chi* in your free time. Maybe you'd like to work as an accountant in Sydney and surf on the weekends. What about a job as a nurse in Chicago, a manager in Bangalore, or an engineer in Montreal?

Whatever your dream, now may be the time to go for it. Before you do, take this quiz to see if you have what it takes to work and live abroad.

Circle the statement that describes you best.

(1) **a.** I want adventure in my life.
b. I like trying new things.
c. I'm a little uncomfortable in new situations.
d. I prefer to stay close to home.

(2) **a.** I will eat almost anything.
b. I like trying different foods.
c. I prefer foods that are familiar to me.
d. I won't eat strange food.

(3) **a.** It's fun trying to figure out how to communicate in a new language.
b. Communicating in a new language is a good experience.
c. Having to use a new language to communicate is kind of scary.
d. It's a pain in the neck trying to understand a different language.

(4) **a.** I make new friends easily.
b. It takes a while for me to make new friends.
c. It's hard for me to make friends.
d. I'm shy and do not have many friends.

(5) **a.** I think difficult situations can be good learning experiences.
b. I work hard to make difficult situations better.
c. I complain a lot in difficult situations.
d. If a situation is too difficult, it's probably more trouble than it's worth.

Now figure out your score. Give yourself:

3 points for each **a.**
2 points for each **b.**
1 point for each **c.**
0 points for each **d.**

Score _____

If your score was:
13–15 points Do it! You'll love working and living overseas.
10–12 points It may be difficult, but working abroad will be a good experience for you.
7–9 points You may have to work hard to have a good experience.
0–6 points Don't do it! You'll be ready to head home after one week.

SOURCE: www.transitionsabroad.com

Do you have what it takes to work and live abroad? Why or why not?

....

....

2 Complete each opinion with an expression from the box. More than one answer is possible for each item.

It's a pain in the neck.	It's more trouble than it's worth.	I can't get enough of it.
I've had about enough of it.	I can't get over how much I enjoy it.	

1. The food here is delicious. ....

2. The weather is terrible here. ....

3. It's too difficult to get there, and there isn't a lot to see. ....

4. I have to work hard to understand what people are saying. ....

5. Being here is so much fun. ....

LESSON 1

3 Complete each sentence with the gerund or infinitive form of the verb in parentheses.

a. Don't forget (call) .... your mother on her birthday.

b. Stop (eat) .... sweets and fatty foods.

c. Remember (make) .... time for just the two of you.

d. I'll never forget (meet) .... my boss for the first time.

e. Every now and then, you should stop (tell) .... the people you know how much they mean to you.

Now match each sentence above with a topic below. Write the letter on the line.

1. .... health   3. .... family   5. .... romance

2. .... friends   4. .... work

4 Challenge. Answer the questions about yourself.

1. What will you never forget about your childhood?

   Example: *I'll never forget baking holiday cookies with my grandmother.* ....

   ....

   ....

2. When you're eighty years old, what do you think you'll remember about your life now?

   Example: *I'll remember going to the beach with my friends.* ....

   ....

   ....

5 Write a tip or reminder for each person. Use <u>remember</u>, <u>forget</u>, or <u>stop</u> with a gerund or an infinitive. Use the phrases in parentheses.

1. ....
   (buy coffee)

2. ....
   (wish your wife happy anniversary)

3. ....
   (work so much)

4. ....
   (turn off your cell phone)

LESSON 2

6 Complete the conversation. Write the letter on the line.

A: Have you met our new neighbors, the Lovinas?

B: ....
   1.

A: Well, the husband is friendly. He seems like a nice guy.

B: ....
   2.

A: She's never home. Everyone says she's a workaholic.

B: ....
   3.

A: She works in advertising, I think. She's a manager.

B: ....
   4.

A: Well, the least we can do is keep an open mind.
   She might turn out to be really likeable.

a. And the wife? I wonder what she's like.

b. So, she's a boss . . . I hope she's not anything like *my* boss!

c. No, I haven't had a chance yet. What are they like?

d. Really? What does she do?

In Japan, 76 percent of people work more than 40 hours per week. In Germany, 44 percent of people work more than 40 hours per week.

SOURCE: www.nationmaster.com

7 Read the descriptions of Type A and Type B personalities. Then answer the questions.

www.personality.com

File   Edit   Links   Tools   Help   Chat

Back   Forward   Reload   Stop   Home   Search

TYPE A

A determined, impatient, and sometimes angry personality. People with Type A personalities work hard to succeed and to get what they want. They are busy, often stressed out, and don't like to wait. They eat, talk, walk, and drive fast. They might seem unfriendly and difficult to get along with. Workaholics and tyrants may have Type A personalities.

TYPE B

The opposite of Type A personality. The Type B personality is easygoing, patient, and friendly. People with Type B personalities are able to relax and have fun. They live a more balanced life. Someone who is a sweetheart, a team player, or a people person may have a Type B personality.

1. Do you know someone who has a Type A personality? ....

2. What is this person like? Write three examples to support your opinion.

....

....

....

3. Describe your own personality. Are you more like a Type A or a Type B personality?

....

....

....

8 What qualities would you like the people in your life to have? Complete the sentences with adjectives from the box.

easygoing	fun	helpful	polite	reliable	smart
fair	funny	lovable	outgoing	serious	talkative
friendly	hardworking	modest	professional	silly	

1. I would like a boss who's ....

2. I would like co-workers who are ....

3. I would like a spouse who's ....

4. I would like classmates who are ....

5. I would like friends who are ....

6. I would like neighbors who are ....

7. I would like a teacher who's ....

8. I would like to be more ....

9 **Complete the conversation with your own words.**

A: Have you had a chance to meet .... ?

B: No, I haven't. I wonder what .... like.

A: Well, everyone says ....

B: Yeah, but you can't believe everything you hear. ....

LESSON 3

10 **Read each adjective. Does it describe an optimistic or a pessimistic perspective? Write O for optimistic or P for pessimistic.**

1. .... down

2. .... defeated

3. .... hopeful

4. .... positive

5. .... negative

6. .... cynical

Now read each statement. Write O for optimistic or P for pessimistic.

1. .... The glass is half full.

2. .... The glass is half empty.

3. .... Times are hard now, but life will get better.

4. .... Life will always be difficult and painful.

5. .... The world is unjust and unfair.

6. .... There's beauty, love, generosity, and goodness in the world.

11 **Complete each suggestion with the gerund or infinitive form of the verb in parentheses.**

1. Remember (look) .... on the bright side.

2. Stop (expect) .... the worst.

3. Don't forget (see) .... goodness in the world.

4. Stop (believe) .... that life will always be difficult and painful.

5. Remember (avoid) .... negative thinking.

6. Don't forget (try) .... to see a solution.

12 Reading Warm-up. **Answer the questions.**

1. Do you know someone who is very optimistic? Who? ....

2. Do you know who Lance Armstrong is? What do you know about him?

....

....

13 Reading. **Read the article about Lance Armstrong. Then answer the questions.**

VOL. 55

The Power of Optimism

Martin Seligman has been studying optimists and pessimists for 25 years. He's a psychologist and the author of bestselling books that help people to be more optimistic. In his studies of world-class athletes and top performers in the business world, Seligman found that optimists perform better when they encounter difficult situations than pessimists do. According to Seligman, "When pessimists come up against an obstacle, they often quit; when optimists meet an obstacle, they try harder." An optimist stays in the game and instead of seeing a problem, looks for a solution.

One world-class athlete who stayed in the game and is a perfect example of the power of optimism is the cyclist Lance Armstrong. In 1996, Armstrong was diagnosed with advanced testicular cancer that had spread to his lungs and brain. His doctors were not optimistic, but he was. Instead of feeling down and defeated by his serious condition, Armstrong felt challenged and prepared for his future. He found chemotherapy treatments that would not damage his lungs permanently (because a world-class cyclist needs strong lungs). He rode his bicycle 80 to 100 kilometers a day, even though he was so sick that it was difficult for him to get out of bed. And, he had his sperm frozen so that he could have children someday, even though he was single at the time.

Armstrong survived cancer and won the Tour de France seven times. He has three children, a boy and twin girls. Lance Armstrong has been called a "hope machine" and is an inspiration for those of us who need help being optimistic.

SOURCES: www.coachginger.com
Learned Optimism: How to Change Your Mind and Your Life, Martin Seligman (New York, Pocket Books, 1998)

1. What was Lance Armstrong's difficult situation? ....

2. How did he respond to this problem? ....

....

3. Did he succeed? ....

4. Were his hopes realistic? Explain your answer. ....

....

14 Think of a problem you have or a difficult situation you're facing. What's the problem or situation?

....

....

Now try to "see a solution." What are three things you could do to make the situation better?

1. ....

2. ....

3. ....

15 Match the perspectives with their definitions.

1. .... optimistic
2. .... pessimistic
3. .... realistic

   a. expecting that bad things will happen in the future or that a situation will have a bad result

   b. believing that good things will happen in the future, or feeling confident that you will succeed

   c. perceiving and responding to situations in a practical way, according to what is actually possible

What's <u>your</u> perspective? Explain your answer. ....

....

Challenge. How does the realist see the glass of water?

....

"Keep a green tree in your heart and perhaps the singing bird will come."
— Chinese proverb

LESSON 4

16 **What About You?** Answer the questions about your own experiences.

1. Describe an experience that <u>broadened your horizons</u> — or made it possible for you to learn, understand, and do new things. ....

....

2. Describe a <u>rewarding</u> experience you've had — an experience that made you feel happy and satisfied because you were doing something useful, important, or interesting, even if you did not earn much money. ....

....

3. Describe an experience that caused you to <u>see the big picture</u> — or made you realize what was really important in your life. ....

....

17 After completing Student's Book page 11 in class, write what you remember about a classmate's life-changing experience.

Grammar Booster

A Circle the gerund or infinitive form of the verb to correctly complete each sentence.

1. Mr. Banks often urges his wife **coming / to come** home from work earlier.

2. He wants her **spending / to spend** more time with her family.

3. She promises **trying / to try**, but she's really not capable of **slowing / to slow** down.

4. She's sorry **disappointing / to disappoint** her family, but she's also worried about **advancing / to advance** in her career.

5. Mrs. Banks knows it's important **living / to live** a balanced life, but she keeps **working / to work** late and **bringing / to bring** work home on the weekends.

6. She plans **taking / to take** some time off next month, but don't be surprised if demands at work prevent her from **doing / to do** so.

B Complete each sentence with your own gerund or infinitive phrase. Refer to Student's Book pages A3 and A4 if you need to.

1. I look forward to ....

2. I miss ....

3. I'm fortunate ....

4. I struggle ....

5. I can't stand ....

6. My parents encouraged me ....

7. .... is relaxing for me.

8. It's my dream ....

9. I'm tired of ....

10. I'm studying English ....

C List three ideas under each of the topics below.

1. **Activities you enjoy**

....

....

....

2. **Your goals**

....

....

....

3. **Good memories**

....

....

....

4. **To-do list for this week**

....

....

....

Now use your lists to complete the sentences. Use gerunds or infinitives. Make sure the items in each series are parallel.

Example: I enjoy *skiing, running, and painting* ....

1. I enjoy ....

2. I intend ....

3. I recall ....

4. I need ....

Writing: Describe optimists or pessimists

Step 1. Prewriting. Brainstorming ideas. Write words and phrases related to each perspective.

Optimists	Pessimists
think positively	*think negatively*

Use your ideas to write a topic sentence for each perspective. (Remember: The topic sentence **introduces** the topic and the focus of the paragraph.)

1. Optimists: ....

2. Pessimists: ....

Choose one of your topic sentences. Write three to five supporting sentences. (Remember: The supporting sentences give **details**, **examples**, and **other facts** related to the topic sentence.)

1. ....

2. ....

3. ....

4. ....

5. ....

Step 2. Writing. Write your topic sentence and supporting sentences from Step 1 in the form of a paragraph. End with a concluding sentence. (Remember: The concluding sentence **restates** [gives the same information in different words] the topic sentence or **summarizes** the paragraph.)

....

....

....

....

....

....

....

Step 3. Self-Check.

☐ Does your paragraph have a topic sentence?

☐ Do the supporting sentences in your paragraph all relate to the topic?

☐ Do you have a concluding sentence?

UNIT 2

Musical Moods

PREVIEW

1 Try to name an artist for each musical genre.

1. Pop: ....
2. Rock: ....
3. Urban dance: ....
4. World: ....
5. Latin: ....
6. Jazz: ....
7. Classical: ....

2 Complete the chart.

What types of music do you listen to when you're . . .
1. studying?
2. eating in a restaurant?
3. dancing?
4. feeling down?
5. commuting (by car, bus, train, etc.)?

3 Complete the conversation about musical tastes. Use your own words.

A: So, what's in your CD collection?

B: ....

A: Let's put something on.

B: How about .... ?

A: What's it like?

B: ....

10

4 **What About You?** Answer the questions.

1. What was the last CD you bought? ....

2. Circle the adjectives you'd use to describe the CD.

annoying	different	exciting	offensive	surprising	uplifiting
brilliant	dull	fun	playful	traditional	
cynical	energetic	haunting	romantic	unpredictable	

3. Which songs on the CD do you like the most? The least? ....
....

5 **Read the online music review.**

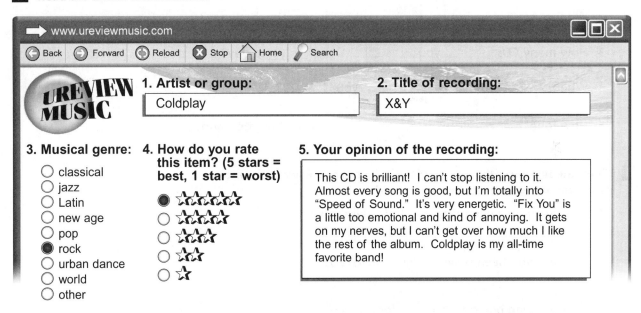

Now complete a review of the CD you chose in Exercise 4.

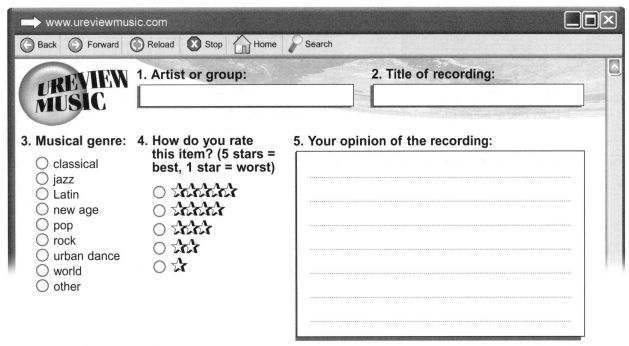

LESSON 1

6 For each description, name a song, a band, or a singer you know.

1. A song with a great dance beat: ....

2. A band with a unique sound: ....

3. A song with a catchy melody: ....

4. A singer with an amazing voice: ....

5. A song with fantastic lyrics: ....

7 Complete the questions with the simple past tense or the present perfect continuous form of the verb in parentheses. Then answer the questions.

1. What .... you .... to lately? ....
                            (listen)

2. What song .... you .... in your head all day? ....
                                (hum)

3. How many CDs .... you .... to yesterday? ....
                                    (listen)

4. When .... you .... your first CD? What was it? ....
                        (buy)

5. How long .... you .... to your favorite band? ....
                            (listen)

8 Check the sentences that are grammatically correct. Rewrite the incorrect sentences, using a correct form of the verb.

1. ☐ I've already been listening to Shakira's new CD.

   ....

2. ☐ Have you been playing any music lately?

   ....

3. ☐ He's been going to concerts for a while.

   ....

4. ☐ She's been going to five concerts this month.

   ....

5. ☐ I've seen Vanessa-Mae in concert twice.

   ....

6. ☐ How many times have you been listening to that song?

   ....

7. ☐ Have you been playing my favorite song yet?

   ....

LESSON 2

9 Check the statements that you agree with.

1. ☐ I can't imagine what my life would be like without music.
2. ☐ Listening to music is how I stay productive.
3. ☐ Music is what helps me unwind.
4. ☐ Music is a way for people to communicate with whomever they meet.
5. ☐ Music is a way for me to express what's in my heart.

10 Complete each noun clause with your own words.

1. I wonder who ....
2. I don't understand why ....
3. I'm not sure when ....
4. I don't know where ....
5. I have no idea what ....
6. Can you tell me which ....?
7. I can't imagine how ....

11 Read each situation. Then use noun clauses to complete the sentences in your own words.

1. Your friend invites you to a concert. You need more information. You ask him *when the*
   concert is and who's playing ....

2. You need to buy a gift for your nephew. You ask his mother ....
   ....

3. You're discussing music with some friends. You say that to you, listening to music is ....
   ....

4. Your colleague has just met a famous musician. You want to know ....
   ....

12 Read about the role of music in Adam Reed's life. Underline the eight noun clauses.

I'm not sure when I started really listening to music. I think I was about 14. I was totally into pop music then. Now pop music gets on my nerves. I listen to urban dance music mostly, and jazz or classical when I'm working or studying. My taste in music has changed over the years, but the role of music in my life has not changed. I've been listening for almost ten years now, and I can't imagine what I would do without music. Listening to music is how I spend my free time, and it's what helps me focus and get things done. It's how I relax and how I have fun with my friends. I believe that life would be dull and empty without music.

Adam Reed
San Francisco, California, USA

Now write a short paragraph about the role of music in your life. Why do you listen to music? What types of music do you listen to? How has your taste changed? Try to use noun clauses.

_____

_____

_____

_____

_____

_____

_____

LESSON 3

13 Do you know someone who's gifted? What does this person do well? Describe his/her personality. What are some of this person's positive qualities? Negative qualities?

....

....

....

14 **Reading.** Answer the question. Then read the biography on page 15.

Have you ever heard of Ray Charles? What do you know about him?

....

....

Ray Charles

"I was born with music inside me."

They called him "The Genius"—"the *only* genius in the [music] business," according to singer Frank Sinatra. What made him a genius is the original way in which he combined the diverse genres of jazz, rhythm and blues, gospel, and country. He broke down the walls that had always existed between musical genres, creating groundbreaking music that has had a huge influence on the course of rock and pop. It has been said that his music can "break your heart or make you dance." His name was Ray Charles, and he was known as "the father of soul."

Ray Charles was born in 1930, into a poor family in the southeastern United States. At age five, he gradually began to lose his vision and was totally blind by age seven.

Charles had shown an interest in music since the age of three. At seven, he left home to attend the Florida School for the Deaf and Blind. There he learned to read, write, and arrange music in Braille and play the piano, organ, saxophone, clarinet, and trumpet. While he was at the school, his mother died. At fifteen, he left school and began working as a traveling jazz musician in Florida, and later in Washington state.

In 1950, Charles moved to Los Angeles, where he found his own unique sound. He combined jazz and blues with gospel music to create his first big hit recording, "I Got a Woman." On "I Got a Woman," Charles began to sing in a more emotional, intense, and exciting voice. He later said, "When I started to sing like myself . . . when I started singing like Ray Charles, it had this spiritual and churchy, this religious or gospel sound." This recording made him famous and marked the beginning of a new musical genre, "soul."

Although Charles had discovered his sound and success, he didn't stop trying new things.

Always energetic, he explored new genres and brought his unique style to new audiences. In the 1960s, he had both country and pop hits, with songs like "Georgia on My Mind" and "Hit the Road, Jack."

Throughout his life, Charles continued to write and perform. He also made television and movie appearances. His participation in the 1985 release of "We Are the World" brought a renewed interest in his work.

To this day, Ray Charles remains one of the most important influences on popular music. His passionate singing and intelligent combining of different musical genres is the ideal that many musicians continue to measure their work by.

Ray Charles died on June 10, 2004, at the age of 73. A notorious ladies' man, he is survived by 12 children, 18 grandchildren, and 1 great-grandchild. In response to the news of his death, singer Aretha Franklin said, "He was a fabulous man, full of humor and wit . . ." Ray Charles possessed all of the positive qualities of a creative personality—he was gifted, energetic, imaginative, and passionate—without displaying the negative qualities that often accompany creative genius. He was not difficult or egotistical. In fact, he was quite humble. In 1983 he said, "Music's been around a long time, and there's going to be music long after Ray Charles is dead. I just want to make my mark, leave something musically good behind."

Sources: www.pbs.org, www.en.wikipedia.org, www.swingmusic.net

List at least six adjectives from the reading that describe Ray Charles's music.

....

....

....

Now list five adjectives from the reading that describe Ray Charles's personality.

....

....

....

15 Match the words and phrases from the reading with their definitions.

1. .... groundbreaking
2. .... blind
3. .... Braille
4. .... gospel
5. .... soul
6. .... ladies' man
7. .... humble

a. a type of music with jazz, blues, and gospel influences that often expresses deep emotions

b. a form of raised printing that blind people can read by touching

c. original and important; showing a new way of doing or thinking about things

d. not considering yourself better than others

e. not able to see

f. a man who enjoys and attracts the company of women

g. a style of religious music associated with the southern U.S.

16 Write a short description of Ray Charles's music, based on the reading.

....

....

....

17 Challenge. What do Ludwig van Beethoven and Ray Charles have in common? How are they different? Fill in the diagram to compare them.

Beethoven Ray Charles

egotistical *gifted musicians* *humble*

LESSON 4

18 Complete the sentences with the correct participial adjectives. Use the present or past participle of the underlined verb.

1. Classical music <u>soothes</u> her infant son.

   a. Classical music is .... to her infant son.

   b. Her infant son is .... by classical music.

2. Jazz <u>interests</u> Robert.

   a. Robert thinks jazz is ....

   b. Robert is .... in jazz.

3. Her piano playing <u>amazes</u> me.

   a. I'm .... by her piano playing.

   b. Her piano playing is ....

4. The song's lyrics <u>touched</u> Samantha.

   a. Samantha was .... by the song's lyrics.

   b. Samantha found the song's lyrics to be very ....

5. Pop music <u>bores</u> Eric because it's so predictable.

    a. Eric is .... by predictable pop music.

    b. Eric thinks pop music is .... and predictable.

6. Concerts <u>excite</u> Alex and Sophie. They're going to one this Saturday.

    a. Alex and Sophie think concerts are ....

    b. Alex and Sophie are .... about the concert on Saturday.

19 **Circle the correct adjective and then complete each sentence with your own words.**

1. I'm (soothed / soothing) by ....

2. I find .... to be very (entertained / entertaining).

3. I try to avoid .... because it's so (depressed / depressing).

4. I was (disappointed / disappointing) when I found out that ....

5. For me, ... is really (relaxed / relaxing).

6. I'm (pleased / pleasing) that ....

20 **Read the advertisement. Then answer the questions.**

Little Genius CDs | Classical music for infants and toddlers

Music that babies love— but that doesn't get on moms' and dads' nerves!

Babies are soothed by classical melodies selected and arranged for their little ears. And when babies stop crying, parents are more relaxed, too!

But that's not all these CDs have to offer. Research has shown that listening to classical music promotes babies' intellectual development and can make them better at reading and math. As they listen, babies' abstract thinking skills and spatial intelligence are improved. Creativity and imagination are also stimulated. And you can start preparing your "Little Genius" before she's even born! These CDs are highly recommended listening for mothers-to-be.

This music has been successful with babies all around the world. Since there are no lyrics, the CDs are truly international. Try them for yourself and witness your own baby's amazing responses. You won't be disappointed!

1. According to the ad, what are five benefits of *Little Genius* CDs?

....

....

....

....

....

2. What's your opinion? Do you think listening to music is beneficial for babies?

....

....

Grammar Booster

A Choose the correct verb form(s) to complete each sentence. In some sentences, two or more verb forms are correct.

1. He _____ to pop music when he was a teenager.

   ☐ listened   ☐ has listened   ☐ has been listening

2. They _____ new-age music all day, and it's starting to get on my nerves.

   ☐ played   ☐ have played   ☐ have been playing

3. By the time I got to the concert, my favorite singer _____.

   ☐ already performed   ☐ had already performed   ☐ had already been performing

4. He _____ that music video last night on TV.

   ☐ saw   ☐ has seen   ☐ has been seeing

5. She _____ on the lyrics for her new song for hours, but now she's taking a break for dinner.

   ☐ worked   ☐ has worked   ☐ has been working

B Find the error in each sentence. Rewrite the sentence, using a correct verb form.

1. What did you listen to lately?

   ....

2. Sarah Cho has been playing that CD for me yesterday.

   ....

3. I've been watching that video four times already.

   ....

4. I was buying that DVD yesterday.

   ....

5. How many concerts have you been going to?

   ....

6. The performance already began by the time we arrived.

   ....

7. When we got to the ticket window, the concert already sold out.

   ....

8. Many people have been downloading world music last year.

   ....

C Complete the sentences with your own words. Use appropriate verb forms.

1. When I began this class, I had already _____.

2. Before I traveled to _____, I had never _____.

3. I had never seen _____ until _____.

4. I bought the _____ CD after _____.

5. By the time I got home last night, _____.

D Read each pair of sentences. Then write one sentence with a similar meaning, using the past perfect continuous.

1. He worked at Datatech for 35 years. Then he retired.

   He had been working at Datatech for 35 years when he retired.

2. She slept for only four hours. Then her alarm clock went off.

   _____

3. They drove their car for ten years. Then it broke down.

   _____

4. I waited for 45 minutes. Then the train arrived.

   _____

5. We lived in London for five years. Then we decided to move to Dublin.

   _____

E Complete each statement in your own way.

Example: Many people believe that *there is life on other planets* _____.

1. Many people believe that _____.

2. My friend argues that _____.

3. Experts recommend that _____.

4. Some people claim that _____.

5. The newspapers report that _____.

Now give your opinion of each statement, using a noun clause as a noun complement.

Example: [The belief . . .] *The belief that there is life on other planets makes sense to me.*

1. [The belief . . .] _____

2. [The argument . . .] _____

3. [The recommendation . . .] _____

4. [The claim . . .] _____

5. [The report . . .] _____

Writing: Describe a friend or a relative

Step 1. Prewriting. Clustering ideas. Create an idea cluster about a friend or relative you know well.

   a. Write the person's name inside the center circle below.

   b. Use the idea cluster to describe the person. Write ideas that come to mind in the circles around the main circle. You can include personality traits, interests, accomplishments, personal qualities, occupation, etc.

   c. Use the circles connected to each of those circles to expand or give details about your ideas. Try to write something in each circle, but it's OK if some circles are empty.

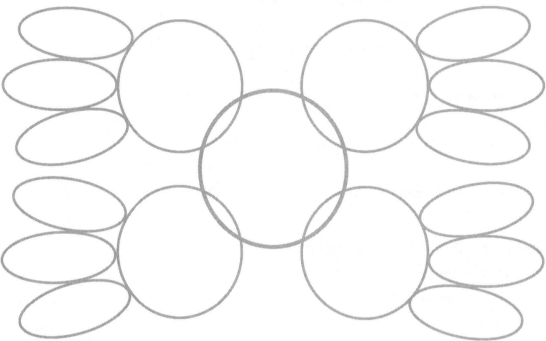

Step 2. Writing. Write a paragraph describing your friend or relative, using the information from your cluster. Make sure to use parallel structure.

....

....

....

....

....

....

....

....

....

Step 3. Self-Check.

☐ Did you use parallel structure with pairs or series of nouns, adjectives, and adverbs?

☐ Did you use parallel structure with the clauses, phrases, and tenses?

☐ Does the topic sentence introduce the topic of the paragraph?

Money Matters

PREVIEW

1 **How can you spend less and save more? List some ideas.**

1. ....

2. ....

3. ....

4. ....

5. ....

1. Bring lunch to work instead of buying it.
2. Take the bus to work instead of driving.
3. Remember to pay credit card bills on time. Avoid late charges!

2 **Read each statement. Check the statements that are good financial advice.**

1. ☐ Keep track of your expenses.

2. ☐ If you don't have enough money for something, use your credit card to treat yourself.

3. ☐ Buy financial planning software.

4. ☐ Cut back on your spending.

5. ☐ Live beyond your means.

6. ☐ Wait until you're older to start saving.

7. ☐ Make sure your income is more than your expenses.

8. ☐ Pay the least possible amount on your credit card bills each month.

9. ☐ Put some money away in savings each month.

10. ☐ If you're feeling down, go shopping.

3 **Answer the questions.**

1. What's a minor indulgence (something small and unnecessary) that you spend money on regularly? (For example, a daily cup of coffee or a weekly magazine.) ....

2. How much does this indulgence cost? ....

3. Calculate how many times per year you spend money on it. (For example, a cup of coffee each weekday: 5 days x 52 weeks = 260 times per year.) ....

4. Multiply the cost (your answer to question 2) by the number of times (your answer to question 3). How much money do you spend in a year on your small indulgence? ....

5. Were you surprised by the results? Can you think of something else you'd like to spend that money on? ....

4 Read the article.

Financial Planning
Five Benefits of Keeping a Budget

1. A budget allows you to spend money on things you really need or want. A budget requires you to keep track of your expenses. You see where your money actually goes and plan where to cut back on spending. The money you used to spend daily on little things like coffee or taxis can go toward something more important.

2. A budget can keep you out of debt. With a budget, you know whether or not you're living within your means. If you use credit cards, this may not be obvious. You might have extra cash at the end of each month and think that you're OK. But, if you're not paying your credit card bills in full, you're probably living beyond your means.

3. A budget can make you better prepared for emergencies. A budget requires you to put some money away in savings. So, if you find yourself in a difficult situation or faced with unexpected expenses, you'll have some extra money you can fall back on.

4. A budget can help you reach your savings goals. Whatever you are saving for, you need a plan that tells you how much you have, how much you need to spend, and how much you can save.

5. A budget gives you peace of mind because it allows you to stop worrying about how you're going to make ends meet.

SOURCE: www.financialplan.about.com

Now answer the questions.

1. According to the article, why is it important to keep track of your expenses?

....

2. According to the article, why can using credit cards be a problem?

....

3. Why can a budget make you better prepared for emergencies?

....

4. Which benefit from the article do you think is the most important? Why?

....

5 Respond to the e-mail. Write three suggestions for how the person could budget his money to save for a TV.

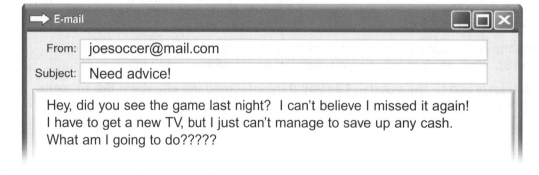

➡ E-mail	⬓◻✕
From:	joesoccer@mail.com
Subject:	Need advice!

Hey, did you see the game last night? I can't believe I missed it again! I have to get a new TV, but I just can't manage to save up any cash. What am I going to do?????

....

....

....

....

LESSON 1

6 Answer each question about your financial goals. Then, for each answer, do the following:

    a. Write a sentence about what you will do to reach your goal. Use <u>expect</u>, <u>hope</u>, <u>intend</u>, or <u>plan</u> with an infinitive.

    b. Write a sentence about when your goal will be reached. Use the future perfect.

Example: What's something expensive that you hope to buy? *a laptop computer*

    a. *I intend to put away $100 in savings each month.*

    b. *I will have saved enough to buy a laptop by next March.*

1. What's something expensive that you hope to buy?

    a.

    b.

2. Do you have a debt you'd like to pay off? What is it?

    a.

    b.

3. What is one way you can cut back on your spending and save more each month?

    a.

    b.

7 What will you have done by the year 2020? Write a short paragraph. Use the future perfect or <u>expect</u>, <u>hope</u>, <u>intend</u>, or <u>plan</u> and the perfect form of an infinitive.

Example: *By the year 2020, I will have finished law school. I expect to have bought a house by then. I hope to have gotten married and started a family...*

LESSON 2

8 Look at the pictures. Why do the people regret their purchases? Complete each explanation with a reason from the box.

is so hard to operate	takes up so much room	is so hard to put together
just sits around collecting dust	costs so much to maintain	

1. "I bought a guitar last summer. I really intended to learn how to play it, but I haven't picked it up for months now. It ...."

2. "I was so excited to get my new PDA. But it .... Who has thumbs small enough to push those tiny buttons? Not me! What a pain!"

3. "We bought a beautiful crib for our baby, but it's in pieces all over the floor. Unfortunately, the instructions are in Italian, and it ...."

4. "I ordered a new computer online, but I had no idea the monitor would be so big. It .... on my desk. I should have bought a laptop."

5. "I wish I hadn't bought this boat. I don't use it very often, and it .... Between the fuel, the docking fees, and the costs to service and clean it, I'm not sure it's worth it."

9 For each item in Exercise 8, write a sentence about the buyer's remorse. Use the inverted form of the past unreal conditional.

1. *Had he known it would just sit around collecting dust, he wouldn't have bought a guitar.*

2. ....

3. ....

4. ....

5. ....

10 After completing the Conversation Starter on Student's Book page 31, write a statement expressing buyer's remorse about the purchase listed there or about another purchase. Use the inverted form of the past unreal conditional.

LESSON 3

11 Read the following excerpts from the radio call-in show on Student's Book page 32. Try to determine the meaning of the underlined phrases from their context.

Steve:	"I'm afraid I'm really having problems <u>making ends meet</u> . . . I earn a good living, but it seems like no matter how much money I make, I can't seem to catch up."
Lara:	"Do you <u>put anything away for a rainy day?</u>"
Steve:	"You mean savings? No way. There's never enough for that."
Lara:	"Steve, what about debt? Are you <u>maxing out</u> on your credit cards?"
Steve:	"Well, yes, I do use credit cards, if that's what you mean."
Lara:	"Are you drowning in credit card bills, or have they been fairly reasonable so far?"
Steve:	"Well . . . I guess I'd have to say I've been <u>drowning in debt</u>."
Lara:	"Steve, if you want to <u>keep your head above water</u>, you've got to <u>live within your means</u>. That means spending less than you're making, not more."
Lara:	"If you feel like your finances are out of control, then you need to <u>take the bull by the horns</u> and take control of your finances."

Now match the phrases on the left with the definitions on the right. Write the letter on the line.

1. .... make ends meet

2. .... put something away for a rainy day

3. .... max out

4. .... drown in debt

5. .... keep your head above water

6. .... live within your means

7. .... take the bull by the horns

a. owe so much money that your financial situation is almost impossible to deal with

b. have just enough money to buy what you need

c. use something to its limit or so much that there is nothing left

d. manage to deal with all your debts or some other problem, but it's so difficult that you almost can't do it

e. to save something, especially money, for a time when you will need it

f. to take control of a difficult situation

g. to spend only the money or income that you have, no more

12 Circle the letter of the correct choice to complete each statement.

1. Spendthrifts generally live _____ their means.

   a. below   **b.** within   **c.** beyond

2. Big spenders are more likely to _____.

   a. be drowning in debt   **b.** be frugal   **c.** stick to a budget

3. Cheapskates generally _____.

   a. use credit cards often   **b.** have a lot of stuff   **c.** keep track of their expenses

4. Big spenders are usually _____.

   a. generous   **b.** stingy   **c.** frugal

5. Thrifty people are more likely to _____.

   a. be wiped out by   **b.** stick to a budget   **c.** let their bills get out of hand
   a job loss

13 Do you know someone who's a big spender, a spendthrift, or a tightwad? Describe his/her spending habits. Give examples.

> The world record for owning the most credit cards is held by Walter Cavanagh of Santa Clara, California, USA. He has 1,397 cards, which together are worth more than $1.65 million in credit.
>
> SOURCE: www.guinnessworldrecords.com

LESSON 4

14 Reading Warm-up. Complete the chart with information about a charity with which you are familiar.

Name of charity	Who they help	What they do
CARE	poor people all over the world	work to reduce poverty and solve problems in poor communities—through education, health care, etc.

Have you ever donated money to a charity? What was the name of the organization or cause? Why did you make a donation?

15 Reading. **Read the article.**

World Wildlife Fund

The World Wildlife Fund (WWF) is known worldwide by its panda logo. WWF has been working for almost 50 years in more than 100 countries around the globe to conserve nature and the diversity of life on Earth. With more than 5 million members worldwide, WWF is the world's largest privately-financed conservation organization. It leads international efforts to protect animals, plants, and natural areas. Its global goals are:

1. to save endangered species—especially giant pandas, tigers, threatened whales and dolphins, rhinos, elephants, marine turtles, and great apes.
2. to protect the habitats where these endangered species and other wild animals live.
3. to address threats to the natural environment—such as pollution, over-fishing, and climate change.

Doctors Without Borders

Doctors Without Borders (Medecins Sans Frontieres, or MSF) is an international independent humanitarian organization that provides emergency medical assistance in almost 70 countries. Each year, MSF medical and non-medical volunteers participate in more than 3,400 aid missions. These international volunteers work with more than 16,000 people hired locally to provide medical care. They often work in the most remote or dangerous parts of the world to do things such as provide health care, get hospitals up and running, perform surgery, vaccinate children, operate feeding centers, and offer psychological care. MSF gets medical attention to people who need it in cases of:

1. war or armed conflict.
2. epidemics of infectious diseases such as tuberculosis, malaria, and AIDS.
3. natural disasters.
4. non-existent health care in remote areas.

The United Nations Children's Fund

The United Nations Children's Fund (UNICEF) is active in 157 countries and territories around the world. The organization works to improve the lives of children worldwide. Its mission is to ensure every child's right to health, education, equality, and protection. UNICEF's priorities are:

1. ensuring quality basic education for all children, especially girls.
2. reaching every child with vaccines and other life-saving health services.
3. building protective environments to keep children safe from violence, abuse, and exploitation.
4. preventing the spread of HIV/AIDS among young people and from parent to child and providing care for those already affected.
5. giving each and every child the best start in life—through health services, good nutrition, safe water, and early learning activities.

SOURCES: www.worldwildlife.org, www.doctorswithoutborders.org, www.unicef.org

Now complete the chart with information from the reading.

Name of charity	Who they help	What they do

16 To which of the three charities on page 27 would you consider making a contribution? Is there one you wouldn't want to give money to? What are your reasons for donating or not donating?

....

....

....

> " Charity begins at home
> but should not end there. "
> —Scottish proverb

SOURCE: www.charityvillage.com

Grammar Booster

A What are your plans? For each item, write a sentence about what you will probably be doing. Use the future continuous.

1. Next Monday I ....

2. This weekend I ....

3. Next year I ....

4. Five years from now I ....

5. At this time next week I ....

B Imagine your life in ten years. Where will you be living? What are you going to be doing? Write a paragraph, using the future continuous. When the future continuous is not possible, use the simple future tense.

C Look at the two schedules. Write sentences comparing the activities of Tom and Tina Lee for each day. Use a time clause with <u>while</u> and the future continuous.

Tom Lee

Thursday	work
Friday	work
Saturday	clean the house
Sunday	do laundry

Tina Lee

Thursday	pack for weekend trip with friends
Friday	lie on the beach
Saturday	go horseback riding
Sunday	play tennis

1. Thursday: _While Tom Lee is working, Tina Lee is going to be packing for a trip._

2. Friday: ....

3. Saturday: ....

4. Sunday: ....

D Complete the chart with three of your hobbies or activities and the year in which you started each.

Hobby / activity	When started

Now use the information in the chart to complete the sentences, using the future perfect continuous.

Example: By the year 2010, _I will have been collecting stamps for 20 years_ .

1. By the year 2020, ...

2. By next year, ...

3. By the time I ...., I ....

Writing: Describe a new charitable organization

Step 1. Prewriting. Listing ideas. Choose an idea for a new local charity. Think of a name and long-term goal for your charity. Then complete the chart.

Name: ....

Long-term goal: ....

> **Some ideas**
> - An organization to improve city parks
> - An after-school program for young children
> - A fund to provide housing for the homeless
> - An organization to help stray animals
> - A soup kitchen
> - Your own idea: ....

The mission of People for City Park is to make the park a clean, safe, and fun place for families to spend time outdoors. First, we plan to clean up the park. We will post signs in the community and ask for volunteers. Next, we intend to ask local nurseries to donate new trees, plants, and flowers for the park. Then, we hope to raise money for new playground equipment. We will place collection jars in cafes, restaurants, and shops. In the end, we expect to have collected enough money and bought new equipment for children to play on by next summer.

	Goal or step	Plan	Completion date
First,			
Next,			
Then,			
In the end,			

Step 2. Writing. Write a paragraph, using ideas from your chart. Your topic sentence should state your charity's long-term goal. Use time order words and expressions to organize the sequence of steps in your paragraph.

....

....

....

....

....

....

....

....

Step 3. Self-Check.

☐ Did you use time order words or expressions in the paragraph?

☐ Does the sequence of events in the paragraph make sense?

☐ Does the topic sentence introduce the topic of the paragraph?

UNIT 4

Looking Good

PREVIEW

1 Look at the hairstyles. Then answer the questions.

a bob · an afro · a Caesar cut · a Mohawk · a quiff · a mullet · a shag cut · a bouffant

1. Do you find any of these hairstyles attractive? Which ones? ....

2. Do you find any of these hairstyles unattractive? Which ones? ....

3. Do any of the hairstyles look modern, like you might see them in a fashion magazine today? ....

4. Which hairstyles are attention-getting? ....

5. Which hairstyles look like they take a lot of time to maintain? ....

6. Would you consider any of these hairstyles for yourself? Which one(s)? ....

2 Complete the sentences about your favorite outfit.

1. I love to wear my ....

2. These clothes are formal / casual. (Circle one.)

3. If I wore this outfit to ...., I would be underdressed.

4. If I wore this outfit to ...., I would be overdressed.

5. If I wore this outfit to ...., I would be appropriately dressed.

LESSON 1

3 Read the opinions of casual business dress. Check the statements with which you agree.

1. ☐ What's important is to act like a professional. If you're confident and good at your job, you can be just as effective in jeans and a nice shirt as in a suit and tie.

2. ☐ I think casual dress is appropriate for most offices, as long as one's appearance is clean and neat.

3. ☐ I believe that when people dress like professionals, they act more professionally.

4. ☐ I think dress-down day is a pain in the neck. I never know what to wear. What does "business casual" really mean?

5. ☐ People have taken casual dress codes too far! A number of companies have actually had to introduce "business formal days."

6. ☐ I don't think casual dress creates a good image for a company, especially if the company does business internationally.

7. ☐ Casually dressed employees are better workers because people are more productive when they're comfortable.

"I think Charlie is taking Casual Fridays a bit too far!"

SOURCE: www.CartoonStock.com

4 Now summarize the opinions in Exercise 3. Complete each statement below with a quantifier from the box.

each	several	half of	two	a number of
every	three	many	most	a couple of
some	four	one	a few	a majority of

1. .... person expressed an opinion about business casual dress.

2. .... people think business casual is a good idea.

3. .... people think business casual is a bad idea.

4. .... people think that dress and behavior are related.

5. .... person thinks business casual is annoying.

5 Now rewrite statements 1–4 from Exercise 4, using different quantifiers with similar meanings.

1. ....

2. ....

3. ....

4. ....

Challenge. Judging from the statements in Exercise 3, do you think casual business dress is on the way out? ....

LESSON 2

6 **What Do You Think?** Comment on each of the fashions shown. Use the adjectives listed or your own adjectives. Where possible, use two adjectives.

chic	elegant	flashy	old-fashioned	sloppy	tacky
classic	fantastic	in style	out of style	striking	tasteful
eccentric	fashionable	loud	shocking	stylish	trendy

①  ②  ③  ④

1. *These pearls are elegant and chic.*   3. ....

2. ....   4. ....

⑤  ⑥  ⑦  ⑧

5. ....   7. ....

6. ....   8. ....

7 **Match each word or expression with its opposite. Write the letter on the line.**

1. .... conform   a. tacky
2. .... classic   b. subdued
3. .... elegant   c. trendy
4. .... flashy   d. cheap
5. .... fashionable   e. stand out
6. .... shocking   f. tasteful
7. .... well made   g. old-fashioned

In the summer of 2005, both the Japanese and Chinese governments asked office workers to dress down to save energy. A majority of Japanese companies complied with the "Cool Biz" no-tie, no-jacket campaign to reduce air-conditioner use. In Japan, about 210 million kilowatt hours of electricity were saved, reducing carbon dioxide emissions by about 79,000 tons.

SOURCE: www.japantimes.co.jp

8 List an article of clothing, a pair of shoes, or an accessory you have that can be described by each adjective.

1. Trendy: _____

2. Elegant: _____

3. Striking: _____

4. Out of style: _____

5. Comfortable: _____

6. Classic: _____

9 Challenge. Read the quote from 1930s fashion designer Elsa Schiaparelli. Then answer the questions.

> 66 *Ninety percent [of women] are afraid of being conspicuous and of what people will say. So they buy a gray suit. They should dare to be different.* 99

1. Rewrite Ms. Schiaparelli's fashion advice in your own words.

_____

_____

2. Do you think this is good fashion advice for people (not just women) today? Why or why not?

_____

_____

LESSON 3

10 Think about people you know—friends, relatives, classmates, colleagues, etc. Write statements about things they do to make themselves more attractive. Use quantifiers and ideas from the box or your own ideas.

body piercing	hair coloring	nail extensions
braids	hair transplants	permanents
contact lenses	hair removal	sideburns
cosmetic surgery	long hair	skin tanning
facials	makeup	tattoos
false eyelashes	manicures	

Several men I know have long hair.

_____

_____

_____

_____

11 **Answer the questions.**

1. Do you think that most people are happy with their appearance, or that a majority would like to change their appearance?

2. What would you consider doing to change your appearance?

3. How far is too far? Which ways of changing one's appearance do you think are inappropriate, tacky, or shocking?

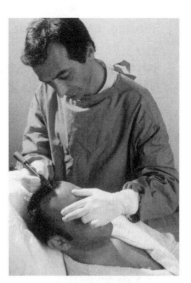

LESSON 4

12 **Reading Warm-up. Look at the ad. Then answer the questions.**

1. How would you describe the man in this ad?

2. Do you think that the man in this ad reflects how most men look?

3. Do you think men are more or less self-conscious about how they look than women are?

13 Reading. **Read the article.**

Boys and Body Image

Most people realize that unrealistic ideals of beauty in the media have negatively affected the body image of women and girls. However, not as many are aware of the pressure on men and boys to conform to an ideal body type that television, movies, and magazines have started to define for them. Males are becoming more self-conscious and self-critical. They compare themselves to media images of muscular, well-built men and are not satisfied with how they look.

Half man and half god, Adonis was considered the ideal of masculine beauty by ancient Greeks.

The trend in advertising to use the male body to sell a variety of products—from clothes to exercise equipment—has led to an increase in negative body image and low physical self-esteem among men and boys. Although the majority of teenagers with eating disorders are girls, researchers believe that the number of boys affected is increasing. Also, like girls, teenage boys who think they're overweight are more likely to try smoking as a way to lose weight.

This new ideal of male beauty has also created some problems that are unique to men and boys. In an effort to attain the muscular bodies of the shirtless men in ads, many are turning to obsessive exercising and weight lifting. In the United States, the number of men who exercise has increased more than thirty percent since the start of the 1990s. While exercise is, of course, a healthy habit, exercising excessively is not. Some men spend so many hours at the gym that they don't have time for family and friends.

Researchers have defined a new body-image disorder, termed muscle dysmorphia, that is the reverse of the extreme dieting that has been a problem among girls and young women. Men with this disorder worry that they are too thin and small. As a result, they engage in extreme exercise and use a variety of products that promise bigger muscles and more energy. Some of these products—such as anabolic steroids—are dangerous. Abuse of these muscle-building drugs can cause serious health problems such as heart disease, liver cancer, and depression.

Research has shown that Western men are much more concerned with looking muscular than Asian men. Steroids are available legally and without a prescription in Beijing, but steroid abuse is generally not a problem in China. According to researcher Harrison Pope of Harvard University, "the Chinese idea of masculinity has more to do with inner strength—strength of character and intellect."

SOURCES: www.mediascope.org, www.infoplease.com, www.healthyplace.com

Now complete the statements with words from the box.

1. Advertisers use images of .... men to sell their products.

2. These images of perfect male bodies are an .... ideal.

3. They have caused many men to become more ....

4. As a result, a lot of men now suffer from low ....

5. Some of these men try to improve their appearance in ways that are ....

> dangerous
> self-esteem
> muscular
> unrealistic
> self-conscious

14 Answer questions about the article.

1. According to the article, where do we see images that now define male beauty? ....

....

2. How has the modern ideal body type affected Western men's self-image? ....

....

3. What problems are some men having as a result? ....
....

4. What do you think Western men could learn from Chinese men about self-image? ....
....

Grammar Booster

A Read each statement. Check the meaning of the quantifier in each sentence.

	Some	Not many / Not much
1. Few people were dressed appropriately for the event.	☐	☐
2. There are a few really good books on fashion here.	☐	☐
3. I've got a little money put away for a rainy day.	☐	☐
4. I have little interest in pop music.	☐	☐
5. There are few hairstyles that look good on me.	☐	☐
6. There's a little cake left, if you'd like a piece.	☐	☐

B Add _of_ to the sentences that need it.

1. Several ˄ his co-workers wear suits to work.
   of

2. A few friends are coming over for dinner on Friday night.

3. A few my friends are going to a movie tonight.

4. Both dresses look great on you.

5. A majority people still dress up to go to the theater.

6. This is the most traffic I've ever seen on this road.

7. Each the employees voted on whether or not to dress down on Fridays.

C Complete each sentence with a phrase from the box. Change the verb as necessary to agree with the subject.

be quite good	have tattoos	wear contact lenses
be self-confident	dress casually	

1. Most of my friends ....

2. A lot of pop music ....

3. Several of my classmates ....

4. One of my family members ....

5. None of the people I know ....

Writing: *Compare ways people make themselves more attractive*

Step 1. Prewriting. Organizing ideas. Choose one of the topics from the box.

> • Compare and contrast what you and someone you know well do
>   to make yourselves more attractive.
>
> • Compare and contrast what people today do to make themselves
>   more attractive with what they did twenty years ago.
>
> • Compare and contrast what celebrities do to make themselves
>   more attractive with what average people do.

Complete the diagram below. Label the circles with the people you're comparing. Think about what people do (or did) to make themselves more attractive. List the differences in each circle and the similarities in the middle.

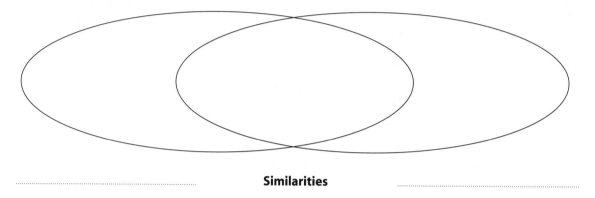

.... **Similarities** ....

Step 2. Writing. Write two paragraphs comparing and contrasting ideas within the topic you chose, referring to your notes in the diagram.

> • In your first paragraph, write about the similarities. Remember to use connecting words such as
>   <u>like</u>, <u>similarly</u>, and <u>too</u> / <u>also</u>.
>
> • In your second paragraph, write about the differences. Remember to use connecting words such as
>   <u>but</u>, <u>however</u>, and <u>whereas</u> / <u>while</u>.

....

....

....

....

....

....

....

....

Step 3. Self-Check.

☐ Did you correctly use connecting words for comparing?

☐ Did you correctly use connecting words for contrasting?

☐ Does each paragraph have a topic sentence?

Community

PREVIEW

1 Think about a city you have lived in or visited. Then complete the chart with your opinions.

City: _____	
Things you like about the city	
Things you dislike about the city	
Trends (general changes taking place) in the city	
Things that could be done to improve life in the city	

2 Read the e-mail message.

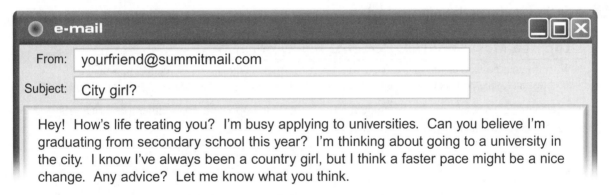

From: yourfriend@summitmail.com

Subject: City girl?

Hey! How's life treating you? I'm busy applying to universities. Can you believe I'm graduating from secondary school this year? I'm thinking about going to a university in the city. I know I've always been a country girl, but I think a faster pace might be a nice change. Any advice? Let me know what you think.

Now respond to the e-mail message. Do you think a move to the city is a good idea? Explain your opinion. Describe some advantages and disadvantages of life in the city. If you can, give advice on living in a city.

To: yourfriend@summitmail.com

Subject: RE: City girl?

LESSON 1

3 Combine each pair of sentences, using a possessive with a gerund.

1. He sleeps in class. What do you think about it?

   What do you think about his sleeping in class?

2. Julie's husband checks his PDA constantly. She can't stand it.

3. Patricia's co-workers call her Patty. She resents it.

4. They complain all the time. I'm so tired of it.

5. We take calls during dinner. Our father objects to it.

6. I hum while I work. Do you mind?

7. You are late so often. Mr. Yu objects to it.

4 Read the list of annoying office behaviors.

Top Ten Most Annoying Personal Behaviors at Work

What do your co-workers do that gets on your nerves? We recently asked our readers to e-mail us the most annoying personal behaviors of their officemates. Here are the ten most popular responses:

1. Chewing, smacking, and popping gum
2. Humming, whistling loudly, or listening to the radio in a shared work area
3. Interrupting conversations
4. Smoking at work
5. Inappropriate jokes, language, or comments
6. Inappropriate dress—either too casual or too shocking
7. Looking at the clock or at one's watch repeatedly during a meeting
8. Wearing too much perfume or cologne
9. Playing with objects on someone else's desk
10. Gossiping and complaining constantly

SOURCE: www.bizjournal.com

Now answer the questions.

1. Which behavior from the list do you find most annoying?

2. Can you think of any annoying workplace behaviors that aren't on the list?

3. Do you know someone who engages in one of these behaviors? How do you feel about it? Write a sentence, using a possessive with a gerund.

4. Write a sentence asking for permission to do one of the things listed.

5. Write a sentence politely asking someone not to do one of the things listed.

5 Judge the appropriateness of each behavior below. Write sentences, using adjectives from Student's Book page 53 or your own adjectives.

1. Using a hand-held phone while driving: *It's unsafe to use a hand-held phone while driving.*

2. Taking a call in a movie theater: ....

3. Turning your cell phone off in class: ....

4. Having a loud, personal conversation on the train: ....

....

5. Talking on the phone while shopping: ....

6. Turning your phone to silent mode in a restaurant: ....

....

7. Leaving your phone on during a flight: ....

Cell-phone use at public cultural events — such as plays, movies, concerts, and art exhibits — is now against the law in New York City. The penalty for violating the law is a fifty-dollar fine and removal from the theater, museum, etc. The law was passed in 2003 after two famous actors reacted to cell-phone users during Broadway performances. In mid-performance, Kevin Spacey turned to a member of the audience who had answered a cell phone and said, "Tell them you're busy." Laurence Fishburne wasn't as polite. When an audience member answered a phone during one of his performances, he yelled, "Turn your @#?!* phone off!"*

SOURCES: www.wired.com, www.playbill.com

LESSON 2

6 Offer acceptable alternatives for each inappropriate behavior. Use <u>either . . . or</u>.

1. Littering: *People should either throw their garbage in a trash can or hold on to it until they find one.*

2. Talking during a movie: ....

3. Playing loud music on a bus: ....

4. Gossiping: ....

5. Eating in class: ....

7 Rewrite each sentence, using <u>neither . . . nor</u> and the antonym of the adjective.

1. Listening to loud music and getting in and out of your seat constantly are inconsiderate on a flight. *Neither listening to loud music nor getting in and out of your seat constantly is considerate on a flight.*

2. Leaving a cell phone on and putting your feet up on the seat in front of you are discourteous in a movie theater. ....

....

3. Talking on a cell phone and smoking while driving are irresponsible. ....

....

4. Talking or laughing while the teacher is talking is disrespectful. ....

....

5. Touching the art and taking flash photography in a museum are inappropriate. ....

....

---

* Symbols such as @#?!* are used to politely denote curse words.

8 Read the pet peeves of visitors to a website.

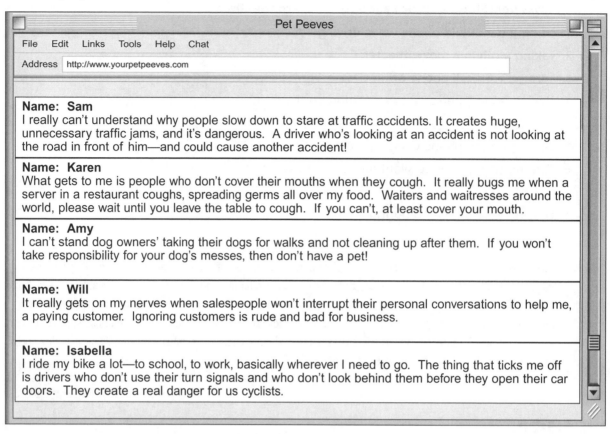

Now rate the pet peeves according to how annoying they are to you. Number them from 1 (most annoying) to 6 (least annoying).

.... drivers who slow down to stare at traffic accidents

.... servers who don't cover their mouths when they cough

.... dog owners who don't clean up after their dogs

.... salespeople who don't interrupt their personal conversations to help you

.... drivers who don't use their turn signals

.... drivers who don't look behind them before they open their car doors

9 Challenge. Now read the pet peeves in Exercise 8 again. Write a sentence summarizing each person's opinion. Use the paired conjunctions in parentheses.

1. Sam's opinion (not only . . . but also): _Not only does slowing down to stare at traffic_
   accidents create huge, unnecessary traffic jams, but it's also dangerous.

2. Karen's opinion (either . . . or): ....

   ....

3. Amy's opinion (either . . . or): ....

   ....

4. Will's opinion (not only . . . but also): ....

   ....

5. Isabella's opinion (neither . . . nor): ....

   ....

10 **What About You?** What's your pet peeve? Post a message to the message board.
Use the messages in Exercise 8 as a guide.

_____
_____
_____
_____

LESSON 3

11 Check the community service activities that you or someone you know has done.

☐ plant flowers or trees   ☐ collect signatures

☐ pick up trash   ☐ volunteer

☐ mail letters   ☐ make arrangements to donate your organs

☐ make phone calls   ☐ donate money

☐ raise money   ☐ other: _____

Now write sentences.

Example: Write about two activities you or someone you know has done. Use <u>not only</u> . . . <u>but also</u>.

Not only have I raised money, but I've also volunteered.

1. Write about two activities you or someone you know has done. Use <u>not only</u> . . . <u>but also</u>.

_____

2. Write about two activities you haven't done. Use <u>neither</u> . . . <u>nor</u>.

_____

3. Write about two activities you'd like to do. Use <u>either</u> . . . <u>or</u>.

_____

12 **Reading Warm-up.** Describe your ideal vacation. Where would you go?
What would you do? Where would you stay?

13 Reading. Read about the service organization started by husband and wife Bud Philbrook and Michele Gran.

Bud Philbrook and Michele Gran were married in 1979. Instead of taking a honeymoon cruise to the Caribbean, they decided to spend a week in a rural village in Guatemala, where they helped raise money for an irrigation system. When they returned to their home in St. Paul, Minnesota, USA, the local newspaper wrote a story about their unusual honeymoon. Soon, people started contacting them, asking how they could plan a similar trip. Philbrook said, "We knew there was a need in rural communities around the world, and now we were learning people wanted to do this."

In 1984, the couple founded Global Volunteers, a nonprofit agency for people who want to spend their vacation helping others. Now the organization sends about 2,000 people each year to community development programs in twenty countries on six continents. These short-term volunteer service projects are focused on helping children and their families.

Volunteers are invited by local community leaders to work on projects that community members have identified as important. Not only do volunteers work side by side with local people, but they also live in the community. In most cases, no special skills are required. Anyone who wants to be of service and to learn about other cultures can volunteer. Global Volunteers' working vacations are popular with people of all ages. There are young, single volunteers and retired volunteers.

More recently, Global Volunteers has started offering programs for families with children as young as five. Some Global Volunteers community service opportunities include:

- helping to build clinics and community centers in mountain villages in Costa Rica.
- caring for infants with special needs in a rural hospital in Romania.
- working with orphaned and abandoned children in India.
- teaching conversational English in a large city or rural village in China.

SOURCE: www.globalvolunteers.org

Now answer questions about the article.

1. Where did Bud Philbrook and Michele Gran go on their honeymoon? ....

2. What did they do? ....

3. Why do you think they decided to spend their honeymoon in this way? ....

   ....

4. What effect did their story have on some people who read it? ....

   ....

5. What did Bud Philbrook and Michele Gran do as a result of people's interest in their trip?

   ....

14 What About You? Would you consider a volunteer vacation? Answer the questions.

1. In my opinion, a volunteer vacation would be ....

   a. a life-changing experience   **c.** more trouble than it's worth

   b. an adventure   **d.** kind of scary

   Explain your answer: ....

2. Some Global Volunteers live with local families. How comfortable would you be doing the same thing?

a. very comfortable   c. a little uncomfortable

b. somewhat comfortable   d. very uncomfortable

Explain your answer: ....

3. At what stage in your life would you want to go on a volunteer vacation?

a. young and single   c. married with a family

b. married without kids   d. retired

Explain your answer: ....

4. Which of the community services listed in the article would you want to do? Why?

....

5. Would you prefer to volunteer in a rural area or in a city? Why? ....

....

LESSON 4

15 **Reading.** **Look back at** *The Advent of the Megacity* **on Student's Book page 58. What is Dr. Perlman's opinion of planned cities?**

....

Now read about Canberra, Australia.

Canberra: A Planned City

Are planned cities too sterile? Not according to most people who live in or visit Canberra, Australia. With a population of just over 323,000, it's not a megacity—but it is Australia's largest inland city and its capital. Opinions of the entirely planned city cite plenty of pros and not a lot of cons. According to the travel guide Lonely Planet, it's "a picturesque spot with beautiful galleries and museums, as well as excellent restaurants, bars, and cafes."

One of the world's greenest cities, Canberra is surrounded by nature reserves, and a great deal of city land was set aside for parks and gardens. Canberra is proof that—with proper planning—the environment can be preserved in densely populated cities and towns.

Canberra also has excellent infrastructure. With wide roads that use

roundabouts, rather than traffic lights, to regulate the flow of traffic, the city offers the shortest average commute times in Australia. Most city roads also have bike lanes, making cycling an important form of transportation in Canberra.

As a result of careful planning, Canberra offers the benefits of city living without the urban problems such as pollution and traffic. Not only does Canberra have clean air and water and good roads, but it also has affordable housing (cheaper than Sydney or Melbourne) and an abundance of health-care facilities. As the seat of Australia's government, Canberra has low unemployment and high education and income levels. It is a relatively safe city, with no murders reported in the 1999/2000 financial year. Canberra shows that planned cities can be great places to live and work.

SOURCES: www.up.edu.ph, www.education.nationalcapital.gov.au

16 Look back at the reading on page 45 and mark each statement about Canberra
True or **False**. Provide information from the article to support your choice.

True   False

1. ☐   ☐   Canberra suffers from a lack of culture and entertainment. ....

2. ☐   ☐   Transportation is a problem in Canberra. ....

3. ☐   ☐   Canberra has high levels of pollution. ....

4. ☐   ☐   Housing is not a problem for most people in Canberra. ....

5. ☐   ☐   A high percentage of people in Canberra cannot find work. ....

6. ☐   ☐   Crime is low in Canberra. ....

17 List one aspect of life in Canberra that appeals to you. Explain your answer.

....

....

18 **Challenge.** If you were going to design a city, what would be important
to you? Choose three urban problems from the box. Provide ideas about
how each problem might be prevented or alleviated through planning.

crime	corruption	disease	discrimination
overpopulation	pollution	poverty	inadequate public transportation
lack of housing	unemployment	other:	

Problem	Ideas
Unemployment	*Job training, encourage employers to locate in city*
1.	
2.	
3.	

> Hippodamus, a Greek architect of the 5th century B.C., is often considered the father of
> city planning. He designed the city of Miletus, using a grid plan for the layout of streets.
> (A grid is a pattern of straight lines that cross each other and form squares.)

Source: www.wikipedia.org

Grammar Booster

A Rewrite each sentence, using the word in parentheses. Make verb changes as necessary.

1. John Coltrane was a great jazz musician, and so was Miles Davis. (too)

   John Coltrane was a great jazz musician, and Miles Davis was too.

2. The restaurant doesn't allow smoking, and neither does the bar. (not either)

3. Her company has adopted a casual dress code on Fridays, and his has too. (so)

4. Shorts aren't appropriate in the office, and neither are jeans. (not either)

5. She was annoyed by his behavior, and we were too. (so)

6. We've decided to volunteer, and so have they. (too)

7. Dave Clark doesn't like the city, and we don't either. (neither)

8. We're not going on vacation this summer, and they're not either. (neither)

B Use the diagram below to compare two cities that you know. Consider things like traffic, weather, population, natural setting, architecture, infrastructure, and tourist attractions. Write similarities where the circles overlap and differences in the areas that do not overlap.

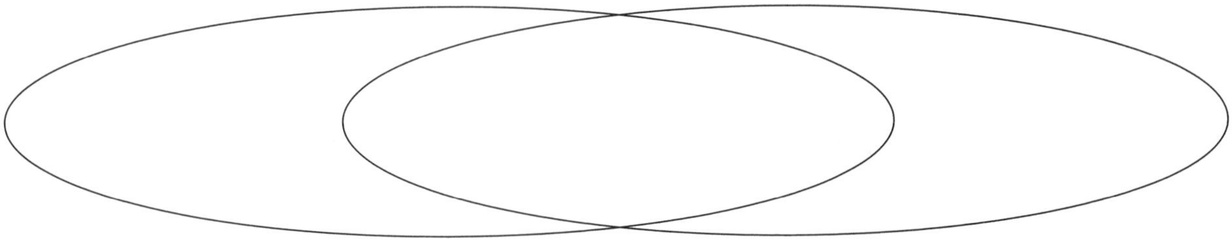

City: _____ Similarities City: _____

Now use the information from the diagram to write sentences about ways in which the two cities are similar. Use conjunctions with <u>so</u>, <u>too</u>, <u>neither</u>, and <u>not either</u>.

1. _____
2. _____
3. _____
4. _____
5. _____

C Use short responses with <u>so</u>, <u>too</u>, <u>neither</u>, or <u>not either</u> to agree with the statements.

1. **A:** I don't really like the fast pace of life in the city.

   B: ....

2. **A:** I'm really annoyed by smoking in restaurants.

   B: ....

3. **A:** I try to be courteous about using my cell phone.

   B: ....

4. **A:** I can't understand why people talk during movies.

   B: ....

5. **A:** I speak up when something bothers me.

   B: ....

6. **A:** I don't have time to get involved with my community.

   B: ....

7. **A:** I would consider donating my organs.

   B: ....

Writing: An e-mail letter to an international website

Step 1. Prewriting. Listing ideas. Think about how visitors to your country generally behave, both positive and negative aspects. List reasons why their behavior is either positive or a problem. If it is a problem, list how you would like behavior to change.

....

....

....

....

....

....

....

....

....

....

....

....

WRITING MODEL

http://www.GlobalCourtesy.com/soundoff

I am writing to complain about tourists' littering in our country. Not only is it inconsiderate, but it also detracts from the ability of everyone—tourists and locals alike—to enjoy all that our country has to offer.

Tourists come to our country from all over the world to enjoy our beaches, museums, and monuments. I have noticed many of them throwing candy wrappers, cigarette butts, and other things on the ground, rather than in trash cans. It is rude for them to expect the people who live here to clean up after them.

I urge all tourists who visit our country to please be considerate of your hosts and to clean up after yourselves. That way we can all enjoy your visit.

Sincerely,
Sasha Pilcher

Step 2. Writing. Use your notes to write an e-mail letter to an international tourism website. Remember to state how you feel about the behavior and, if appropriate, how you would like behavior to change.

....

....

....

....

....

....

....

....

....

....

....

....

Step 3. Self-Check.

☐ Did you use the proper salutation and closing?

☐ Are the tone and language in the letter appropriate for the audience?

☐ Did you use regular spelling and punctuation and avoid abbreviations?

UNIT 6

Animals

PREVIEW

1 **Answer the questions.**

1. Write your own description of your personality. Refer to Student's Book page 62 for adjectives if you need to. _____

   _____

2. If you had to pick any animal to match your personality, what animal would it be?

   _____

3. What characteristics do you and this animal share? _____

   _____

2 **Match each animal with the adjective that best describes it.**
Write the letter on the line.

a. strong
b. quiet
c. brave
d. hairy
e. blind
f. slow
g. fat
h. playful

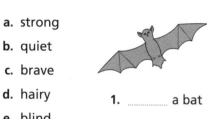

1. _____ a bat

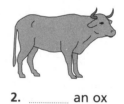

2. _____ an ox

3. _____ a mouse

4. _____ a kitten

5. _____ a lion

6. _____ a pig

7. _____ a gorilla

8. _____ a snail

3 A **simile** is an expression that compares two things, using the words **like** or **as**. Use your answers from Exercise 2 to write animal similes with **as**. Follow the example.

1. *as blind as a bat*   5. _____

2. _____   6. _____

3. _____   7. _____

4. _____   8. _____

50

4 Look back at your answers in Exercise 1. Complete the sentence about yourself with a simile.

I'm _____ .

Now use some of the similes from Exercise 3 to describe people you know, famous people, or fictional characters.

1. *My mother-in-law is as blind as a bat.* _____
2. _____
3. _____
4. _____
5. _____

LESSON 1

5 Complete the sentences in the passive voice with <u>should</u> and a verb from the box. Most verbs will be used more than once.

allow	give	keep	protect	provide	treat

1. Animals on large farms _____ humanely.
2. They _____ with healthy food.
3. They _____ with clean drinking water.
4. They _____ to interact with other animals.
5. The animals _____ space to move around.
6. They _____ from predators.
7. They _____ for illness or injury.
8. They _____ comfortable in extreme weather.

6 In the following passive-voice sentences, use <u>can</u>, <u>can't</u>, <u>might</u>, <u>might not</u>, <u>shouldn't</u>, and <u>don't have to</u> with the verb in parentheses. Use each modal only once.

1. Dogfighting is illegal in all fifty U.S. states. Dogs _____ for fighting in
   (raise)
   the United States.

2. Animals _____ for sport or entertainment. Hunting, animal fighting,
   (harm)
   animal racing, and use of animals in circuses should be illegal in all countries.

3. Animals _____ for their hides and fur. It's not necessary, because there
   (kill)
   are so many man-made materials that can keep people just as warm.

4. The cruel practice of testing cosmetics on animals _____ if everyone
   buys only from companies that don't test on animals.   (eliminate)

5. Pets _____ if there were more laws protecting them.
   (mistreat)

6. Alternatives to animal testing _____ in the next decade.
   (develop)

7 What can be done to promote the humane treatment of animals? List some ideas.

....

....

LESSON 2

8 **Reading.** Read about the advantages and disadvantages of owning different popular pets.

FINDING THE BEST PET FOR YOU

Take time to learn all you need to know about the animal of your choice before bringing one home.

CATS

Cats are independent and easy pets to care for. And, as long as you aren't buying a purebred, they are economical pets, too.

Cats require little actual day-to-day care. They clean and groom themselves, tend to be self-reliant, and are usually happy to stay out of your way. But they can also be cuddly, playful, affectionate creatures—when they are interested.

Finding a kitten is usually easy, and they are often free.

DOGS

Dogs are generally eager to please, affectionate, and loyal, but they demand lots of time and attention. They need plenty of exercise and thrive on interaction with their owners. Daily walks, frequent baths, and feeding are a must.

Dogs range in price from free to quite expensive for some breeds. If you decide to buy a purebred, research the various dog breeds to find the best match for your household.

RABBITS

Rabbits love to run, are very sociable and intelligent, and most are quite adorable.

When deciding whether a rabbit is the pet for you, keep in mind that they require daily attention and care, much like dogs. A rabbit should get lots of exercise, live in a dry spot in your home, and get time out of its cage.

Rabbits are not costly to purchase or care for, though it's important to keep fresh hay and leafy greens on hand for them to eat.

HAMSTERS

Hamsters are easy pets for practically any family. They are amusing, affable, and cute. Hamsters have simple needs and are cheap to buy and to keep. Provide a dry living space outfitted with a gnawing log and a hiding place, and a hamster is content.

BIRDS

Birds have been blessed with lovely voices, though they are not quiet pets. Despite this, they are intelligent companions that are growing in popularity because they are pretty and quite independent.

Caring for birds is not difficult, but they do have special needs. They like to be active and to be challenged, and they must be housed in a place that is not too hot or too cold. Most love human interaction or other bird companions.

They should all be released from their cages periodically to explore their surroundings.

Birds can be quite costly to purchase, depending on which bird you buy, but the cost of caring for a bird is quite low.

SNAKES

If you're the average person, this is not the pet you want. Snakes require careful attention and owners with special knowledge to care for them.

Before you buy a snake, consider that it may grow up to weigh twice what you do and refuse to eat anything but live animals such as mice or insects, which you will need to provide. Temperature and lighting must be controlled, and the snake's enclosure must be secure.

Snakes range from being placid and docile to aggressive, depending on the individual snake. They can be fairly costly to purchase and to maintain.

FISH

Fish fit well in almost any type of household. They're quiet, generally peaceful, and, depending on your tastes, not expensive to buy or to shelter. Care is relatively simple and involves monitoring water and food.

Usually, the biggest expense involves an aquarium, some of which can be very expensive. For those who do not want exotic, pricey fish, a simple, adequately built aquarium will do and costs much less.

SOURCE: www.bankrate.com

Now complete the chart with information from the reading.

Pet	Personality traits	Care / special needs	Cost
Cats	*independent, self-reliant*	*easy to care for*	*economical, often free*
Dogs			
Rabbits			
Hamsters			
Birds			
Snakes			
Fish			

9 **Use information from the chart in Exercise 8 to answer the following questions.**

1. Which pets are low maintenance?

   ....

2. Which pets are high maintenance?

   ....

3. Which pets are costly to buy or care for?

   ....

4. Which pets are inexpensive to buy or care for?

   ....

5. Which pet would be best for your lifestyle? Explain.

   ....

   ....

Researchers have documented many health benefits associated with pet ownership. Owning a pet can help:

- reduce stress
- relieve loneliness and depression
- lower blood pressure
- prevent heart disease
- lower health-care costs
- stimulate exercise
- encourage laughter
- facilitate social contact

SOURCE: www.coloradan.com

Small dog breeds have become trendy in recent years. Celebrities such as Paris Hilton and Geri Halliwell are often spotted with their toy dogs tucked in their purses. As a result of this popularity, designer labels are selling high-end products for dogs—including clothes, collars, and jewelry.

SOURCE: www.coloradan.com

LESSON 3

10 Which character traits are positive? Which are negative? List each in the appropriate place.

clever	gullible	mean	selfish	sincere	vain	wise

Positive character traits

1. ....
2. ....
3. ....

Negative character traits

1. ....
2. ....
3. ....
4. ....

11 Answer the questions.

1. Who's the wisest person you know? What advice has he or she given you?

   ....

2. Describe a time when you did something clever.

   ....

3. Who do you think is a sincere politician?

   ....

4. What is the meanest thing someone has ever said to you?

   ....

5. What is one thing you could do to be less selfish?

   ....

12 Listen again to either the fable of "The Fox and the Crow" (Student's Book page 68) or "The Peacock's Tail" (page 69). Then write the story as well as you can from memory.

Did you know that *gullible* is the only word in the English language that's not in the dictionary? Go ahead, look it up.

If you looked it up, you are definitely gullible.

13 **Reading.** Read the fable of "The Stag with Beautiful Antlers." Then complete the card with information from the story.

ne morning a stag, drinking from a pond, saw his reflection in the water. He thought to himself, "What beautiful antlers I have. Don't I look elegant? But my skinny legs are a sorry sight in contrast! So spindly and bony."

The stag was still admiring his antlers when he heard the baying of hunters' dogs. He dashed away from the pond and ran to hide in the woods. His legs carried him swiftly and surely, but as he passed under a leafy tree, his antlers got caught in its branches.

The stag tried to free his antlers, but each time he shook his head, the more entangled he became. The dogs were getting closer. The stag gave one last, desperate tug and managed to free himself.

Once he was in the woods and able to catch his breath, he thought, "The antlers I admired so much nearly killed me, while the legs I hated so much saved my life."

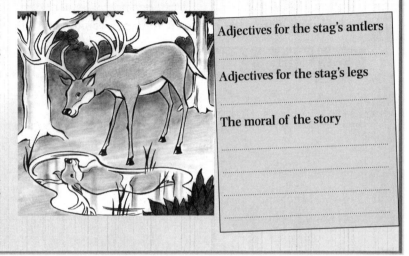

Adjectives for the stag's antlers
....

Adjectives for the stag's legs
....

The moral of the story
....
....
....
....

SOURCE: *Little Book of Fables* (Toronto: Groundwood Books, 2004)

14 **Challenge.** Complete each expression with the correct animal.

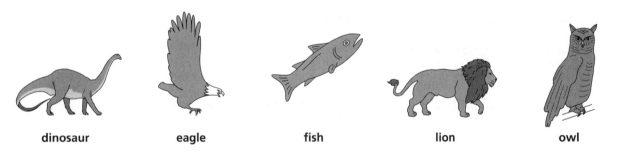

dinosaur   eagle   fish   lion   owl

1. A .... is something very large and old-fashioned that does not work well or effectively anymore.

2. To feel like a .... **out of water** is to feel uncomfortable because you are in an uncomfortable place or situation.

3. Someone who is ....-**eyed** is very good at seeing or noticing things.

4. A **night** .... is someone who enjoys staying awake late at night.

5. Someone who is brave is ....**hearted**.

15 Write your own sentences, using three of the animal expressions from Exercise 14.

Example: _I would feel like a fish out of water if I moved to the country._

1. ....
2. ....
3. ....

LESSON 4

16 Use information from the article on Student's Book page 70 to complete the chart.

Animals at risk of extinction	Where they live	Problems affecting their habitats	The WWF's conservation efforts

17 Answer the questions.

1. Do you know of any other animal that is endangered or whose habitat is being destroyed?

....

2. Where does this animal live? ....

3. What is the cause of this animal's problems? ....

4. Is anything being done to preserve this animal? What can be done? ....

....

5. Do you think action should be taken to protect this animal? Why or why not? ....

....

....

According to The World Conservation Union, a total of 15,589 species of plants and animals are at risk of extinction. One in three amphibians and almost half of all freshwater turtles are threatened. Also, one in eight birds and one in four mammals are endangered.

Grammar Booster

A Circle the letter of the modal that best completes each sentence.

1. I _____ have a pet parrot, but they require too much care.

    a. had better   **b.** would like to   **c.** am able to   **d.** should

2. If you don't mind, I _____ eat out tonight.

    a. wouldn't   **b.** don't have to   **c.** would rather not   **d.** must not

3. _____ Hillary play the violin well?

    a. Should   **b.** Must   **c.** May   **d.** Can

4. I'm sorry, but I _____ come to the meeting tomorrow.

    a. must not   **b.** won't be able to   **c.** couldn't   **d.** don't have to

5. Your sister's a tennis player? She _____ be very athletic.

    a. must   **b.** could   **c.** should   **d.** may

6. We _____ go skiing this weekend. We haven't decided yet.

    a. shouldn't   **b.** can't   **c.** had better not   **d.** might not

7. You _____ feed the animals—it's against the rules!

    a. don't have to   **b.** might not   **c.** had better not   **d.** aren't able to

8. I _____ take this class. It's required.

    a. may   **b.** could   **c.** have to   **d.** can

B Complete each sentence with a modal. More than one answer may be possible in each sentence.

1. You _____ turn on the TV while you wait, if you'd like.

2. It _____ snow tomorrow.

3. _____ I please borrow your pen for a moment?

4. If we leave at 4:00, there _____ be a lot of traffic.

5. We _____ check the weather before we go hiking.

6. If you don't want to see a movie, we _____ go out to eat instead.

7. My mother-in-law _____ have liked to go to Ireland, but they went to France instead.

8. He _____ have been very happy when he found out about his promotion.

9. You _____ smoke in this restaurant; it's prohibited.

10. He _____ come to the party last night because he had to work.

C **Complete each conversation in your own way. Use a modal.**

1. **A:** I passed Ellie on the street yesterday, and she didn't say hello.

   B: *She may not have seen you.*

2. **A:** It's too warm in here.

   B: ....

3. **A:** I don't feel like cooking tonight.

   B: ....

4. **A:** I don't know where to go on vacation this year.

   B: ....

5. **A:** Class was cancelled yesterday.

   B: ....

6. **A:** I've had this cold for three weeks now.

   B: ....

7. **A:** I'm a little hungry.

   B: ....

8. **A:** My brother wants to get a pet.

   B: ....

Writing: Express an opinion on animal conservation

Step 1. Prewriting. Planning your argument. Read the question below. State your opinion and list your arguments. Try to include examples, facts, or experts' opinions to support your opinion. Then list possible opposing arguments.

> **Is animal conservation important?**

Your opinion: ....

Your arguments	**Possible opposing arguments**
1.	1. ....
2.	2. ....
3.	3. ....

Step 2. Writing. Write a paragraph arguing your opinion from Step 1. Remember to include a topic sentence at the beginning of the paragraph and a concluding sentence at the end.

....

....

....

....

....

....

....

....

....

....

....

....

Step 3. Self-Check.

☐ Did you state your point of view clearly?

☐ Did you provide examples, facts, or experts' opinions to support your point of view?

☐ Did you discuss opposing arguments?

☐ Did you include a topic sentence and a concluding sentence?

Advertising and Consumers

PREVIEW

1 **Answer the questions.**

1. Do you have a favorite TV commercial, billboard, magazine ad, or radio ad?
   What product is it for? ....
   ....

2. Describe the ad. What type of ad is it? What do you like about it? ....
   ....
   ....

3. Do you use the product? Why or why not? ....
   ....

2 **What advertising have you been exposed to recently? List the brands or products you remember for each type of advertising.**

TV commercials: ....

Internet pop-ups: ....

Magazine ads: ....

Billboards: ....

Radio ads: ....

Ads on trains, buses, or blimps: ....

Now look at your lists. Which is the most effective way for advertisers to get their messages to you?

....

3 **Which expressions are positive reactions to a product? Which are negative? Check positive or negative.**

	positive	negative
1. Now that's something I'd like to get my hands on.	☐	☐
2. Sounds like a waste of money to me.	☐	☐
3. I think it could really come in handy.	☐	☐
4. You've got to be kidding.	☐	☐
5. What on earth for?	☐	☐

LESSON 1

4 Read each statement and then suggest the best place for each person to shop in your city or town. Use the vocabulary from Student's Book page 76.

I want to pick up some cheap sunglasses before we go sightseeing today. It would be a waste of money to buy designer ones. I'd just lose them!

I'd like to get some coffee, take a walk in this beautiful weather, and check out the new fall fashions.

1. *The open-air market on Fifth Street would be a good bet, if you don't mind haggling.*

2. ....

I've been saving up for a new digital camera. I'd like to check out a couple of different places before I buy one.

I don't really need anything, but I wouldn't mind just looking around. I actually find shopping relaxing.

3. ....

4. ....

5 Look online for something you're interested in buying. Record the prices you find on different websites. Comment on shipping costs, available brands, customer service, etc.

What are you shopping for? ....

Any particular brand? ....

Website: ....
Price: ....
Comments: ....

Website: ....
Price: ....
Comments: ....

Website: ....
Price: ....
Comments: ....

Which website has the best buy? ....

6 **Reading.** **Read the advice on shopping in Tokyo. Then complete the statements and answer the questions.**

TOKYO SHOPPING GUIDE

Below are descriptions of some of the best places to shop in Tokyo.

SOUVENIRS

"100-Yen" Shops
You can find 100-yen shops around many train stations and in some shopping areas. 100-yen shops are stores where most items cost 100 yen or less. In 100-yen shops, you can buy chopsticks, tableware, fans, kites, origami paper, calligraphy sets, "Hello Kitty" items, and much, much more! If you're looking for cheap souvenirs, 100-yen shops are the places to go.

Nakamise Shopping Arcade
This colorful, lively outdoor shopping street leads to the oldest temple in Tokyo. The walkway has been lined with souvenir shops

and local food stands for centuries. You'll find paper umbrellas, kimonos, rice cakes, sweets, and much more. Prices are, for the most part, reasonable.

Oriental Bazaar
Oriental Bazaar is the largest and most famous souvenir shop in Tokyo. It has four floors, and the higher you go, the more expensive the items get. Here you can satisfy all of your gift-giving needs at reasonable prices.

ELECTRONICS

Akihabara
Looking for the latest electronic gadgets? Check out the Akihabara district. It's the place to find the newest cell phones, TVs, *manga* anime CD-ROMs, even miniature robot pets. And it's one of the few places in Tokyo where you can try haggling.

CLOTHING AND ACCESSORIES

Ginza
The Ginza is a famous high-end shopping district in Tokyo. It's full of upscale department stores and expensive designer boutiques. The fashions tend to be more conservative here. For younger and trendier styles, go to Shibuya or Harajuku.

SOURCE: www.tokyoessentials.com

1. .... are the best places to find inexpensive souvenirs in Tokyo.

2. Bargaining is generally not a part of Japanese shopping culture, but one place where it's acceptable is ....

3. At .... , you might find a plastic samurai sword that's a steal in the basement and a traditional kimono that's a good deal on the top floor.

4. Prices are a bit steep here. If you're looking for a bargain, ... is probably not the place to shop.

5. To pick up a few souvenirs, try some local snacks, and do a little sightseeing at the same time, ... is a good bet.

6. Of the places listed in the guide, where would you be most interested in shopping? Why?

....

7. Where would you like to browse? Why? ....

LESSON 2

7 Think of something that happened to you or that you heard about recently that blew you away, got on your nerves, cracked you up, or choked you up. What was it? Why did it make you feel that way?

....

....

....

8 Complete each sentence with the passive form of a gerund or an infinitive. Use verbs from the box.

ask	entertain	ignore	treat
call	force	inform	

1. Pam doesn't want .... about new products.

2. Alex can't stand .... by telemarketers.

3. I enjoy .... by funny commercials.

4. We hate .... to watch ads before movies.

5. I appreciate .... to join this company.

6. Scott hates ....

7. My daughter dislikes .... like a baby.

9 How do you feel about these forms of advertising? Write sentences with passive forms of gerunds or infinitives. Use verbs from the box or your own verbs.

can't stand	don't appreciate	like	prefer
dislike	don't like	love	resent

1. Spam: *I don't appreciate being sent e-mail ads that I don't want.* ....

2. Ads before movies: ....

3. Pop-up ads: ....

4. Direct mail: ....

5. Telemarketing calls: ....

6. Magazine ads: ....

7. Free product samples: ....

8. Product placement in movies: ....

LESSON 3

10 Complete each sentence with a word from the box.

endorse	imply	promote	prove

1. My kids are really going to want to get their hands on those sneakers now that their favorite baseball player has agreed to .... them.

2. I would buy the more expensive brand of toothpaste if the company could .... that it's more effective at fighting cavities.

3. I heard First Choice Pizza is giving away free slices tonight to .... its chain of restaurants.

4. The ads .... that their competitor's cars are unsafe.

11 Look again at the list of advertising techniques on Student's Book page 80. Can you think of ads that use these techniques? Complete the chart for as many of the techniques as you can.

> In 1991, the Swedish government banned advertising directed at children under the age of twelve.
>
> SOURCE: www.en.wikipedia.org

Advertising Technique	Product	How the technique is used
Example: Provide facts and figures	ZX-10 MP3 player	The manufacturer states how many songs it holds, how little it weighs, and how many hours it can play.
1. Provide facts and figures		
2. Convince people to "join the bandwagon"		
3. Play on people's hidden fears		
4. Play on people's patriotism		
5. Provide "snob appeal"		
6. Associate positive qualities with a product		
7. Provide testimonials		
8. Manipulate people's emotions		

Which of these techniques do you think is most effective? Why? ....

LESSON 4

12 Reading Warm-up. **Answer the questions.**

1. Do you enjoy shopping? ....

2. Do you feel comfortable shopping alone? ....

3. How often do you go shopping? ....

4. What do you buy for yourself? ....

5. Do you see a difference between men's and women's attitudes toward shopping?

....

13 Reading. **Read about the shopping habits of North American men.**

Shift in North American Men's Shopping Habits

According to a study commissioned by the men's magazine *GQ*, the shopping habits of North American men are changing significantly. In contrast to the traditional image of men as unwilling shoppers who aren't comfortable shopping for their own clothes, the new findings suggest that men now shop as a leisure activity, and that they make the majority of their own clothing purchases.

Men are becoming independent and more confident shoppers. They're well-informed, willing to shop alone, and no longer dependent on their wives, girlfriends, or sisters to make their purchasing decisions for them.

In addition, the study found that men shop more often than in the past and are increasingly likely to buy certain products for themselves—especially electronics, casual clothing, watches, and fragrance or grooming products.

Among the findings of the 2005 survey:
- 84 percent of men purchase their own clothes—compared with 65 percent in 2001.
- 52 percent of the surveyed stores reported having male customers who shop at least once a month—compared with 10 percent in 2001.
- Male customers shop at the surveyed stores an average of 18 times a year—compared with 5 times a year in 2001.
- Men's tendency to purchase products for themselves increased most for electronics (64 percent increase), casual clothing (62 percent), men's watches (53 percent), and fragrances/grooming products (50 percent).
- The average age of male apparel shoppers is 30–39.

SOURCE: www.men.style.com

Now answer questions about the article.

1. According to the study, how are the shopping habits of North American men changing?

....

....

2. Do you think men's shopping habits are changing in a similar way in your country? Try to give examples to explain your answer.

....

....

3. Do you think the shift in men's shopping habits described in the article is a positive or a negative development? Explain your answer.

....

....

14 **Reading Warm-up.** **Answer the questions.**

1. What country do you think does the most online shopping? ....

2. What do you think is the most popular online purchase? ....

15 **Reading.** **Read about Internet shopping habits.**

Upward Trend in Global Online Shopping

According to a recent survey by AC Nielsen, more than 627 million people—one-tenth of the world's population—have shopped online. Books were the most popular purchase, with 212 million people reporting books as among the last three items they bought on the Internet. Books were followed by DVDs and video games, airline tickets, clothing/shoes/accessories, CDs and music downloads, electronic devices, computer hardware, and hotel reservations and tour bookings.

Among the 21,000 people from North America, Europe, Latin America, the Asia Pacific region, and South Africa who were surveyed, the Germans and the British turned out to be the world's most frequent online shoppers. In the month before the survey, Germans made an average of seven purchases, Britons six. In general, European countries had the highest average purchases, followed by Canada and Asian Pacific countries, with an average of five. U.S. online shoppers made four purchases on average. Latin American shoppers made the fewest purchases, an average of three.

Why do European consumers shop online? One of the main attractions of Internet shopping for Germans is the ability to buy at any time of the day or night, as store hours in Germany are limited by law. British consumers similarly cite convenience, while Italians think online shopping is fun (according to a survey by GfK Ad Hoc Research Worldwide).

In countries with widespread Internet access, some reasons people give for *not* shopping online include the expense of surfing, nervousness about using credit cards online, worries about companies collecting information about their shopping likes and dislikes, and reluctance to purchase goods from retailers they don't know.

SOURCES: www.home.businesswire.com, www.clickz.com

Now answer the questions.

1. Were you surprised by the most popular online purchase? ....

2. Why do you think people buy more books than any other product online? ....
....

3. Do any of the reasons listed for <u>not</u> shopping online concern you? Why or why not? ....
....

16 Complete the chart by listing some advantages and disadvantages of shopping online.

Advantages	Disadvantages
It's easier to comparison shop.	

17 Check the items that you have purchased online.

☐ books   ☐ CDs or music downloads

☐ DVDs or video games   ☐ electronic devices

☐ airline tickets   ☐ computer hardware

☐ clothing / accessories / shoes   ☐ hotel reservations or tour bookings

Now circle the items you've purchased in the last month. How many online purchases do you think you've made in the last month? ....

18 Answer the questions.

1. Describe consumer shopping habits in your country—including online shopping. Do you see differences between older and younger shoppers? Between women and men?

....

....

....

2. Describe your own shopping habits. Are you a compulsive shopper? Do you ever indulge yourself? How often? Do you ever make impulse buys, or do you wait and shop when there is a sale?

....

....

....

Grammar Booster

A Use the past gerund or infinitive form of the verbs in the box to complete the sentences. Use the passive voice where necessary. Refer to pages A3 and A4 in the Student's Book if you need to.

fool	have	sell
give	meet	steal

1. She was excited about .... her favorite actor.

2. He was thrilled .... the award.

3. I disliked .... by that ad.

4. He admitted .... money from the company.

5. She was pleased .... the extra time to shop.

6. The store claimed .... over 10,000 books that year.

B Combine each pair of sentences. Write one sentence, using a past form of a gerund or infinitive.

1. She was offered the position. She was pleased.

    She was pleased to have been offered the position.

2. He went to a conference last week. He mentioned it.

    ....

3. I wasn't told about the meeting. I resent it.

    ....

4. She missed the appointment. She made an excuse.

    ....

5. The manager gave the client the wrong information. The manager apologized.

    ....

6. She's finished her degree already. I didn't expect it.

    ....

7. He received a promotion. He was proud.

    ....

8. We missed the train. We had a good reason.

    ....

9. She used her corporate credit card for personal expenses. She was ashamed.

    ....

10. I was offended by her remarks. I pretended not to be.

    ....

Writing: Explain an article you've read

Choose one of the following articles to summarize:

- *Boys and Body Image*, Workbook page 36
- *Who Defines Beauty?* Student's Book page 46
- *Protecting Our Natural Inheritance*, Student's Book page 70
- An article you've read outside of class

Step 1. Prewriting. Identifying main ideas. Read the article you've chosen and underline or highlight the important parts. Then read the article again and list the main ideas below. (The article you have chosen may have fewer than six paragraphs.)

Main idea of paragraph 1:	
Main idea of paragraph 2:	
Main idea of paragraph 3:	
Main idea of paragraph 4:	
Main idea of paragraph 5:	
Main idea of paragraph 6:	

Step 2. Writing. Combine the main ideas to write your summary. Be sure to paraphrase what the author says, using your *own* words. Your summary should have one or two sentences for every paragraph in the original article.

....

....

....

....

....

....

....

....

....

....

....

....

Reporting verbs:

argue   report

believe   say

conclude   state

point out

Step 3. Self-Check.

☐ Is your summary a lot shorter than the original article?

☐ Does your summary include only the author's main ideas?

☐ Did you paraphrase the author's ideas?

☐ Did you include your opinion of the article? If so, rewrite the summary without it.

Family Trends

PREVIEW

1 Read each situation. Then write a sentence summarizing what happened. Use one of the expressions from the box for each situation.

have a falling out	shape up	things work out
patch things up	talk back	

1. Last night after dinner I asked Jack to wash the dishes. He said, "No way, Mom. You wash the dishes." Can you believe he spoke to me like that?

    ....

2. Did you hear about the big fight Eva and Lana had? Lana got really upset, and they haven't talked for a couple of weeks now.

    ....

3. Tomas came over last night. When I opened the door, he handed me flowers and said, "I'm sorry, Rachel." We talked for a long time and realized that we'd both made mistakes.

    ....

4. Jason used to come in late and leave early, take long lunches, and miss meetings. Now he's here every morning at 7:00 on the dot, works late, and never misses a meeting. That talk with the boss must have really had an impact!

    ....

5. Anna and Mike Gunn had a difficult time making ends meet after Mike's accident. He couldn't go back to work. But now Anna has a job as a consultant, and Mike's a stay-at-home dad. They just bought a new car last week!

    ....

2 How can parents raise well-behaved kids who won't turn into troublemakers? Write sentences using <u>should</u> or <u>shouldn't</u>.

Should	Shouldn't
Kids should be given clear rules to follow.	*Kids shouldn't be criticized constantly.*

LESSON 1

3 Rewrite each sentence with a repeated comparative so that the sentence describes a trend. (Some sentences can be rewritten more than one way.)

1. People are moving to cities to find work.

   More and more people are moving to cities to find work.

2. People are spending long hours at work.

   People are spending longer and longer hours at work.

3. Men are getting involved in caring for their children.

4. People are spending time with their extended families.

5. Mothers are staying home to take care of their children.

6. Couples are choosing to remain childless.

7. Young adults are moving out of their parents' homes.

8. Adolescents receive adult supervision.

4 Complete the sentences, using double comparatives. Use the correct form of each word from the box.

develop	few	good	less	low	more

1. _____ people work, _____ time they spend with their families.

2. _____ a country is, _____ the healthcare system.

3. _____ the birthrate, _____ children there will be to care for older members of society.

few	good	high	long	more	old

4. _____ education you get, _____ your salary will be.

5. _____ the health-care system, _____ people live.

6. _____ people are when they get married, _____ children they are likely to have.

5 Complete each double comparative. Use your own ideas.

1. The longer I live, ...

2. The harder you work, ...

3. The more that you read, ...

4. The better I get to know people, ...

5. The more things change, ...

Now compare your sentences with these famous quotes.

"The longer I live, the
more beautiful life becomes."
—**FRANK LLOYD WRIGHT,** architect
(1869 –1959)

"The harder you work,
the luckier you get."
—**SAMUEL GOLDWYN,** movie producer
(1882–1974)

"The more that you read, the more things
you will know. The more that you learn,
the more places you'll go."
—**DR. SEUSS,** children's book author (1904 –1991)

"The better I get to know men,
the more I find myself loving dogs."
—**CHARLES DE GAULLE,** French leader
(1890 –1970)

"The more things change,
the more they are the same."
—**ALPHONSE KARR,** author
(1808 –1890)

**Choose one of the quotes and describe what it means. How does it apply to
your life and/or to the world today?**

....

....

....

....

Of the 35 richest countries,
in only three – Iceland,
New Zealand, and the
United States – are women
having enough babies to
replace the existing
population.

SOURCE: *The Economist,* Dec. 21, 2000

LESSON 2

6 **What do you think parents should do if their teenaged kids start smoking?**
Read each idea and decide how effective you think it would be.

Parents should . . .	ineffective	somewhat effective	very effective
accept that there's not much they can do.	O	O	O
talk to their kids about the health risks of smoking.	O	O	O
ask their kids questions to find out why they are smoking.	O	O	O
ground them.	O	O	O
let their kids know that they disapprove of their smoking.	O	O	O
talk to their kids about other negative effects of smoking, such as poor sports performance, smelly clothes and hair, bad breath, and yellow teeth.	O	O	O
allow their kids to make their own mistakes.	O	O	O
explain how the tobacco industry's advertising targets young people to become smokers.	O	O	O
have their kids visit people who have lung cancer.	O	O	O
not make a big deal about a little bit of rebellious behavior.	O	O	O
quit smoking themselves if they are smokers.	O	O	O

What do you think is the best idea? Why? ....

....

According to worldwide smoking statistics compiled by the World Health Organization:

- About one in five young teenagers (aged 13–15) smokes.
- Between 80,000 and 100,000 children, roughly half of whom live in Asia, start smoking every day.
- Around 50 percent of those who start smoking as adolescents go on to smoke for 15 to 20 years.
- Teenagers are heavily influenced by tobacco advertising.
- About a quarter of youth alive in the Western Pacific Region will die from the effects of smoking.

SOURCE: www.wpro.who.int

7 Read the teen blog entries and describe the teens' or their parents' behavior. Use the vocabulary from Student's Book page 90.

🔙 Back   ➡ Forward   🔄 Reload   ❌ Stop   🏠 Home   🔍 Search

1. Posted: 10:09 AM

Princess5574

Hey! It's my birthday! When I woke up this morning, I went downstairs and opened the gifts my parents had left for me. I got some jewelry, some clothes, a new laptop – nothing special. I was a little disappointed. But when I walked out of the house, I found my real present in the driveway! My sports car – exactly the one I had asked for. I can't wait to drive it to my party on Saturday.

REPLY

2. Posted: 11:48 AM

Nolife312

They gave you a car? My parents won't even let me learn how to drive, or go anywhere in anyone else's car – or ride my bike down the street! I need to be able to hang out with my friends, go to the movies, maybe even go to a party every once in a while. I love my parents, but they're ruining my life!

REPLY

3. Posted: 1:02 PM

Norules721

Well, at least your parents care about what you do. My parents let me go where I want, do what I want, come home when I want. They don't mind if I invite the whole school over for a party. I know they love me, but I wish they would stop trying to be "cool" and act more like parents.

REPLY

---

1. *Princess is spoiled. Her parents are* ....

2. ....

3. ....

---

8 What About You? Check the sentences that describe your upbringing.

Lenient upbringing	Strict upbringing
○ My parents did things for me that I could or should have done for myself.	○ My parents made me do many things for myself.
○ My parents did not expect me to do many chores or to help much around the house.	○ I had to do a lot of chores around the house.
○ I was allowed to have almost any clothes I wanted.	○ I had to use my own money to buy clothes.
○ My parents gave me too much freedom.	○ I wasn't given very much freedom.
○ My parents allowed me to take the lead or dominate the family.	○ My parents used physical punishment to discipline me.
○ My parents did not enforce their rules.	○ My parents set a lot of rules for me to follow.

Do you think you were spoiled as a child? Were your parents too strict? Or did you grow up with a nice balance between strictness and leniency? Explain and try to give examples.

....

....

....

What should parents do (or not do) to raise kids who aren't spoiled? List some ideas.

....

....

....

LESSON 3

9 **Match the words with their definitions. Write the letter on the line.**

1. .... frustration
2. .... involvement
3. .... courtesy
4. .... maturity
5. .... obedience

a. willingness to do what someone in a position of authority tells you to do

b. the quality of behaving in a sensible way and like an adult

c. the act of taking part in an activity or event, or the way in which you take part in it

d. the feeling of being annoyed, upset, or impatient, because you cannot control or change a situation or achieve something.

e. polite behavior that shows that you have respect for other people

10 **Challenge. Circle the letter of the best choice to complete each sentence.**

1. His parents intend for him to get married as soon as he finishes college. That is their ....

   a. explanation   **b.** importance   **c.** expectation   **d.** impatience

2. Carl Brooks is almost thirty-eight years old and still living in his parents' home. His parents resent his ....

   a. dependence   **b.** dependability   **c.** development   **d.** difference

3. Her parents don't think she should change jobs again. They worry about her long-term financial ....

   a. mobility   **b.** security   **c.** lenience   **d.** confidence

4. Dana Wolf doesn't like her daughter's new boyfriend. She thinks he's lazy and disrespectful. She can't understand her daughter's .... to him.

   a. attractiveness   **b.** consideration   **c.** involvement   **d.** attraction

11 Answer the questions.

1. What is a "generation gap"?

   ....

2. What developments (political, technological, social, etc.) do you think have contributed to the generation gap between your generation and that of your parents?

   ....

   ....

3. In what ways are your generation and that of your parents similar?

   ....

   ....

LESSON 4

12 Reading Warm-up. How are the responsibilities of caring for children different from those of caring for the elderly? How are they the same?

   ....

   ....

13 Reading. Read the article.

The Sandwich Generation

In the United States and Canada they've been termed the sandwich generation—people caught between the needs of their growing children and their aging parents, having to care for both. Factors giving rise to the sandwich generation include the fact that people are having children later in life, combined with longer life expectancies. Whatever the cause, this new responsibility places many demands on these caregivers' time and energy and leaves little space for attending to their own needs.

Some members of the sandwich generation are parents in their 30s or 40s caring for young children. For example, Pamela Bose, 40, has a three-year-old and a nine-year-old. She has recently taken over the care of her widowed mother. One minute she is worrying about getting the children to school on time; the next, she is checking to make sure that her mother has remembered to take her medicine. "I spend so much time keeping up with their competing demands that I end up not devoting enough time to anyone, let alone making time for myself," says Bose.

(continued on page 77)

The Sandwich Generation *(continued)*

Other members of the sandwich generation are parents in their 40s or 50s caring for teenaged or adult children. Nowadays more adult children are living at home while they're in college and even afterward, as they get established and figure out what they want to do. Also, an increasing number of adult children are returning home to live after a divorce or job loss.

The longer adult children remain dependent on their parents, the more people find themselves in the sandwich generation. Patricia Rivas is one of these people. She and her husband David both have careers. They have a teenaged son, a recently divorced daughter with a two-year-old child, and an elderly father who has early dementia and is requiring more and more care, all living in the same household.

Most sandwich-generation caregivers are women. Increased female labor-force participation means that many of these women are balancing not only care for their children and parents but also their own careers. Without a doubt, trying to meet all of these obligations at the same time is stressful. It's not surprising that sandwich-generation members report an increase in depression, sleeplessness, headaches, and other health problems. While many are happy about the chance to help care for their parents, they also feel guilty about not doing more.

As sandwich-generation members try to respond to everyone else's needs, it's important that they not ignore their own needs. As these caregivers struggle to give their young children attention and patience, their older children support and guidance, their elderly parents not only the physical care they need but also opportunities for social interaction and inclusion in family life, it is also important that they make some time for their own relaxation, something that is more often than not overlooked.

SOURCE: www.health24.com

Now answer the questions, using information from the article.

1. What is the "sandwich generation"?

   ....

2. How is the term "sandwich" appropriate to describe this generation?

   ....

3. Name three trends that are responsible for the development of the "sandwich generation."

   ....

   ....

   ....

4. What are some problems that sandwich-generation members experience?

   ....

   ....

5. Why is being a member of the sandwich generation especially stressful for women?

   ....

   ....

14 Look back at the article on pages 76–77. Find the nouns that correspond to the verbs and adjectives below. Write them on the lines.

1. responsible: ....
2. participate: ....
3. obligate: ....
4. depress: ....
5. sleepless: ....
6. patient: ....
7. guide: ....
8. interact: ....
9. include: ....
10. relax: ....

> Life expectancy in India and the People's Republic of China was around 40 years in the middle of the 20th century. By the end of the century, it had risen to around 63 years.

SOURCE: www.en.wikipedia.org

> In the U.S., approximately 44 percent of people between the ages of 45 and 55 have children under 21 and also have aging parents or in-laws.

SOURCE: www.imdiversity.com

15 Do you know anyone who is caring for their children and/or an elderly family member? Describe the person's situation. What challenges is he or she facing?

Grammar Booster

A **Read each pair of statements. Then complete each sentence, using a comparative, superlative, or comparison with as . . . as.**

1. Today's hike is 5 km. But our hike yesterday was 7 km.

   Today's hike is *shorter than yesterday's hike* .

2. A cheetah can run 96 km per hour. A greyhound can run 64 km per hour.

   A greyhound can't run _____ .

3. I am 24 years old. My brother is 20, and my sister is 18.

   Of the three of us, I am _____ .

4. Park City is 5 km from here. Greenville is 10 km from here.

   Greenville is _____ .

5. His parents are very strict. My parents are not very strict.

   My parents are _____ .

6. Mr. Plant has two children. Mr. Lane has four children.

   Mr. Plant has _____ .

7. I paint well. Ten years ago, I didn't paint well.

   I paint _____ .

8. There are five people in my family. There are five people in Irene Lee's family too.

   There are _____ .

9. My commute to work is 14 km. My colleague Mrs. Young has a 20 km commute, and my other colleague, Mr. Davis, travels 30 km to work.

   Of the three of us, I have _____ .

10. My grandmother is 80 years old. My grandfather is 78 years old.

    My grandfather isn't _____ .

B **Compare people and things you know. Use comparatives or as . . . as.**

Example: two friends—adventurous

   Megan is more adventurous than Matthew.

1. two friends—adventurous

   _____

2. two movies—funny

   _____

3. two books—long

   _____

4. two stores—expensive

   _____

5. two TV shows—good

   _____

(continued on page 80)

6. two singers—sing well

....

7. two family members—work hard

....

C **Complete each statement. Use your own idea in the first blank and a superlative in the second.**

1. *Liver*.......................... is *the worst*.......................... thing I've ever eaten.

2. .... is .... person I've ever met.

3. .... is .... place I've ever been.

4. .... is .... thing I've ever done.

5. .... is .... thing I've ever bought.

6. .... is .... thing I've ever said.

D **Challenge. Read each sentence. Then write a sentence with similar meaning, using a comparative, a superlative, or _as . . . as_.**

1. At 421 meters, the Jin Mao Building in Shanghai is very tall.

The Jin Mao Building in Shanghai is more than 400 meters tall.

2. The population of Greenland is only 59,827.

....

3. The movie we watched last night was so depressing.

....

4. Alexis McCarthy is becoming a very good violin player because she practices daily.

....

5. Sometimes he watches TV, but usually he reads.

....

6. The new French restaurant on City Avenue looks expensive, but it's really not.

....

Writing: Compare your generation with that of another family member

Choose a family member of a different generation from you, write about how your generations are different and how they are similar. (But, before you do, identify and correct the error in the previous sentence.)

Step 1. Prewriting. Organizing ideas. After you've chosen a family member of a different generation, label the circles in the diagram with your name and the family member's name. Then write differences between your two generations in each circle and similarities in the middle. Write quickly and don't worry about spelling, punctuation, etc.

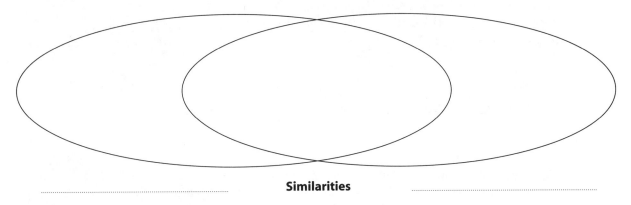

Similarities

Step 2. Writing. Write one or two paragraphs comparing the two generations you chose. Include a topic sentence that expresses your main idea. Avoid run-on sentences and comma splices.

Step 3. Self-Check.

☐ Did you write any run-on sentences? Comma splices? If so, correct them.

☐ Do all the sentences support the topic sentence?

☐ Are the paragraphs interesting? What could you add to make them more interesting?

History's Mysteries

PREVIEW

1 Read the stories below. Rate the probability that each is true.

1. A couple was on vacation in Australia, driving through the bush, when they accidentally hit a kangaroo. They decided to prop the kangaroo up and take a photo. To add a bit of humor, they dressed it up in the husband's jacket.

   As it turned out, the kangaroo was only stunned, not dead, and it hopped away with the jacket on. In the jacket pocket were the keys to their rental car and all their vacation money.

It's probably true.   It could be true.   I have no idea.   It can't be true.

2. A college student stayed up late studying for a math final exam. He overslept and arrived late for the test. He found three problems written on the board. He solved the first two pretty easily but struggled with the third. He worked frantically and figured out a solution just before the time was up.

   That night the student received a phone call from his professor, who told him that the third problem wasn't a test question. Before the test had started, the professor had explained that it was a problem previously thought to be unsolvable. But the student had solved it!

It's probably true.   It could be true.   I have no idea.   It can't be true.

3. A man was jogging through the park one day when another jogger lightly bumped him and excused himself. The man was just a little annoyed—until he realized that his wallet was missing. He immediately began chasing the jogger who'd bumped into him. He caught up to him and tackled him, yelling, "Give me that wallet!" The frightened "thief" handed over a wallet and quickly ran off.

   When the man got home, his wife asked him if he'd remembered to stop at the store. Anxious to tell his story, the man said that he hadn't, but that he had a good excuse. Before he finished, his wife said, "I know—you left your wallet on the dresser."

It's probably true.   It could be true.   I have no idea.   It can't be true.

Sources: www.warphead.com, www.snopes.com

2 Now put the conversation about the third story in order. Write numbers on the lines.

.... What? You've heard it before?

.... What happened?

.... It's a story that people pass on, about something unusual that happened to an ordinary person. A lot of people believe them, but they're usually not true.

___1___ You'll never guess what happened to a friend of a friend's husband.

.... Yeah, I have. The jogger took the other guy's wallet and then got home and realized he had left his wallet at home. It's an urban legend.

.... Wow. I had no idea. It seemed believable.

.... Well, he was jogging in the park, and this guy bumped into him. He thought the guy had stolen his wallet, so he chased him and tackled him . . .

.... What's an urban legend?

.... Don't tell me you buy that story!

3 Challenge. Do you know any urban legends or fantastic stories? Write one of them below.

....

....

....

....

....

....

LESSON 1

4 Read the questions below and answer the ones you can. If you don't know the answer, either guess (using <u>I'll bet</u> ...) or use phrases from Student's Book page 100 to say that you don't know.

1. Is someone with a <u>sanguine</u> personality optimistic or pessimistic? ....

2. Who composed *Swan Lake*? ....

3. Who's the richest person in the world? ....

4. What is the French term for high fashion? ....

5. What city has the world's largest subway system? ....

6. How long does the average elephant live? ....

7. When was the first TV commercial broadcast? ....

8. What country has the highest life expectancy? ....

5 Report on each person's phone message. Use indirect speech. Follow the example.

"Hey. It's Jack. I'm stuck in traffic. I'll be there as soon as I can."

1. _Jack said (that) he was stuck in traffic and (that) he would be there as soon as he could._

"Hi. It's Melanie. I have another meeting at 8:30. I may be late."

2. ....

"Hi. This is Allison. I can't come in today. My son isn't feeling well."

3. ....

"Hello. It's Alex. I have to make some copies. I'll be there by 9:15."

4. ....

6 Read the situation below. Then, for each of the times listed, write a sentence about what could have happened. Use the vocabulary from Student's Book page 101.

Your friend was supposed to arrive on the 8:05 train. You are waiting outside the station, but she still isn't there.

Example: (8:10) Not certain: _Maybe she's getting her luggage._

1. (8:10) Not certain: ....
2. (8:15) Somewhat certain: ....
3. (8:20) Almost certain: ....
4. (8:35) Very certain: ....

LESSON 2

7 Read the statements and check whether each speaker is <u>not certain</u>, <u>almost certain</u>, or <u>very certain</u>. Then rewrite each sentence, using a perfect modal in the passive voice. Use the appropriate degree of certainty.

	not certain	almost certain	very certain	
1.	☑	☐	☐	It's possible that language was developed to allow humans to hunt in groups more effectively.

Language may have been developed to allow humans to hunt in groups more effectively.

| **2.** | ☐ | ☐ | ☐ | Maybe the dinosaurs were killed by climate changes. |

| **3.** | ☐ | ☐ | ☐ | Probably the giant stone statues on Easter Island were carved by the ancestors of the Polynesian people who live there today. |

| **4.** | ☐ | ☐ | ☐ | Most likely Amelia Earhart was killed when her plane ran out of fuel and went down in the Pacific Ocean. |

| **5.** | ☐ | ☐ | ☐ | Clearly the fire was started intentionally. |

| **6.** | ☐ | ☐ | ☐ | There's no question the ship was sunk by a collision with an iceberg. |

8 Reading Warm-up. Look at the picture and caption. Then speculate about what happened to the *Mary Celeste*, using the perfect form of the modal <u>may</u> in the passive voice.

The *Mary Celeste* was discovered drifting off the coast of Portugal in 1872. There was no one aboard.

Example: *The crew may have been washed overboard by a giant wave.*

Your speculation: _____

9 **Reading.** Read more about the circumstances surrounding the disappearance of the *Mary Celeste*'s crew and passengers.

The *Mary Celeste*

On November 7, 1872, the *Mary Celeste* sailed under the command of Captain Benjamin Briggs—known as an honest and fair man. He, his wife, young daughter, and a crew of seven departed from New York City for Genoa, Italy, carrying a cargo of alcohol. They were never seen again.

On December 4, another ship spotted the *Mary Celeste* drifting off the coast of Portugal. A few men from the ship boarded the *Mary Celeste* to offer help. Although there was some damage, it was not extensive, and the ship was seaworthy. The cargo and a six-month supply of food and water were still on board the ship. However, nine of the 1,700 barrels of alcohol were empty, and the lifeboat and all of the

passengers and crew were missing. The last entry in the logbook was dated November 24, 1872.

Many theories have been proposed to explain the mystery of the disappearance of the *Mary Celeste*'s crew and passengers. Here are some of them:

• The crew killed Captain Briggs and his family and escaped in the lifeboat.

• The nine barrels of alcohol had leaked. Afraid the fumes would cause an explosion, Captain Briggs ordered everyone into the lifeboat. The lifeboat got separated from the ship, and its occupants drowned or died at sea.

• A giant octopus snatched the crew one by one from the deck of the ship.

SOURCE: www.en.wikipedia.org

Now speculate about the probability of each theory explaining the disappearance of the *Mary Celeste*'s passengers and crew. Use perfect modals in the passive voice. Explain your answers.

1. The theory that the captain was killed by the crew:

   ....

   ....

2. The theory that the crew was forced by alcohol fumes to leave the ship:

   ....

   ....

3. The theory that the crew was snatched from the ship by a giant octopus:

   ....

   ....

LESSON 3

10 Write the words from the box in order from least certain to most certain.

| believable | debatable | provable | questionable | unsolvable |

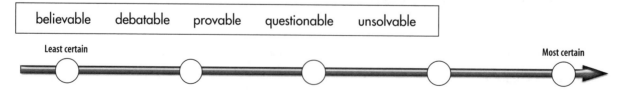

Least certain   Most certain

11 Use the words from Exercise 10 to complete the paragraph.

I recently received an e-mail message of _____ truthfulness. Of course,

1.
whether or not it's a good idea to even open these types of forwarded messages is

_____. However, I did open it. According to the e-mail story, a woman and

2.
her daughter had enjoyed a delicious cookie in the café of a high-end department store in
the United States. The cookie was so good that the woman asked for the recipe. The server
replied that woman could purchase the recipe for "two fifty." The woman agreed and
asked that the charge be added to her credit card bill. When the woman received her bill in
the mail, the charge for the cookie recipe was two hundred and fifty dollars—not two
dollars and fifty cents. I guess a lot of people must find this story _____,

3.
because the message keeps getting forwarded. Personally, I don't buy the story. Of course,
whether or not the story is true is not an _____ mystery. It's easily

4.
_____. All you would have to do is go to the store's café and ask to buy the

5.
cookie recipe—and pay in cash.

SOURCE: www.bl.net

12 **Challenge.** **Have you received similar types of e-mail messages, or have you
ever heard a story that you thought was questionable? Write the story below.
How believable is it? Is it provable?**

....

....

....

....

....

LESSON 4

13 **Reading Warm-up.** **Read the excerpt from the poem "The Puppet."**

. . . if only I had a scrap* of life . . .
I wouldn't let a single day go by without
saying to people I love that I love them.

I would convince each woman [and] man that
they are my favorites, and I would live in
love with love.

*scrap = a small piece of something

Speculate about the poem's author. Check the statement that you think is most likely.

☐ The author is in love.

☐ The author is dying.

☐ Other: _____

Gabriel García Márquez's Final Message

A poem signed with Gabriel García Márquez's name appeared in the Peruvian newspaper *La República* on May 29, 2000. The title of the poem was "La Marioneta," or "The Puppet." The newspaper reported that García Márquez had written the poem and sent it to his closest friends as a way to say good-bye to them. Apparently, García Márquez's health was poor and he expected to die soon.

Other newspapers quickly picked up the story. On May 30, many Mexico City newspapers published the poem. The poem appeared on the front page of the Mexican newspaper *La Crónica*. The poem was superimposed on the author's photo, and the newspaper's headline read, "Gabriel García Márquez sings a song to life." The poem quickly spread throughout the world via the Internet. Many people who read the poem were deeply moved. For example, the Indian filmmaker Mrinal Sen told the *Hindustan Times* that,

after reading the poem, he was flooded with memories of his twenty-year friendship with García Márquez.

However, it soon became clear that Gabriel García Márquez was not dying. Although he had been treated for lymphatic cancer in the summer of 1999, the rumors about his failing health were not true. It also became clear that the sentimental poem was not the work of the Nobel-prize-winning author. The poem was actually written by a Mexican ventriloquist named Johnny Welch. He had written the poem for his puppet, "Mofles." No one is sure how his name was replaced by García Márquez's.

Source: www.museumofhoaxes.com

Now answer questions about the article.

1. What did the newspaper articles claim about Gabriel García Márquez?

   ....

2. Which do you think is more likely: The newspapers looked for evidence of the poem's authenticity, or the newspapers rushed to print the poem?

   ....

3. Do you think Johnny Welch was a forger? Explain your answer.

   ....

4. If you'd read the story in *La República*, *La Crónica*, or the *Hindustan Times*, do you think you would have believed it?

   ....

15 Challenge. **How do you think the Internet has affected the spread of questionable claims and stories?**

   ....

   ....

   ....

Grammar Booster

A Read the sentences. Then use <u>said</u>, <u>told</u>, or <u>asked</u> to rewrite each quote as indirect speech.

1. Sonia: "Oh, Robert, I saw Paul at the supermarket."

   Sonia told Robert that she had seen Paul at the supermarket.

2. The salesperson: "Neil, the video cameras may go on sale tomorrow."

3. Stephen: "I have to work tonight."

4. Caroline: "Can I turn on the TV?"

5. Allen: "OK, kids, you have to clean up your toys."

6. Professor Johnson: "Class, did you complete the assignment?"

B Rewrite the quotations as indirect speech. Use reporting verbs from the box. (You will not use all the reporting verbs.)

add	answer	complain	explain	mention	remark	reveal
announce	comment	exclaim	maintain	promise	report	write

1. "The economy will improve." —*The president*

   The president promised that the economy would improve.

2. "My client cannot be guilty of the charges." —*The attorney*

3. "There is no scientific evidence of negative side effects." —*Smith Pharmaceuticals*

4. "The earthquake has left one million people homeless." —*The Daily Journal*

5. "We may have to lay off some employees." —*Strauss-Lyon, Inc.*

6. "My team will make the championships this year!" —*Coach Moore*

7. "There aren't enough services for poor families." —*Anna Graham, Director of City Kids*

Writing: *Write about an interesting experience*

Step 1. Prewriting. **Generating ideas with information questions.**

Think about something interesting that you did or experienced in the past. The experience you've chosen will be your topic. Write information questions about the topic to help generate ideas.

Topic: _____

Who? _____

What? _____

When? _____

Where? _____

Why? _____

How? _____

A New Friend

Last summer I made a new friend while on vacation in Italy. I was hiking in a region called Cinque Terre when I met a man named Flavio. We discovered that we both spoke English, and we began talking. We got along so well that he invited me back to his family's home for lunch. I met his mother, father, and brothers and sisters. His mother made a delicious lunch, and we ate it in their beautiful home overlooking the ocean. I spent a delightful afternoon with Flavio and his family, and by the end of the day we were friends. We still write to each other, and I plan to visit again next year.

Step 2. Writing. Write about the experience, answering your questions from Step 1. Try to include as much information as you can. Choose a title that reflects your main idea.

_____

_____

_____

_____

_____

_____

_____

_____

_____

_____

Step 3. Self-Check.

☐ Did you write any sentence fragments? If so, correct them.

☐ Do you have a clear topic sentence?

☐ Is your writing interesting? Could you add any more details?

Your Free Time

PREVIEW

1 Answer the questions.

1. How does the Internet help people save time? ....
   ....

2. List some ways the Internet takes away from people's free time. ....
   ....
   ....

3. Do you consider surfing the Web a leisure activity? Why or why not? ....
   ....
   ....

2 What About You? Complete the survey.

About how much time do you spend on the Internet each day? ....
What do you do on the Internet? Check all the activities you engage in.

    ◯ e-mail   ◯ music

    ◯ news   ◯ chat/instant messaging

    ◯ games   ◯ information searches

    ◯ shopping   ◯ surfing

    ◯ banking   ◯ other: ....

Do you think you spend too much time online? ....

If you didn't have Internet access, what would you spend more time doing?

....

....

Factoid South Koreans spend more time surfing the Web than any other nation, at an average of 16 hours and 17 minutes spent each month.

SOURCES: www.bizjournals.com, www.acnielsen.com

3 Challenge. **Look at the graphs. What happens as people spend more time on the Internet? Write sentences about each graph, using double comparatives. Refer to Student's Book page 88 if you need to review double comparatives.**

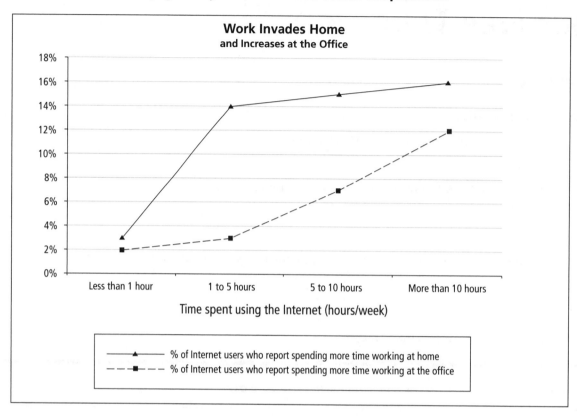

Work Invades Home
and Increases at the Office

Time spent using the Internet (hours/week)

— ▲ — % of Internet users who report spending more time working at home
- - ■ - - % of Internet users who report spending more time working at the office

1. *The more time people spend on the Internet, the more time they spend working at home.*

2. ....

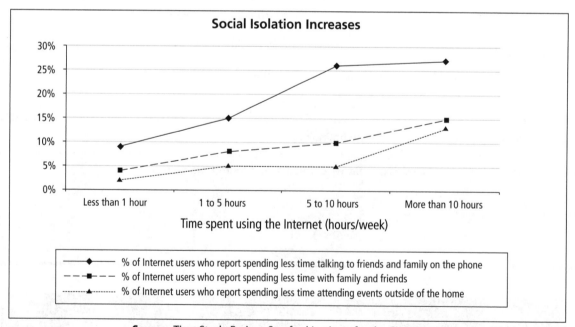

Social Isolation Increases

Time spent using the Internet (hours/week)

— ◆ — % of Internet users who report spending less time talking to friends and family on the phone
- - ■ - - % of Internet users who report spending less time with family and friends
·······▲······· % of Internet users who report spending less time attending events outside of the home

Source: Time Study Project, Stanford Institute for the Quantitative Study of Society (SIQSS)

3. ....

4. ....

5. ....

LESSON 1

4 Give your opinion of the leisure activities below. Use adjectives from the box or your own adjectives.

annoying	challenging	difficult	entertaining	fascinating	interesting	stimulating
boring	costly	dull	exciting	fun	relaxing	unusual

1. Go: *I've never played, but I think Go sounds fascinating.*

2. Karate: ....

3. Chess: ....

4. Aerobics: ....

5. Yoga: ....

6. Ping-pong: ....

7. Embroidery: ....

8. Wood carving: ....

5 Think of an activity that you are interested in taking up and one that you are **not** interested in. Use them to complete the two conversations below.

A: You should give .... a try. I'm sure you'd like it.

You: ....

A: You should give .... a try. I'm sure you'd like it.

You: ....

6 Complete each collocation for leisure activities with the correct verb. Then, circle the adverbs and underline the words or phrases they modify. Finally, write **V** (verb) or **A** (adjective) above each underlined word or phrase.

1. I .... yoga. It's a great workout, and I find it emotionally soothing.

2. I .... video games. I know what you're thinking, but video games do have benefits. My favorite ones are intellectually stimulating.

3. My friends and I .... embroidery. Not only is it a fun way to interact socially, but it also pays off financially. We sell what we make.

4. I .... antiques – mostly furniture. It keeps me busy and active. It's actually a lot more physically demanding than most people realize.

What leisure activity do you do? What are the benefits? Use an adverb in your answer.

....

....

LESSON 2

7 Describe the clothing, shoes, and accessories you're wearing right now. Use as many modifiers as you can.

Example: *I'm wearing my comfortable new green leather boots.*

_____

_____

8 In the circles below are collectors' names and the objects they collect. Surrounding each circle are modifiers describing the most valuable item in each collection. Write a one-sentence description of each item, using the words from the diagram.

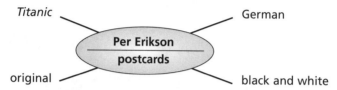

1. _Per Erikson has an original black-and-white German Titanic postcard._

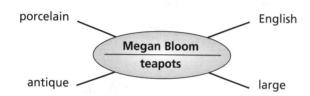

2. _____

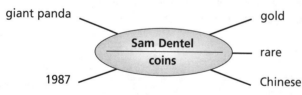

3. (Challenge) _____

Now think of something special that you have. Write the item and words to describe it in the diagram.

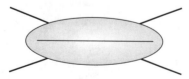

Use the modifiers from your diagram to write a one-sentence description of your item.

_____

9 Complete the second sentence in each pair, using a compound modifier. Remember to hyphenate.

1. This vase is three hundred years old. It's a _____ vase.

2. Yoga classes usually last one and a half hours. They're _____ classes.

3. The diamond in her ring is two carats. She has a _____ diamond ring.

4. The book I'm reading has nine hundred pages. It's a _____ book.

5. The Internet was invented in the twentieth century. It's a _____ invention.

6. That mountain bike costs a thousand dollars. It's a _____ mountain bike.

LESSON 3

10 How do new technological tools make people's lives easier? How do they take away from leisure time? Name one positive aspect and one negative aspect of each of the technologies listed.

Technology	Positive	Negative
cell phones		
PDAs		
laptops		
e-mail		
voice mail		

11 Read the article on Student's Book page 116 again. Then complete the sentence below in three different ways, using double comparatives.

According to the author, the more we use new technological tools, . . .

. . . _____ .

. . . _____ .

. . . _____ .

12 Think about your day yesterday. Answer the questions.

1. How many hours did you spend working or studying? _____

2. How much free time did you have? What did you do? _____

_____

3. If you work, did you work after hours? What technological tools did you use to do your work?

_____

4. Did you talk to any friends yesterday? If so, did you see them in person, talk to them on the phone, or send them an e-mail or an instant message? _____

_____

13 Look at the list of technological tools below. First, circle the ones you have or use. Then, indicate how difficult it would be for you to live without each.

How difficult would it be to live without _____?	not difficult at all	somewhat difficult	extremely difficult
a cell phone	○	○	○
a PDA	○	○	○
a laptop	○	○	○
e-mail	○	○	○
the Internet	○	○	○
voice mail	○	○	○
a fax machine	○	○	○

According to a survey done by the British magazine *Personnel Today* and Websense International, 72% of British companies have dealt with employees' accessing the Internet for personal use.

SOURCE: www.out-law.com

Of the technological tools listed, which would be the most difficult for you to live without? Why?

....

....

14 Reading. Read the article.

Work at Home, Play at Work

Thanks to the Internet and other relatively new technological tools, more and more employees work after hours. They check their e-mail before they go to bed at night, take business calls while out to dinner with friends, and check their PDAs at family picnics. Nowadays, if you're sick, you don't have to take a day off. Why waste a day sleeping and watching movies when, with a laptop and an Internet connection, you can work from home? It seems that the line between work and leisure has become blurry and that more technology for work has meant less time for ourselves.

However, technology has not only helped work invade people's leisure time, but it has also allowed people to engage in leisure-time activities at work. With the computer on your office desk, you can leave work virtually. You can check the score of last night's game, do a little shopping, catch up on the news, order concert tickets, plan a vacation, chat with your friends, or just browse the Web. You can appear to be working hard—plugging away at your computer—when in reality you're reading a fashion magazine online.

According to a recent survey by California-based Websense, more than half of the employees questioned said they spent between one and five hours a day surfing the Internet at work for personal reasons. There are even websites dedicated to keeping bored workers amused while they wait for the end of the work day. A psychotherapist who treats Internet addiction explains, "It's like having a TV at everyone's desk. People can watch whatever they want and do whatever they want."

Perhaps a more definite separation of work and home life would be better not only for employees but also for employers. It's not healthy for workers to have access to work 24/7*. And maybe if employees weren't busy working at night and on the weekends, they wouldn't have to e-mail their friends while they're at work.

* 24/7 = 24 hours a day, 7 days a week

SOURCE: www.post-gazette.com

Now complete each sentence with a word or phrase from the article.

1. If something is not clear, it's ....

2. When something unwanted interferes with your time, it .... your time.

3. If you do something on a computer, rather than in the real world, you do it

....

4. If you're working hard at something, you're .... at it.

5. If you do something all the time, you do it ....

15 **Answer the questions, using information from the article in Exercise 14.**

1. What are some ways people are able to work from home? ....

....

2. What are some ways people are able to engage in leisure-time activities at work?

....

3. What's the author's point of view in the article? ....

....

4. Do you agree with the author's point of view? Why or why not? ....

....

LESSON 4

16 **What's your opinion? Place each of the extreme sports under one of the four categories in the chart.**

bungee jumping	mountain biking	surfing
extreme skiing	rock climbing	waterfall jumping
hang gliding	skydiving	white water rafting

I've already done it.	I can't wait to try it.	It could be fun.	Not a chance!

17 Take the quiz to see if you have a risk-taking personality.

---

www.adventurequiz.com ☐☐✕

QUIZ   Are you a risk taker or a risk avoider?

1. Which type of movie would you rather watch?
   - ○ **a.** scary
   - ○ **b.** funny

2. Which would you rather do at an amusement park?
   - ○ **a.** go on a roller coaster
   - ○ **b.** see a show

3. Which sentence describes you better?
   - ○ **a.** I love trying new things.
   - ○ **b.** I prefer to stick close to home.

4. Which genre of music would you rather listen to?
   - ○ **a.** urban dance
   - ○ **b.** pop

5. What kind of clothes do you wear? Pick one adjective from each pair.
   - ○ **a.** trendy
   - ○ **b.** classic

   - ○ **a.** flashy
   - ○ **b.** subdued

   - ○ **a.** shocking
   - ○ **b.** tasteful

6. Which do you prefer? Pick one choice from each pair.
   - ○ **a.** to stand out in a crowd
   - ○ **b.** to conform

   - ○ **a.** fast-paced city life
   - ○ **b.** slower pace of the country or suburbs

7. What are your shopping habits?
   - ○ **a.** impulse buying
   - ○ **b.** comparison shopping

8. How do you spend your free time?
   - ○ **a.** I find something exciting to do.
   - ○ **b.** I catch up on work and chores.

9. Which would you rather take up?
   - ○ **a.** karate
   - ○ **b.** embroidery

10. Pick the adjective or phrase that best describes you from each of the following pairs.
    - ○ **a.** thrill-seeking
    - ○ **b.** conservative
    - ○ **a.** a troublemaker
    - ○ **b.** well-behaved

    - ○ **a.** rebellious
    - ○ **b.** obedient
    - ○ **a.** self-confident
    - ○ **b.** nervous

    - ○ **a.** aggressive
    - ○ **b.** cautious
    - ○ **a.** energetic
    - ○ **b.** calm

    - ○ **a.** adventurous
    - ○ **b.** prefer routine
    - ○ **a.** outgoing
    - ○ **b.** shy

Count up your score.
How many <u>a</u>'s did you check? _____
How many <u>b</u>'s did you check? _____

0–5 <u>a</u> answers: You probably have a "small T" personality. You don't like thrills and prefer to avoid them. You're among the faint of heart. You prefer certainty and routine. But don't get too set in your ways. A little adventure from time to time would do you some good.

6–11 <u>a</u> answers: You fall somewhere in the middle of the risk-taking continuum. You're probably willing to take some risks from time to time, but maybe prefer to avoid risk in general. Sounds like you live a pretty balanced life.

12–20 <u>a</u> answers: You probably have a "big T" personality. You love thrills and can't get enough of them. You're happiest living on the edge. You like to take risks and do new things. Remember: risk-taking can be the key to success, but it can also get you into trouble. Make an effort to exercise some caution.

How do your quiz results compare with your answer to Exercise B on Student's Book page 118? If they differ, which do you think is more accurate? Explain.

....

....

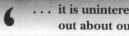

> " . . . it is uninteresting to do easy things. We find
> out about ourselves only when we take risks,
> when we challenge and question.
> —Magdalena Abakanowicz, Polish artist, born 1930

SOURCE: www.wisdomquotes.com

Grammar Booster

A Complete the sentences with appropriate intensifiers.

1. He has a _____ interesting hobby.
2. I find yoga _____ boring.
3. My mother is _____ interested in ancient history.
4. She's _____ good about keeping in touch with her friends.
5. He's a _____ skilled dancer.
6. Our company uses some _____ advanced technology.
7. Mr. James is _____ busy at work right now.
8. She says that playing the guitar is _____ challenging.

B Complete the sentences with adverbs of manner from the box. Use each adverb only once.

angrily	beautifully	fairly	hard	softly	quickly

1. We walked _____, because we were late.
2. Their daughter was sleeping, so they spoke _____.
3. After arguing with his father, he _____ left the room.
4. She's quite a musician. She plays the clarinet _____.
5. You must treat your friends _____.
6. Mrs. Young works _____ all week long.

C Write your own sentences, using the adverbs in parentheses.

1. (well) _____
2. (poorly) _____
3. (suddenly) _____
4. (sadly) _____
5. (slowly) _____

Writing: Comment on another's point of view

Step 1. Prewriting. Developing arguments.

Read the article "Work at Home, Play at Work" on page 96 and underline sentences that you agree with or do not agree with. Then do the following:

- Paraphrase each sentence you underlined.
- Provide the reasons why you agree or disagree.

The author says that technology has allowed people to engage in leisure-time activities at work. I agree because I know a lot of people who use the Internet at work for personal reasons.

....

....

....

....

....

....

....

....

Step 2. Writing.
Write a critique of the article. State your own opinion at the beginning. Use the sentences you underlined and the comments you wrote to support your opinion.

....

....

....

....

....

....

....

....

....

....

....

....

....

....

Step 3. Self-Check.

- ☐ Is your opinion clearly stated?
- ☐ Did you use connecting words to support your reasons and sequence your ideas?
- ☐ Did you use quotation marks when using the author's own words?
- ☐ Did you paraphrase the author's words when you didn't use direct speech?

NELSON MANDELA

NELSON MANDELA

THE AUTHORIZED COMIC BOOK

NELSON MANDELA FOUNDATION

WITH

UMLANDO WEZITHOMBE

W. W. NORTON & COMPANY
NEW YORK · LONDON

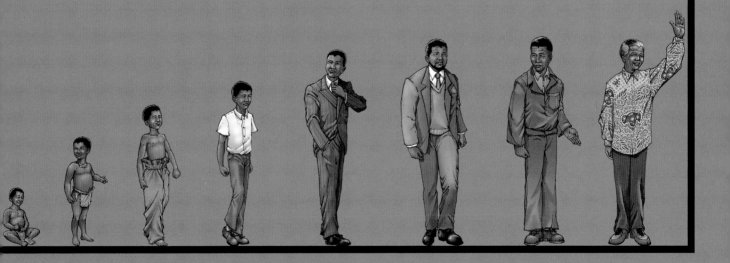

NELSON MANDELA
FOUNDATION
Living the Legacy

The Nelson Mandela Foundation, through its Nelson Mandela Centre of Memory and Dialogue, contributes to the making of a just society by promoting the vision and work of its founder and convening Dialogue around critical social issues. The Centre was inaugurated by Nelson Mandela on September 21, 2004.

Umlando Wezithombe produces accessible educational comic books. The visual medium is used to cross cultural boundaries and deliver material that addresses a range of literacy levels. Umlando specializes in using the visual medium to address awareness on subjects that include history, HIV/AIDS, healthy living, pandemics, and life skills.

Copyright © 2009, 2008 by The Nelson Mandela Foundation
First American Edition 2009
First published by Jonathan Ball Publishers in South Africa in 2008

For information about permission to reproduce selections from this book, write to Permissions, W. W. Norton & Company, Inc., 500 Fifth Avenue, New York, NY 10110

For information about special discounts for bulk purchases, please contact W. W. Norton Special Sales at specialsales@wwnorton.com or 800-233-4830

Manufacturing by RR Donnelley, Shenzhen
Design and reproduction by Umlando Wezithombe
Production managers: Joe Lops and Devon Zahn

Library of Congress Cataloging-in-Publication Data

Nelson Mandela : the authorized comic book / Nelson Mandela Foundation
with Umlando Wezithombe. — 1st American ed.
p. cm.
Includes bibliographical references and index.
ISBN 978-0-393-07082-8 (hardcover : alk. paper) — ISBN 978-0-393-33646-7 (pbk. : alk. paper)
1. Mandela, Nelson, 1918– —Comic books, strips, etc. 2. Presidents—South Africa—Comic books, strips, etc.
3. Political activists—South Africa—Comic books, strips, etc. 4. Presidents—South Africa—Biography—Comic books,
strips, etc. 5. Political activists—South Africa—Biography—Comic books, strips, etc.
I. Nelson Mandela Foundation. II. Umlando Wezithombe (Firm)
DT1974.N47 2009
968.06′5092—dc22
[B]

2009001695

W. W. Norton & Company, Inc.
500 Fifth Avenue, New York, N.Y. 10110
www.wwnorton.com

W. W. Norton & Company Ltd.
Castle House, 75/76 Wells Street, London W1T 3QT

1 2 3 4 5 6 7 8 9 0

CONTENTS

MESSAGE FROM NELSON MANDELA   IX

1 A SON OF THE EASTERN CAPE   1

2 BECOMING A LEADER   25

3 THE BLACK PIMPERNEL   49

4 THE TRIALIST   73

5 PRISONER 466/64   97

6 THE NEGOTIATOR   121

7 PRESIDENT—IN—WAITING   145

8 MR. PRESIDENT   169

INDEX   194

ACKNOWLEDGMENTS   197

MESSAGE FROM NELSON MANDELA*

I am not an expert on the subject of comics. And it would be unwise for me to discuss myself as the main character in the comic. We human beings tend to exaggerate most when we are talking about ourselves. So, I will leave exaggeration to historians and other experts.

Now, my Chief Executive tells me that he is an expert on comics. And he advises me that they have three very important qualities. Firstly, for those, like me, whose eyesight is not what it was, there is the option of simply looking at the pictures. Secondly, you know that you are really famous the day that you discover that you have become a comic character. And thirdly, young people read comics. The hope is that the elementary reading of comics will lead them to the joy of reading good books. That joy has been mine all my life. If the comic reaches new readers, then the project will have been worthwhile.

But we believe that all readers will find something of value in this comic. The artwork in the comic is of a high standard, and we congratulate the team of young artists who worked on it. They have expressed very well the themes and narratives chosen by the historians and writers who guided them. Three themes in particular are given prominence—"tradition," "community," and "story." And it is so that these themes, or values, played an important role in shaping my early life. Indeed, they have been shaping influences throughout my life.

Let me recount a story to illustrate this. Recently a friend of mine pointed out that when I first went to prison the concept of "non-sexism" was hardly known, and yet when I was released twenty-seven years later I was a champion of women's rights. Then he asked: "How did you catch up with the world so fast?" (As you can see, my friends enjoy asking me difficult questions.) The answer, of course, is not simple. One of the few advantages of prison life is that one has the time to read. In prison we read as widely as the circumstances allowed, and we discovered literature which opened our minds and forced us to reexamine some of our views. Prison also gave us time for reflection. And I thought much about the history of the place where I was born and brought up—Thembuland. As I reflected on Thembu history, I was reminded of the many women who played a prominent role in that history. I remembered their stories. I remembered many stories of women having taken leadership positions.

All of us are experts in listening to stories. All of us have the *potential* to be experts in telling stories and in reading stories. It is our hope that the comic will promote this understanding.

N. R. Mandela

---

* This is an edited version of a speech given by Nelson Mandela in Johannesburg on October 28, 2005, at the launch of the comic series on which this book is based.

A SON OF THE EASTERN CAPE

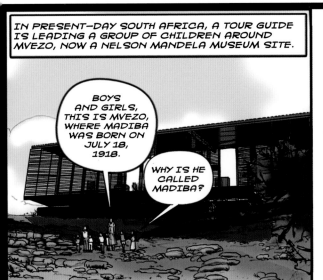

IN PRESENT-DAY SOUTH AFRICA, A TOUR GUIDE IS LEADING A GROUP OF CHILDREN AROUND MVEZO, NOW A NELSON MANDELA MUSEUM SITE.

BOYS AND GIRLS, THIS IS MVEZO, WHERE MADIBA WAS BORN ON JULY 18, 1918.

WHY IS HE CALLED MADIBA?

MADIBA IS NELSON ROLIHLAHLA MANDELA'S CLAN NAME.

NELSON'S FATHER, MPHAKANYISWA GADLA MANDELA, WAS THE CHIEF OF MVEZO. IT IS PART OF THE THEMBU KINGDOM...

...WHICH FORMED PART OF THE GREATER XHOSA NATION.

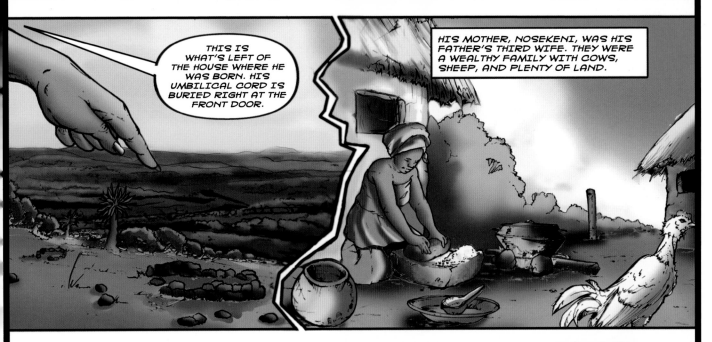

THIS IS WHAT'S LEFT OF THE HOUSE WHERE HE WAS BORN. HIS UMBILICAL CORD IS BURIED RIGHT AT THE FRONT DOOR.

HIS MOTHER, NOSEKENI, WAS HIS FATHER'S THIRD WIFE. THEY WERE A WEALTHY FAMILY WITH COWS, SHEEP, AND PLENTY OF LAND.

THE SOUTH AFRICAN GOVERNMENT CONTROLLED TRADITIONAL CHIEFS. THE GOVERNMENT APPOINTED, DISMISSED, AND ADMINISTERED CHIEFS THROUGH LOCAL MAGISTRATES.

...AND THE YOUNG ROLIHLAHLA'S FATHER WAS IN BIG TROUBLE...

BRING ME MPHAKANYISWA NOW!!

YES SIR!

CHIEF MPHAKANYISWA HAD NOT REPORTED A TRIBAL MATTER TO THE MAGISTRATE AS WAS REQUIRED.

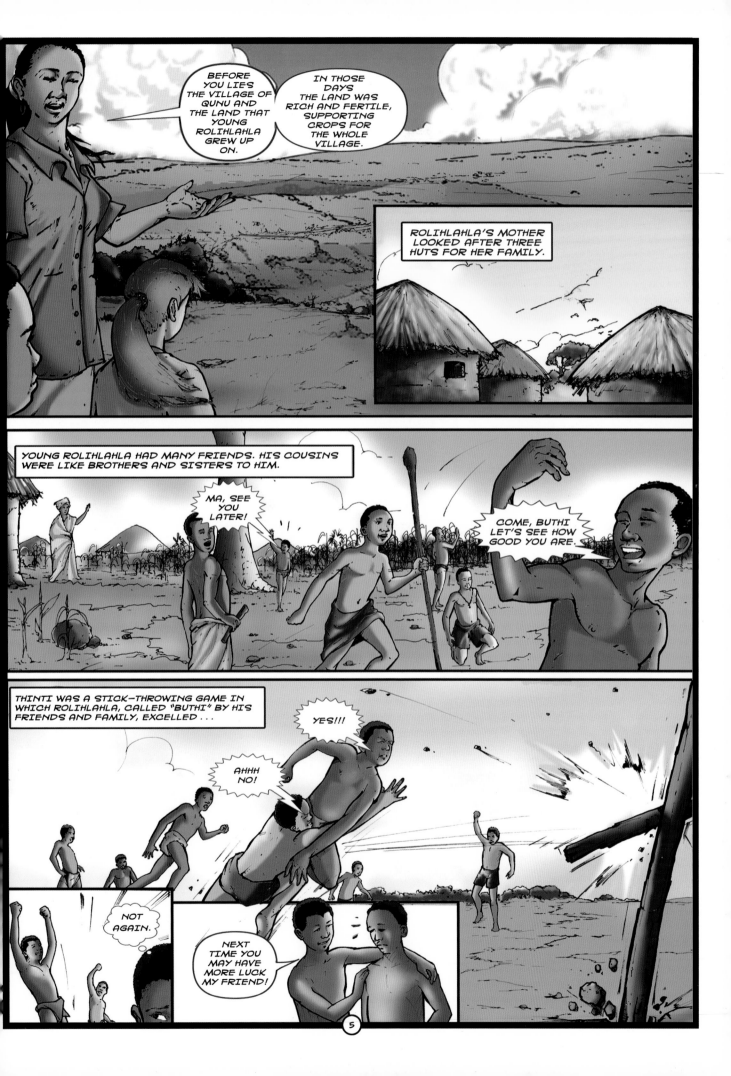

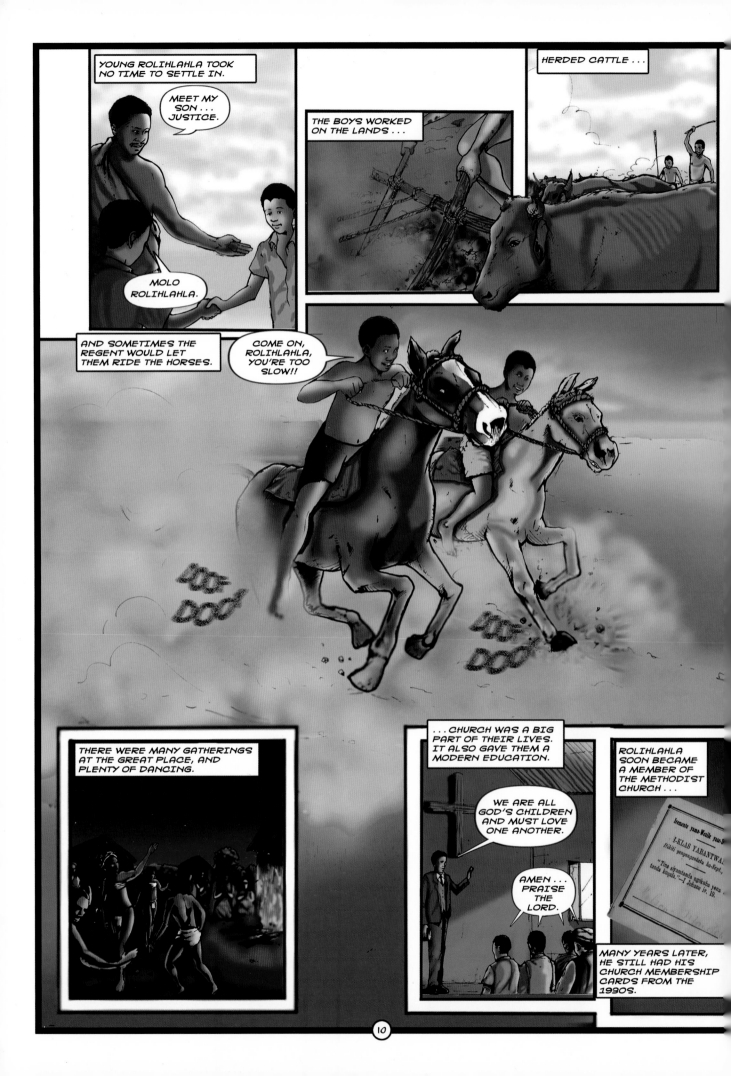

WHEN BIG DECISIONS HAD TO BE MADE, THE CLANS GATHERED AT THE GREAT PLACE.

MY PEOPLE ARE WORRIED . . .

THERE WERE FEASTS AT THESE BIG GATHERINGS.

ALL THAT LISTENING HAS MADE YOU HUNGRY, ROLIHLAHLA!

GRR GE

AT THE GATHERINGS, EVERY VOICE WAS HEARD, AND NO OPINION DISCOUNTED. WOMEN, HOWEVER, COULD ONLY BE OBSERVERS.

IT WAS THE REGENT'S DUTY TO SUM UP ALL THE POINTS OF VIEW AND TO FIND ANSWERS TO PROBLEMS.

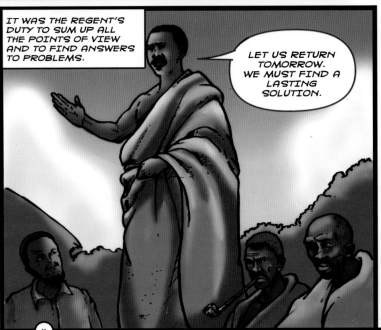

LET US RETURN TOMORROW. WE MUST FIND A LASTING SOLUTION.

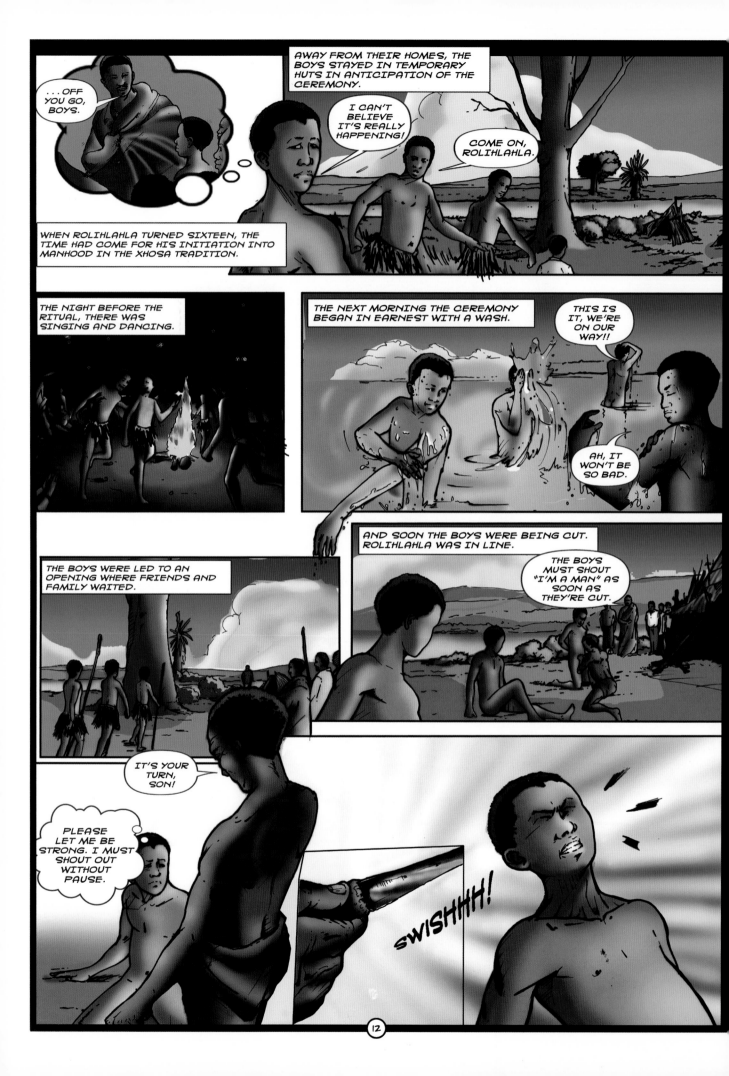

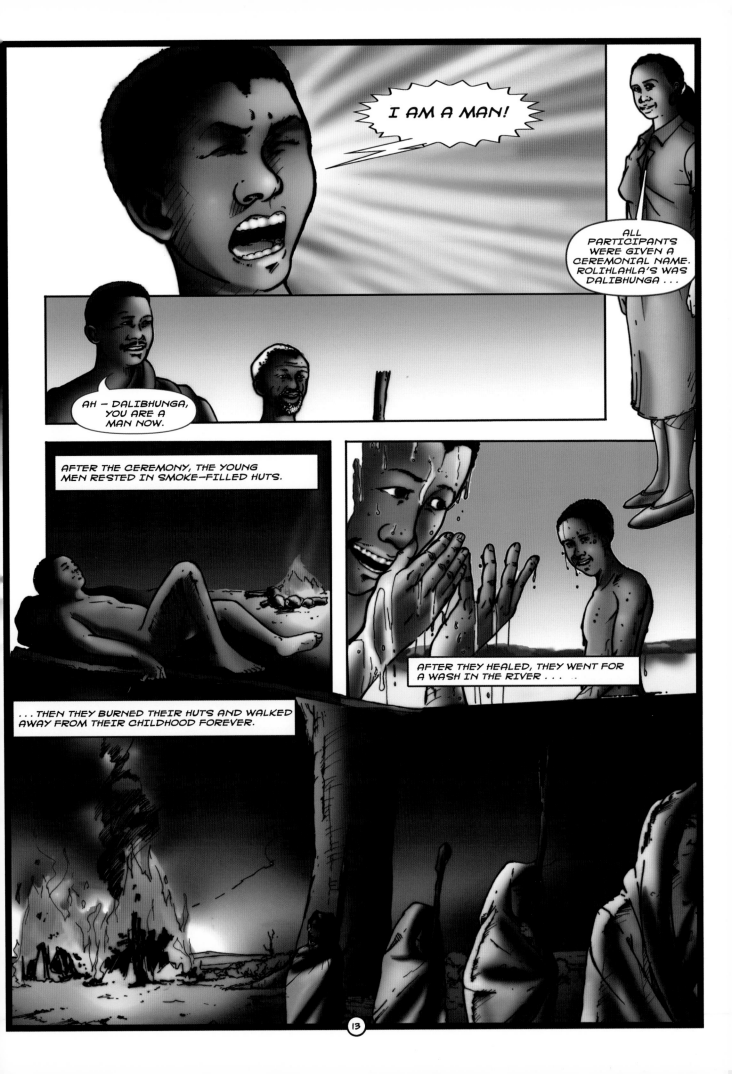

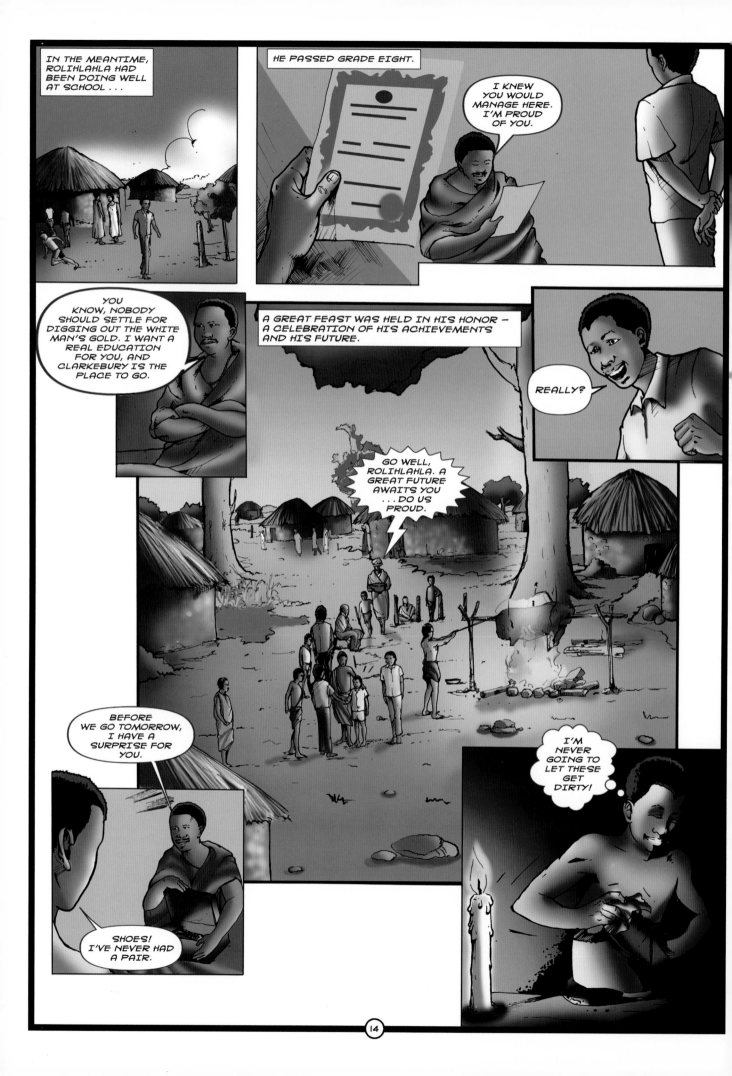

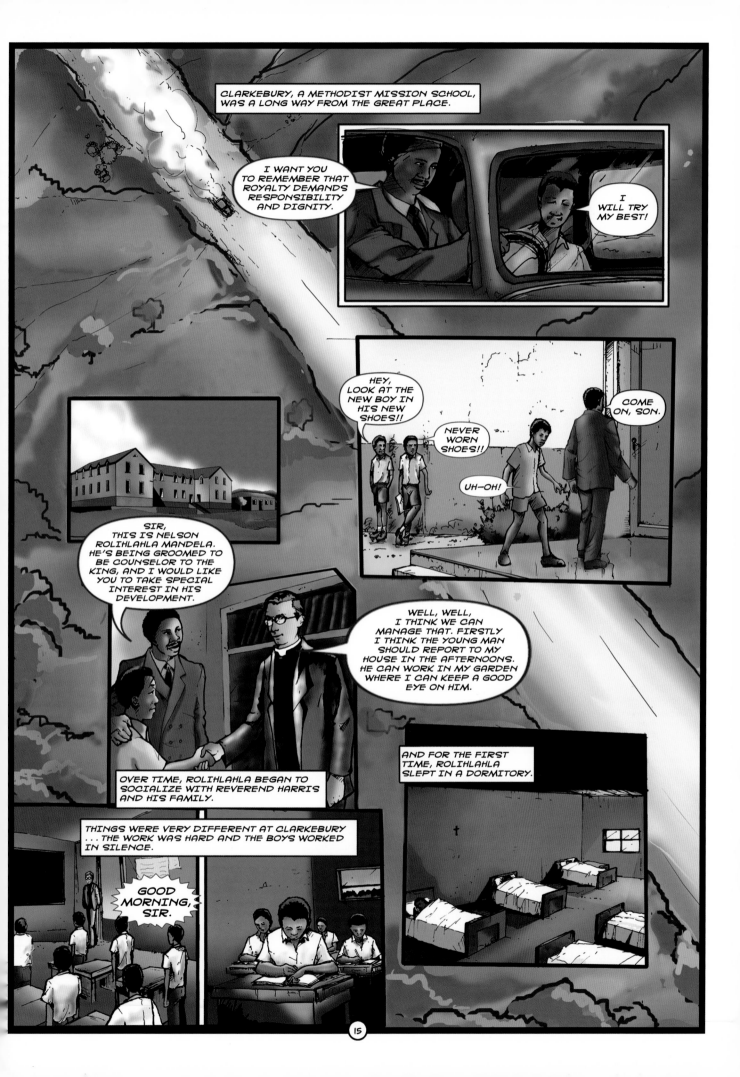

AFTER HEALDTOWN, THE TWENTY-ONE-YEAR-OLD ROLIHLAHLA'S NEXT STEP WAS FORT HARE UNIVERSITY, THE TRAINING GROUND OF MANY INFLUENTIAL AFRICAN LEADERS.

HE STUDIED ENGLISH, POLITICS, ANTHROPOLOGY, ROMAN DUTCH LAW, AND NATIVE ADMINISTRATION.

I'VE BEEN MEANING TO INTRODUCE YOU TWO. I THINK YOU WILL GET ALONG . . .

ROLIHLAHLA NELSON MANDELA, MEET KAISER MATANZIMA.

KAISER MATANZIMA WAS A NEPHEW OF MANDELA'S, AND MUCH LATER HE BECAME A POLITICAL OPPONENT. ROLIHLAHLA ADDRESSED HIM BY HIS CIRCUMCISION NAME, DALIWONGA.

ROLIHLAHLA ALSO MET OLIVER TAMBO AT FORT HARE.

OLIVER, WITHOUT YOU WE WOULD HAVE LOST THAT DEBATE . . .

HE LOVED BALLROOM DANCING, AND SOMETIMES ROLIHLAHLA AND HIS FRIENDS SNEAKED OUT TO PARTIES . . .

MAY I HAVE THIS DANCE?

YOU DANCE BEAUTIFULLY . . .

ON ONE OCCASION, HE DISCOVERED THAT HE WAS DANCING WITH A UNIVERSITY PROFESSOR'S WIFE.

HE ENJOYED SOCIALIZING WITH FRIENDS. DOING SIMPLE THINGS REMINDED HIM OF HOME . . .

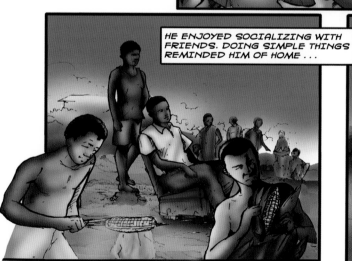

HE PLAYED SOCCER, RAN CROSS-COUNTRY, JOINED THE DRAMA SOCIETY, AND GOT INVOLVED IN STUDENT POLITICS.

IN 1940, ROLIHLAHLA FACED A PERSONAL CRISIS.

THE ONLY WAY TO BRING ABOUT MEANINGFUL CHANGE IS TO BOYCOTT THE STUDENT COUNCIL ELECTIONS!

YES, WE WILL PLAY NO PART . . .

THE PRINCIPAL, DR. ALEXANDER KERR, HAD OTHER IDEAS . . .

I WANT YOUR VOTES BY THE END OF THE DAY.

. . . AND THE MEMBERS OF THE COUNCIL ARE . . .

SIX OF THE STUDENTS WERE ELECTED TO THE COUNCIL.

KNOCK KNOCK

ROLIHLAHLA WAS SUMMONED TO DR. KERR'S OFFICE . . .

MANDELA! IF YOU DON'T TAKE UP YOUR SEAT, YOU WILL HAVE TO LEAVE THE UNIVERSITY . . .

SORRY, SIR, I WON'T BE TAKING UP THE SEAT. I AM STANDING WITH THE BOYCOTT OF THE ELECTION . . .

THINK ABOUT IT, AND LET ME KNOW TOMORROW.

DALIWONGA, I FEEL I AM RIGHT, ALTHOUGH ALL OF THE OTHERS ARE TAKING UP THEIR POSITIONS.

YES, BUT YOU CAN'T GIVE IN, AND THAT COULD BE THE END OF YOUR HOPES TO BE A LAWYER!

A UNIVERSITY EDUCATION WAS A RARE PRIVILEGE GRANTED TO FEW BLACK SOUTH AFRICANS.

BUT I JUST CAN'T DO IT!

YOU ARE MAKING A MISTAKE!

BUT GO AND SPEND THE SUMMER THINKING ABOUT THIS. IF YOU DON'T CHANGE YOUR MIND, DON'T BOTHER COMING BACK . . .

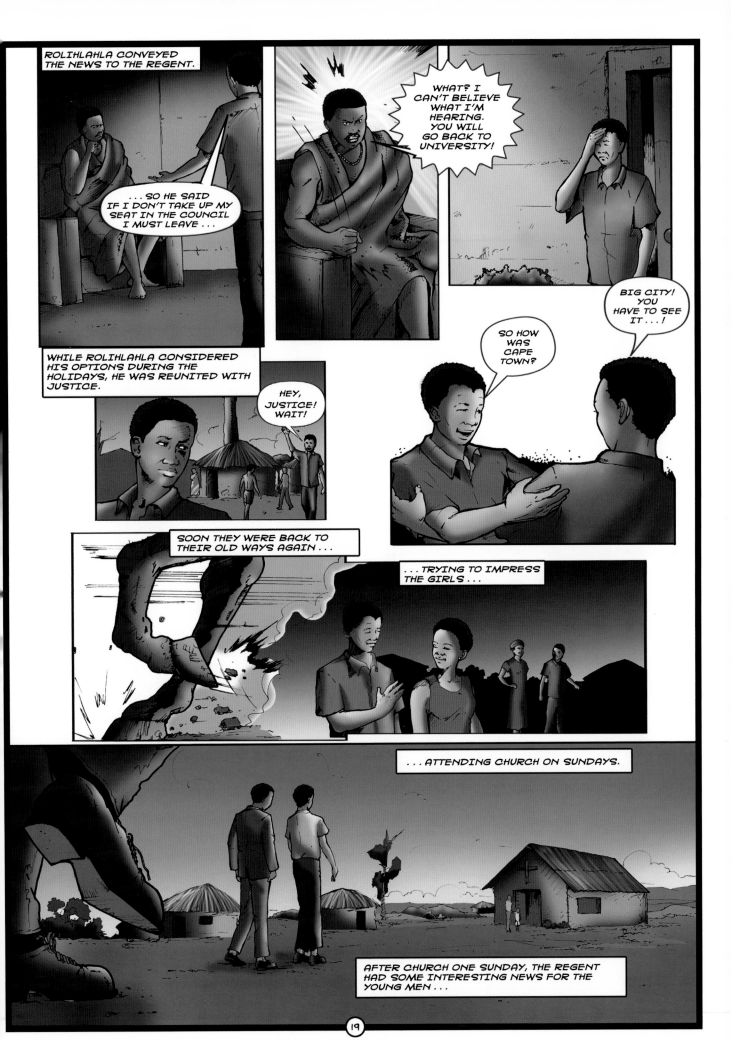

THINGS WERE ABOUT TO CHANGE . . .

THE REGENT HAD ARRANGED FOR THE TWO OF THEM TO GET MARRIED . . .

JUSTICE! ROLIHLAHLA! COME HERE, IT'S TIME WE TALK LIKE MEN!

WHAT!

NOO!

THIS WAS A MOMENT FOR ROLIHLAHLA WHEN TRADITION CLASHED WITH PERSONAL DESTINY.

THIS IS HOW IT WILL BE . . . AND THAT'S FINAL.

THERE IS ONLY ONE THING TO DO . . . WE HAVE TO RUN AWAY.

TO JOHANNESBURG . . .

. . . WE'VE GOT NO TIME TO WASTE.

WHAT ABOUT MONEY?

DON'T WORRY, I HAVE AN IDEA!

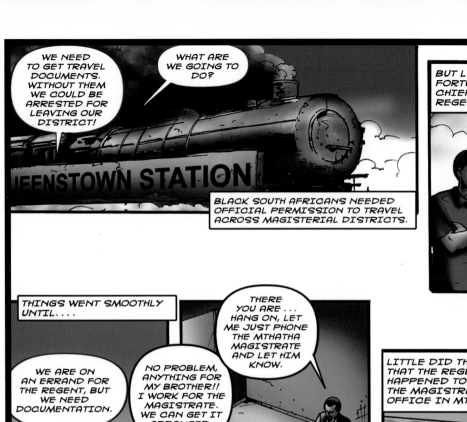

WE NEED TO GET TRAVEL DOCUMENTS. WITHOUT THEM WE COULD BE ARRESTED FOR LEAVING OUR DISTRICT!

WHAT ARE WE GOING TO DO?

QUEENSTOWN STATION

BLACK SOUTH AFRICANS NEEDED OFFICIAL PERMISSION TO TRAVEL ACROSS MAGISTERIAL DISTRICTS.

BUT LUCK WAS ON THEIR SIDE. FORTUNATELY, THEY RAN INTO CHIEF MPONDOMBINI, THE REGENT'S BROTHER.

LET'S ASK HIM . . .

THINGS WENT SMOOTHLY UNTIL. . . .

WE ARE ON AN ERRAND FOR THE REGENT, BUT WE NEED DOCUMENTATION.

NO PROBLEM, ANYTHING FOR MY BROTHER!! I WORK FOR THE MAGISTRATE. WE CAN GET IT ARRANGED.

THERE YOU ARE . . . HANG ON, LET ME JUST PHONE THE MTHATHA MAGISTRATE AND LET HIM KNOW.

LITTLE DID THEY KNOW THAT THE REGENT HAPPENED TO BE IN THE MAGISTRATE'S OFFICE IN MTHATHA.

WHAT? SEND THEM BACK!

YOU HEARD ME . . . ARREST THE BOYS!

I HAVE STUDIED THE LAW, AND I KNOW YOU HAVE NO RIGHT TO STOP US.

JUST GET OUT!

22

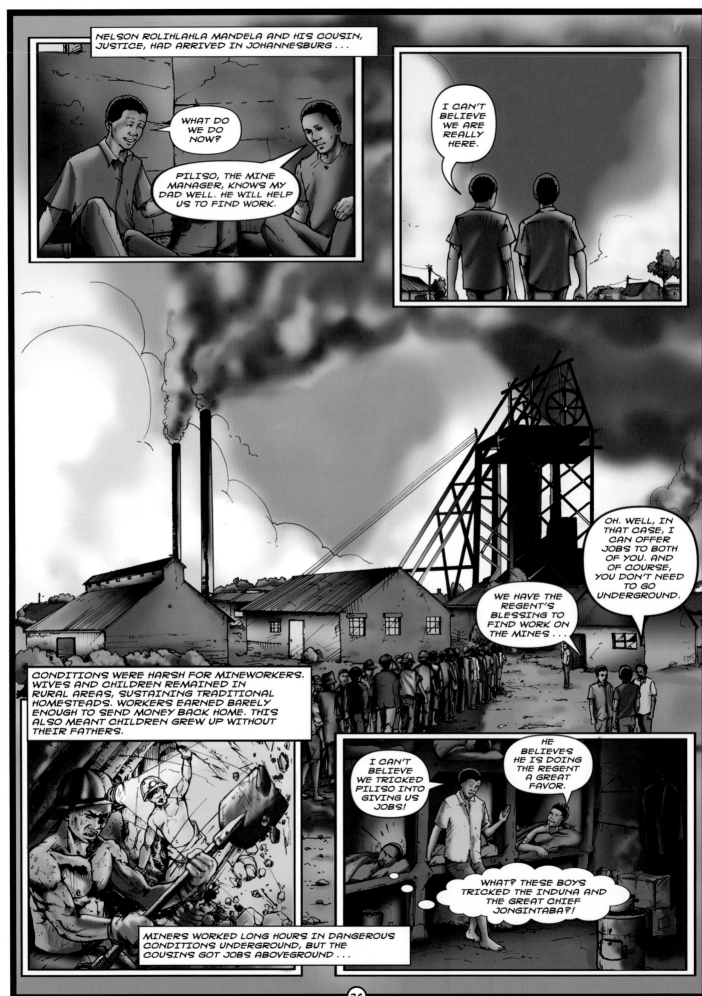

REGENT!

ROLIHLAHLA, I HEAR YOU HAVE FOUND A HOME FOR YOURSELF . . .

THE REGENT VISITED JOHANNESBURG IN 1941.

AFTER I STOLE THE CATTLE, I WAS WORRIED THAT THE BOND BETWEEN US WAS BROKEN.

NO, ROLIHLAHLA, OUR BOND IS STRONG, AND I WILL SUPPORT YOU WHEREVER I CAN. BUT I NEED JUSTICE TO RETURN TO THE GREAT PLACE . . . I AM NOT WELL.

IN THE WINTER OF 1942, THE REGENT DIED. JUSTICE AND MANDELA READ OF HIS DEATH IN THE NEWSPAPER. THE TELEGRAM SENT TO THEM DID NOT ARRIVE.

WE MUST HURRY. WE MAY HAVE ALREADY MISSED THE FUNERAL.

HE LOOKED UNWELL WHEN HE VISITED. I SHOULD HAVE GONE HOME THEN . . .

YES, I SHOULD HAVE APPRECIATED THE REGENT MORE WHEN HE WAS ALIVE. HE TOOK CARE OF ME LIKE I WAS HIS SON.

SADLY, MANDELA AND JUSTICE ARRIVED AT THE GREAT PLACE A DAY AFTER THE REGENT'S FUNERAL . . .

AFTER A WEEK AT THE GREAT PLACE, MANDELA SAID GOOD-BYE TO HIS MOTHER AND TO JUSTICE, TO RETURN TO HIS LIFE IN THE BIG CITY. JUSTICE WAS TO SUCCEED THE REGENT.

BACK IN JOHANNESBURG, RADEBE WAS SURPRISED THAT MANDELA RETURNED.

STAY WELL.

IT IS GOOD TO BE BACK!

I STILL HAVE MANY RIVERS TO CROSS . . .

BUS FARES ARE UP AGAIN. YOU MAY WANT TO THINK OF JOINING THE ALEXANDRA BUS STRIKE.

YES, I CAN RELATE TO THAT. I CAN HARDLY GET BY NOW . . .

IN AUGUST 1949, MANDELA MARCHED WITH 10,000 OTHERS PROTESTING THE INCREASE IN BUS FARES, AND BOYCOTTED THE BUSES.

AFTER NINE DAYS, THERE WAS VICTORY FOR THE COMMUTERS. THEIR UNITY HAD SUCCEEDED. IT SENT A POWERFUL MESSAGE TO THE PEOPLE OF SOUTH AFRICA.

NELSON, COME AND STAY AT OUR HOME UNTIL YOU CAN AFFORD YOUR OWN.

YOU ARE GOOD TO ME, WALTER.

MANDELA AND SISULU WERE BECOMING CLOSE FRIENDS AND DISCOVERING COMMON INTERESTS. MANDELA FELT THE IMMEDIATE WARMTH AND WELCOME AT THE SISULU HOME.

IT WAS THERE THAT MANDELA MET SISULU'S COUSIN, EVELYN MASE, A TRAINEE NURSE FROM ENGCOBO IN THE TRANSKEI. IT WAS LOVE AT FIRST SIGHT.

IN 1943, MANDELA GRADUATED WITH HIS B.A. DEGREE AT FORT HARE. HIS MOTHER, NOSEKENI, HIS NEPHEW, KAISER MATANZIMA, AND THE REGENT'S WIDOW, NO-ENGLAND, WERE THERE TO WISH HIM WELL.

MANDELA DECLINED. HE RETURNED TO THE CITY TO CONTINUE HIS LAW STUDIES AT WITS UNIVERSITY. THIS WAS A DIFFICULT TIME FOR HIM, WITH MANY NEW FRIENDSHIPS, AND MANY HUMILIATIONS.

DALIBHUNGA, YOU ARE NEEDED HERE NOW. WHY DON'T YOU STAY?

MANDELA ARRIVED LATE FOR CLASS ON OCCASION . . .

MANDELA, IF YOU CAN'T EVEN ARRIVE ON TIME, YOU CAN NEVER BE A LAWYER!

I CAN'T SIT NEXT TO HIM. WHO DOES HE THINK HE IS?

MANDELA WAS THE ONLY AFRICAN IN HIS CLASS. HE COULD NOT USE THE SPORTS FIELDS, SWIMMING POOL, CAFETERIA, OR RESIDENCES. THESE WERE FOR WHITES ONLY!

MANDELA HAD A MIX OF EXPERIENCES AT WITS. HE WAS BEFRIENDED BY STUDENTS FROM OTHER RACE GROUPS LIKE RUTH FIRST, GEORGE BIZOS, J. N. SINGH, AND ISMAIL MEER.

LET'S GO GET SOME LUNCH AT MY APARTMENT.

THEY BOARDED A TRAM RESERVED FOR WHITES AND INDIANS ONLY . . .

WE ARE NOT ALLOWED TO CARRY A KAFFIR!

THEY WERE CHARGED WITH INTERFERING WITH THE TRANSPORT SERVICE. BRAM FISCHER, A COMMUNIST PARTY MEMBER, REPRESENTED THEM. FISCHER'S FATHER WAS THE JUDGE PRESIDENT IN THE FREE STATE. THE CASE WAS DISMISSED.

WHAT DO YOU MEAN? DO YOU KNOW THE MEANING OF THAT WORD?

I WILL HAVE YOU ARRESTED AT THE NEXT STOP!

WE WERE LUCKY. THANK GOODNESS THE MAGISTRATE WAS SUCH AN ADMIRER OF BRAM'S FATHER.

DR. XUMA, THE ANC PRESIDENT, OBJECTED TO THE YOUTHS' IDEAS OF MASS ACTION, BUT... IN APRIL 1944 THE YOUTH LEAGUE WAS FORMED WITH ANTON LEMBEDE AS ITS FIRST PRESIDENT...

WE MUST MAKE SURE THAT AFRICANS ARE AT THE FOREFRONT OF OUR STRUGGLE...

NO FOREIGNER CAN EVER LEAD THE AFRICAN PEOPLE... OUR MANIFESTO SAYS THIS CLEARLY...

...THE NAMES OF OUR EXECUTIVE MEMBERS ARE OLIVER TAMBO, WALTER SISULU, NELSON MANDELA...

WHAT?!?

TAMBO AND SISULU KNEW WHY MANDELA WAS BEING CALLED UP...

IT'S A GOOD THING TO GET NELSON INVOLVED. HE IS A STRONG LEADER...

MANDELA'S ROMANCE WITH EVELYN GREW...

YOUR BROTHER HAS GIVEN ME PERMISSION TO REQUEST YOUR HAND IN MARRIAGE...

IT WAS A SIMPLE CEREMONY, HELD AT THE NATIVE COMMISSIONER'S OFFICE IN 1944. THEY COULDN'T AFFORD A BIG WEDDING.

...AT HOME IN ORLANDO, SOWETO.

...HE SAYS NOT TO WORRY ABOUT THE COMMUNISTS OVER-SHADOWING AFRICANS.

I DON'T UNDERSTAND ALL THIS POLITICS.

IN THE FIRST YEAR OF THEIR MARRIAGE, EVELYN GAVE BIRTH TO THEIR SON MADIBA THEMBEKILE – AFFECTIONATELY KNOWN AS THEMBI.

BUT WE NEED TO THINK OF OUR BABY'S FUTURE. THE GOVERNMENT'S LAWS HAVE STOLEN OUR LAND, CREATED SLUMS FOR US, DENIED US SKILLED WORK, AND ARE STOPPING US FROM VOTING. THEY EVEN RULE OUR KINGS.

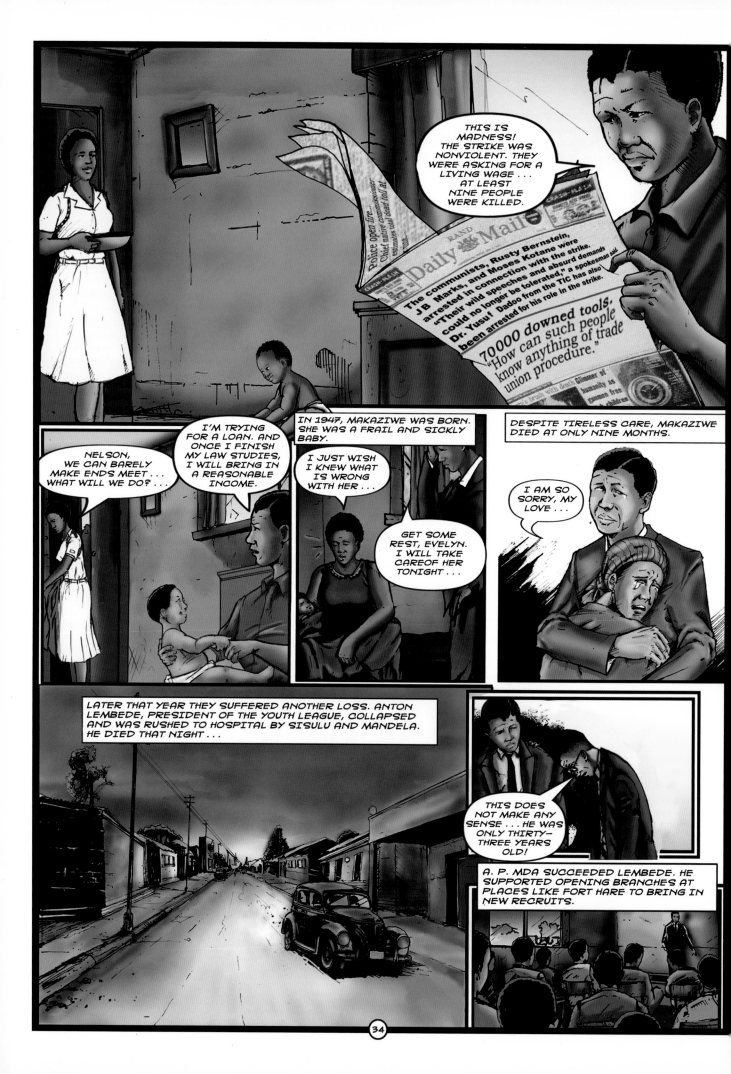

THIS IS MADNESS! THE STRIKE WAS NONVIOLENT. THEY WERE ASKING FOR A LIVING WAGE . . . AT LEAST NINE PEOPLE WERE KILLED.

NELSON, WE CAN BARELY MAKE ENDS MEET . . . WHAT WILL WE DO? . . .

I'M TRYING FOR A LOAN. AND ONCE I FINISH MY LAW STUDIES, I WILL BRING IN A REASONABLE INCOME.

IN 1947, MAKAZIWE WAS BORN. SHE WAS A FRAIL AND SICKLY BABY.

I JUST WISH I KNEW WHAT IS WRONG WITH HER . . .

GET SOME REST, EVELYN. I WILL TAKE CARE OF HER TONIGHT . . .

DESPITE TIRELESS CARE, MAKAZIWE DIED AT ONLY NINE MONTHS.

I AM SO SORRY, MY LOVE . . .

LATER THAT YEAR THEY SUFFERED ANOTHER LOSS. ANTON LEMBEDE, PRESIDENT OF THE YOUTH LEAGUE, COLLAPSED AND WAS RUSHED TO HOSPITAL BY SISULU AND MANDELA. HE DIED THAT NIGHT . . .

THIS DOES NOT MAKE ANY SENSE . . . HE WAS ONLY THIRTY-THREE YEARS OLD!

A. P. MDA SUCCEEDED LEMBEDE. HE SUPPORTED OPENING BRANCHES AT PLACES LIKE FORT HARE TO BRING IN NEW RECRUITS.

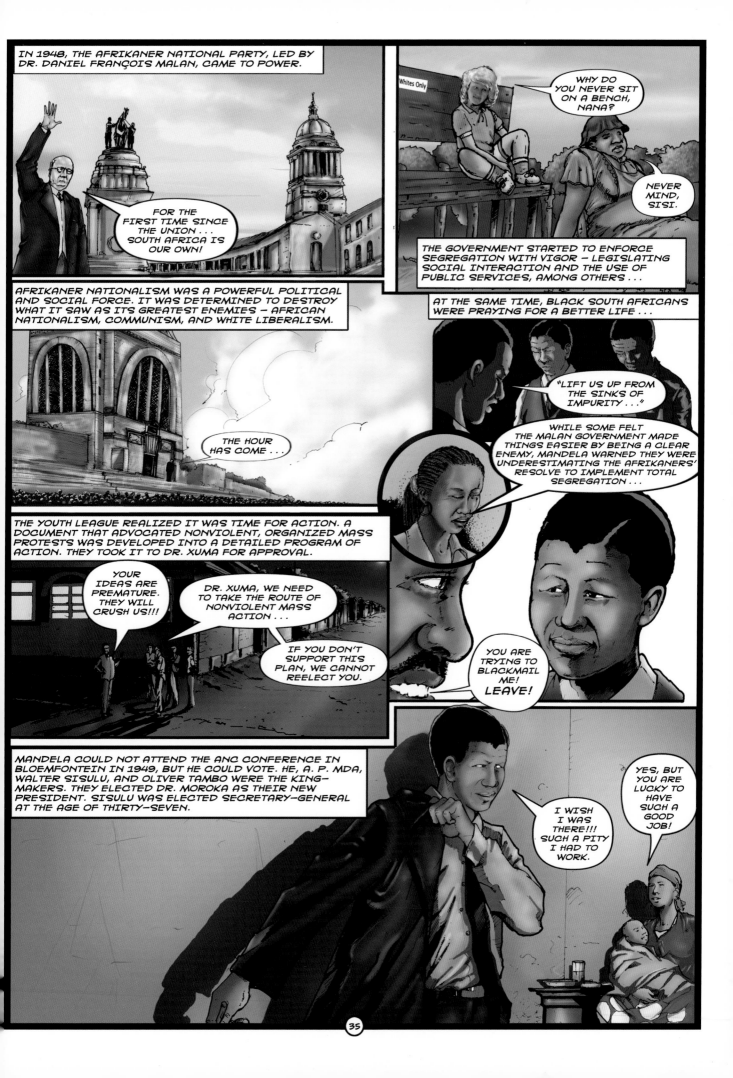

IN 1948, THE AFRIKANER NATIONAL PARTY, LED BY DR. DANIEL FRANÇOIS MALAN, CAME TO POWER.

FOR THE FIRST TIME SINCE THE UNION . . . SOUTH AFRICA IS OUR OWN!

Whites Only

WHY DO YOU NEVER SIT ON A BENCH, NANA?

NEVER MIND, SISI.

THE GOVERNMENT STARTED TO ENFORCE SEGREGATION WITH VIGOR — LEGISLATING SOCIAL INTERACTION AND THE USE OF PUBLIC SERVICES, AMONG OTHERS . . .

AFRIKANER NATIONALISM WAS A POWERFUL POLITICAL AND SOCIAL FORCE. IT WAS DETERMINED TO DESTROY WHAT IT SAW AS ITS GREATEST ENEMIES — AFRICAN NATIONALISM, COMMUNISM, AND WHITE LIBERALISM.

AT THE SAME TIME, BLACK SOUTH AFRICANS WERE PRAYING FOR A BETTER LIFE . . .

"LIFT US UP FROM THE SINKS OF IMPURITY . . ."

THE HOUR HAS COME . . .

WHILE SOME FELT THE MALAN GOVERNMENT MADE THINGS EASIER BY BEING A CLEAR ENEMY, MANDELA WARNED THEY WERE UNDERESTIMATING THE AFRIKANERS' RESOLVE TO IMPLEMENT TOTAL SEGREGATION . . .

THE YOUTH LEAGUE REALIZED IT WAS TIME FOR ACTION. A DOCUMENT THAT ADVOCATED NONVIOLENT, ORGANIZED MASS PROTESTS WAS DEVELOPED INTO A DETAILED PROGRAM OF ACTION. THEY TOOK IT TO DR. XUMA FOR APPROVAL.

YOUR IDEAS ARE PREMATURE. THEY WILL CRUSH US!!!

DR. XUMA, WE NEED TO TAKE THE ROUTE OF NONVIOLENT MASS ACTION . . .

IF YOU DON'T SUPPORT THIS PLAN, WE CANNOT REELECT YOU.

YOU ARE TRYING TO BLACKMAIL ME! LEAVE!

MANDELA COULD NOT ATTEND THE ANC CONFERENCE IN BLOEMFONTEIN IN 1949, BUT HE COULD VOTE. HE, A. P. MDA, WALTER SISULU, AND OLIVER TAMBO WERE THE KING-MAKERS. THEY ELECTED DR. MOROKA AS THEIR NEW PRESIDENT. SISULU WAS ELECTED SECRETARY-GENERAL AT THE AGE OF THIRTY-SEVEN.

I WISH I WAS THERE!!! SUCH A PITY I HAD TO WORK.

YES, BUT YOU ARE LUCKY TO HAVE SUCH A GOOD JOB!

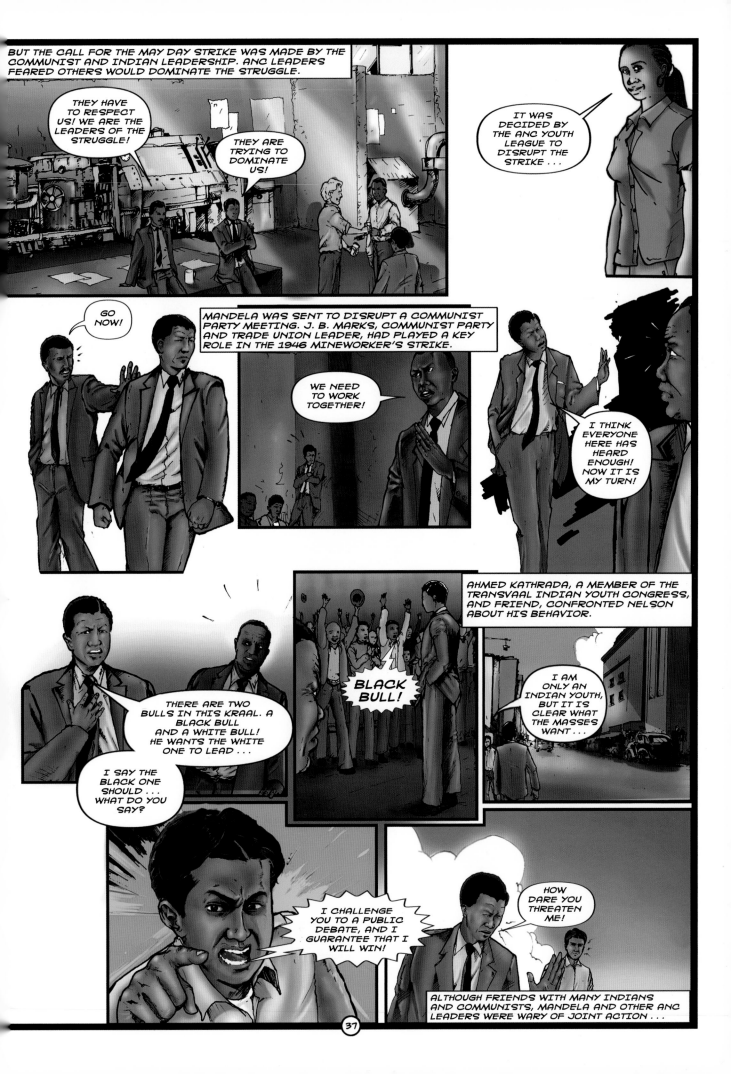

MANDELA AND SISULU HELPED TO TAKE THE INJURED TO HOSPITALS...

I CAN'T BELIEVE WE SURVIVED THAT!

THIS IS A FIERCE ENEMY WE ARE FACING.

THE MAY DAY TRAGEDY STIRRED THE ANC INTO ACTION. IT ASKED OTHER PARTIES TO JOIN IN A NATIONAL DAY OF MOURNING — A STAY-AWAY ON JUNE 26, 1950.

YES, WE ARE OPPOSING THE SUPPRESSION OF COMMUNISM ACT! WE ARE MOURNING FOR OUR BROTHERS AND SISTERS...

NELSON, EVELYN NEEDS YOU...

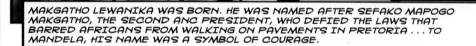

MAKGATHO LEWANIKA WAS BORN. HE WAS NAMED AFTER SEFAKO MAPOGO MAKGATHO, THE SECOND ANC PRESIDENT, WHO DEFIED THE LAWS THAT BARRED AFRICANS FROM WALKING ON PAVEMENTS IN PRETORIA... TO MANDELA, HIS NAME WAS A SYMBOL OF COURAGE.

POLITICS WAS CAUSING MORE AND MORE FRICTION IN THE MANDELA HOME...

I WISH WE COULD GO BACK TO THE TRANSKEI... THEN WE WOULD SEE MORE OF YOU!

I'M SORRY, EVELYN, BUT POLITICS IS NOT A DISTRACTION. IT IS MY LIFE WORK!

JOE SLOVO, A COMMUNIST, TRIED TO CONVINCE THE ANC TO WORK WITH OTHER ORGANIZATIONS IN A UNITED FRONT...

WE ARE GETTING THERE, JOE.

THE PROPOSED STAY-AWAY FAILED IN PARTS OF THE COUNTRY. FOR MANDELA, THE STRUGGLE HAD BECOME ALL-CONSUMING. HE WAS ON THE EXECUTIVE OF THE ANC, WORKED AT LAW FIRMS IN THE CITY, AND EVENTUALLY QUALIFIED AS AN ATTORNEY. EVELYN, ON THE OTHER HAND, WAS CONCENTRATING ON FAMILY, RELIGION, AND NURSING...

THE ANC WAS MOBILIZING IN BLOEMFONTEIN, DECEMBER 1951 . . .

WE HAVE TO START A MASS CAMPAIGN OF CIVIL DISOBEDIENCE . . . DEFYING UNJUST LAWS . . . AND GO TO PRISON IF WE NEED TO!

THIS WAS THE BIRTH OF THE DEFIANCE CAMPAIGN. MANDELA, Z. K. MATTHEWS, ISMAIL MEER, AND J. N. SINGH WERE ASKED TO DRAFT A LETTER TO THE PRIME MINISTER, WARNING HIM OF THEIR PLANS, UNLESS SIX UNJUST LAWS WERE REPEALED . . .

6 UNJUST LAWS
Group Areas Act
Pass Laws
Suppression of Communism Act
e Representation
oters Act
Stock Limitation
antu Authorities

DR. MALAN REACTED THE WAY THEY EXPECTED . . .

YOUR TIME HAS COME . . . YOU ARE OUR VOLUNTEER-IN-CHIEF. YOU HAVE TO TAKE CHARGE OF RECRUITING VOLUNTEERS TO THE CAMPAIGN!

OUR CAMPAIGN IS NONVIOLENT AND DISCIPLINED. MAKE SURE ALL VOLUNTEERS FOLLOW THESE RULES!

TELL THEM RACE DIFFERENCES ARE PERMANENT, NOT MAN-MADE! THE FULL WEIGHT OF THE STATE MACHINERY WILL BE USED TO CRUSH THEIR CAMPAIGN!!!

ALL RACES UNITED AGAINST THE OPPRESSORS!

THE DEFIANCE CAMPAIGN DREW INSPIRATION FROM THE PASSIVE RESISTANCE STRATEGIES OF M. K. GANDHI.

YES, BUT STILL NO VIOLENCE. WE MUST NOT RESIST ARREST. OUR AIM IS TO FILL THEIR JAILS.

WE ARE TIRED OF BEING HUMILIATED BY THE GOVERNMENT!

WALTER SISULU, J. B. MARKS, YUSUF DADOO, AND YUSUF CACHALIA MADE UP THE NATIONAL PLANNING COUNCIL. MANDELA WAS A VISIBLE PRESENCE THROUGHOUT THE CAMPAIGN, TRAVELING FROM PLACE TO PLACE, AND MAKING SURE THAT ALL WAS RUNNING SMOOTHLY. FOR THE FIRST TIME, HE TOOK UP A NATIONAL LEADERSHIP ROLE. VOLUNTEERS WERE SIGNED UP AND THEN ORGANIZED INTO GROUPS TO BREAK THE LAWS TOGETHER.

FOUR DAYS BEFORE THE LAUNCH, 10,000 PEOPLE GATHERED IN DURBAN FOR "THE DAY OF THE VOLUNTEERS." MANDELA DELIVERED A SPEECH ON THE SAME STAGE AS CHIEF ALBERT LUTHULI, PRESIDENT OF THE NATAL ANC, AND DR. NAICKER, PRESIDENT OF THE NATAL INDIAN CONGRESS.

WE WELCOME ALL TRUEHEARTED VOLUNTEERS FROM ALL WALKS OF LIFE, WITHOUT THE CONSIDERATION OF COLOR, RACE, OR CREED ... TO DEFY THESE UNJUST LAWS ...

"I DO HEREBY PLEDGE TO BIND MYSELF TO SERVE MY COUNTRY AND MY PEOPLE... TO PARTICIPATE FULLY AND WITHOUT RESERVATIONS, TO THE BEST OF MY ABILITY..."

WHITES ONLY
SLEGS BLANKES
TICKET OFFICE

"Afrika! Mayibuye... let Africa come back!"

JUNE 26, 1952, PORT ELIZABETH RAILWAY STATION. RAYMOND MHLABA LED VOLUNTEERS THROUGH A WHITES-ONLY ENTRANCE ...

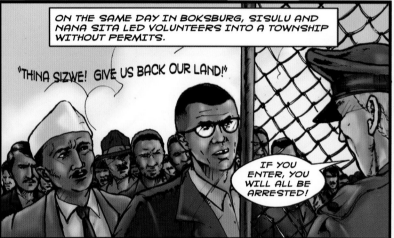

ON THE SAME DAY IN BOKSBURG, SISULU AND NANA SITA LED VOLUNTEERS INTO A TOWNSHIP WITHOUT PERMITS.

"THINA SIZWE! GIVE US BACK OUR LAND!"

IF YOU ENTER, YOU WILL ALL BE ARRESTED!

WHITES ONLY

THE VOLUNTEERS WERE ORDERLY AND WELCOMED ARREST.

OPEN UP THE JAILS, MALAN! WE ARE KNOCKING!

WHAT ARE THESE PEOPLE UP TO?

WHITES ONLY TOILETS

OVER THE NEXT SIX MONTHS, MORE THAN 8,000 PEOPLE WERE ARRESTED. THE JAILS WERE OVERFLOWING. EVEN THOUGH DEFIERS COULD PAY A FINE, THEY REFUSED, AND SERVED FULL SENTENCES – USUALLY FOUR TO SIX WEEKS. THE PEOPLE WERE BECOMING MORE POLITICIZED, AND MEMBERSHIP OF THE ANC INCREASED FROM ABOUT 5,000 TO 100,000.

IN 1950, THE SUPPRESSION OF COMMUNISM ACT HAD BEEN PASSED AND THE COMMUNIST PARTY DISSOLVED. MEETINGS OF MORE THAN TEN PEOPLE WERE ILLEGAL. MANDELA WAS ASKED TO DRAFT A DOCUMENT EXPLAINING HOW THE ANC SHOULD KEEP IN TOUCH WITH THE MASSES IN THE EVENT OF IT BEING OUTLAWED – IT WAS CALLED THE M-PLAN.

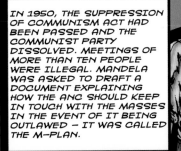

IF YOU CANNOT HOLD MEETINGS PUBLICLY, THEN YOU MUST HOLD THEM IN THE FACTORIES, ON THE TRAMS AND BUSES ... IN EVERY HOME, SHACK, AND EVERY MUD STRUCTURE ... WE MUST NEVER SURRENDER!

THE GOVERNMENT CONTINUED IMPLEMENTING APARTHEID. PLANS FOR BANTU EDUCATION LAWS – AN INFERIOR EDUCATION FOR AFRICANS – AND THE FORCED REMOVAL OF PEOPLE FROM THEIR HOMES IN SOPHIATOWN, AND OTHER AREAS, WERE BEING PUT IN PLACE.

THERE IS NOT A STRAND OF BARBED WIRE BETWEEN MY CONSTITUENCY AND THAT SLUM!

IN 1953, MANDELA'S BANS EXPIRED FOR A SHORT TIME. HE ADDRESSED A MEETING IN SOPHIATOWN ... PEOPLE WERE OUTRAGED AT THE PROSPECT OF BEING FORCIBLY MOVED ...

THESE ARE OUR ENEMIES!

YOU MUST REMEMBER TO EXERCISE DISCIPLINE, NELSON. MILITANCY WILL NOT HELP US NOW. WE HAVE TO AVOID BLOODSHED!

WE WON'T MOVE!

IT IS DIFFICULT WHEN LIVING WITH THIS BRUTALITY EVERY DAY.

SISULU TRAVELED TO CHINA IN 1953 AND EXPLORED THE OPTION OF AN ARMED STRUGGLE, BUT HAD BEEN ADVISED TO CONSIDER THIS ONLY WHEN THERE WERE NO OTHER OPTIONS LEFT.

Ons dak nie ons pella hier

grrr!

THE BULLDOZERS AND POLICE ARE COMING!!

BUT THE REMOVALS WENT AHEAD UNDER THE HEAVY HAND OF THE LAW. IN 1954, THE NATIVE RESETTLEMENT BILL WAS PASSED. IN FEBRUARY 1955, 2,000 POLICE ACCOMPANIED EIGHTY-SIX TRUCKS AND STARTED LOADING UP SOPHIATOWN.

IT FEELS LIKE WE HAVE FAILED OUR PEOPLE ...

WE DID WHAT WE COULD ...

WE WILL NOT MOVE

FATHER TREVOR HUDDLESTON, A CHURCH MINISTER IN SOPHIATOWN, WAS A STAUNCH ALLY OF THE STRUGGLE. HE BECAME A LIFELONG FRIEND OF MANDELA'S. THE DESTRUCTION OF SOPHIATOWN WAS COMPLETED IN 1959.

FOUR ORGANIZATIONS JOINED THE CAMPAIGN FOR A FREEDOM CHARTER – THE ANC, THE INDIAN CONGRESS, THE COLORED PEOPLE'S ORGANIZATION, AND THE CONGRESS OF DEMOCRATS. TOGETHER THEY FORMED THE CONGRESS ALLIANCE AND COLLECTED VIEWS FROM PEOPLE ACROSS THE COUNTRY.

THIS FELLOW WANTS PERMISSION TO HAVE TEN WIVES!

I'LL VOTE AGAINST THAT!

WE THE PEOPLE OF SOUTH AFRICA DECLARE, FOR ALL OUR COUNTRY AND THE WORLD TO KNOW, THAT SOUTH AFRICA BELONGS TO ALL WHO LIVE IN IT, BLACK AND WHITE, AND THAT NO GOVERNMENT CAN JUSTLY CLAIM AUTHORITY UNLESS IT IS BASED ON THE WILL OF THE PEOPLE.

ON JUNE 25 AND 26, 1955, THE CAMPAIGN CULMINATED IN A CONGRESS OF THE PEOPLE, ATTENDED BY THOUSANDS, IN KLIPTOWN, SOWETO. THE FREEDOM CHARTER WAS ADOPTED.

MANDELA OBSERVED FROM A DISTANCE BECAUSE OF HIS BANNING ORDERS.

WE ARE INVESTIGATING A CASE OF TREASON. DO NOT LEAVE UNTIL WE HAVE YOUR NAME AND YOU HAVE BEEN SEARCHED!

EVERYONE WAS CHECKED BY THE POLICE.

WHILE THE AFRIKANERS ARE ENFORCING THEIR EXCLUSIVE POWER OVER ALL OTHER RACES, WE HAVE DECLARED ALL PEOPLE EQUAL!

I CANNOT BE PASSIVE IN THE FACE OF OPPRESSION!

YOU SHOULD SERVE GOD!

YOU NO LONGER SPEND ANY TIME AT HOME . . .

BY NOW, THE COUPLE HAD ANOTHER BABY GIRL; THEY NAMED HER MAKAZIWE, TO HONOR HER SISTER WHO HAD DIED. BUT THEIR MARRIAGE WAS IN TROUBLE . . .

I MUST GO AND VISIT MY FAMILY.

MANDELA'S SECOND BAN EXPIRED. HE TOOK THE OPPORTUNITY TO LEAVE JOHANNESBURG TO SEE HIS FAMILY IN THE TRANSKEI AND TO ORGANIZE FOR THE ANC.

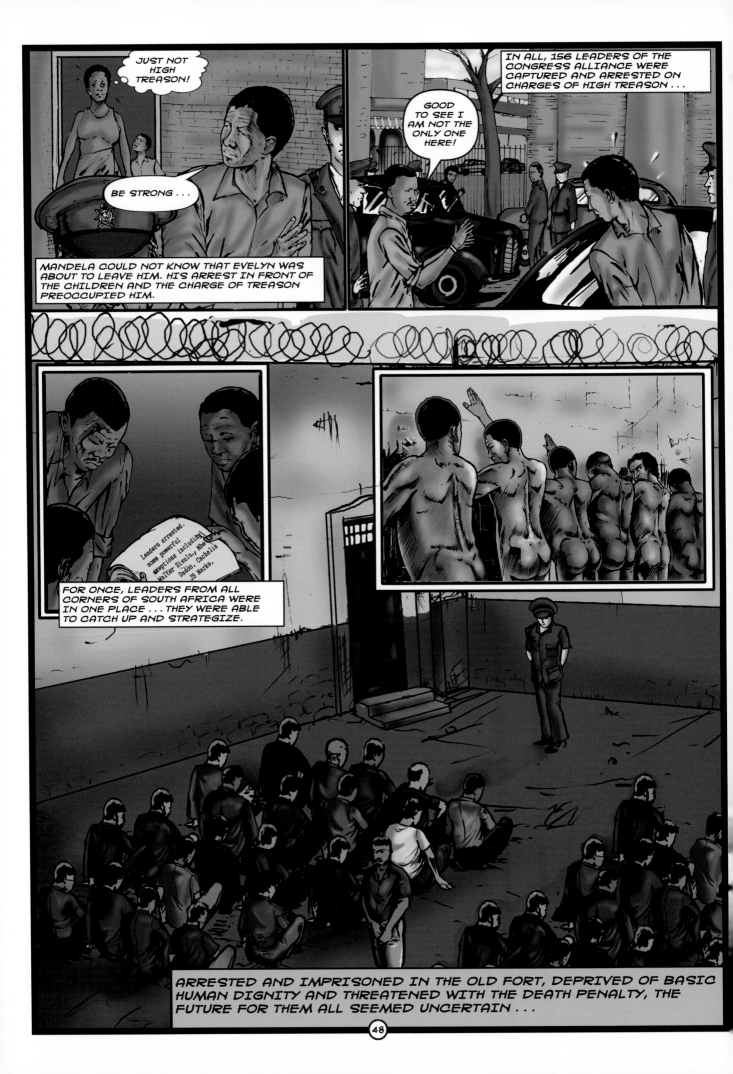

3

THE
BLACK PIMPERNEL

THIS IS THE DRILL HALL
IN JOHANNESBURG, THE PLACE
WHERE THE TREASON TRIALISTS
APPEARED IN COURT. IT WAS
DESTROYED BY TWO FIRES IN
2001 AND 2002. IT IS NOW
RENOVATED, AND 156 PLAQUES
WERE ERECTED IN MEMORY
OF THE TRIALISTS.

THE CAGE WAS REMOVED. WHILE THE TRIAL WENT AHEAD INSIDE, POLICE AND SUPPORTERS CLASHED OUTSIDE: TWENTY-TWO PEOPLE WERE INJURED.

WE STAND BY OUR LEADERS

WE STAND BY OUR LEADERS

WE STAND BY OUR LEADERS

THE DRILL HALL SITE IS NOW A MUSEUM.

ON THE FOURTH DAY OF THE TRIAL, THE PRISONERS WERE RELEASED ON BAIL. TWENTY-FIVE POUNDS FOR AFRICANS, 100 POUNDS FOR INDIANS, AND 250 POUNDS FOR WHITES ... DEMONSTRATING PETTY APARTHEID ...

I SEE I AM 75 POUNDS MORE VALUABLE TO THE COURTS THAN YOU!

WHAT NEXT!

BY NOW, THE MANDELA MARRIAGE WAS OVER ...

IT'S NOT TOO LATE TO SAVE YOUR MARRIAGE ...

NO, WALTER! IT'S OVER.

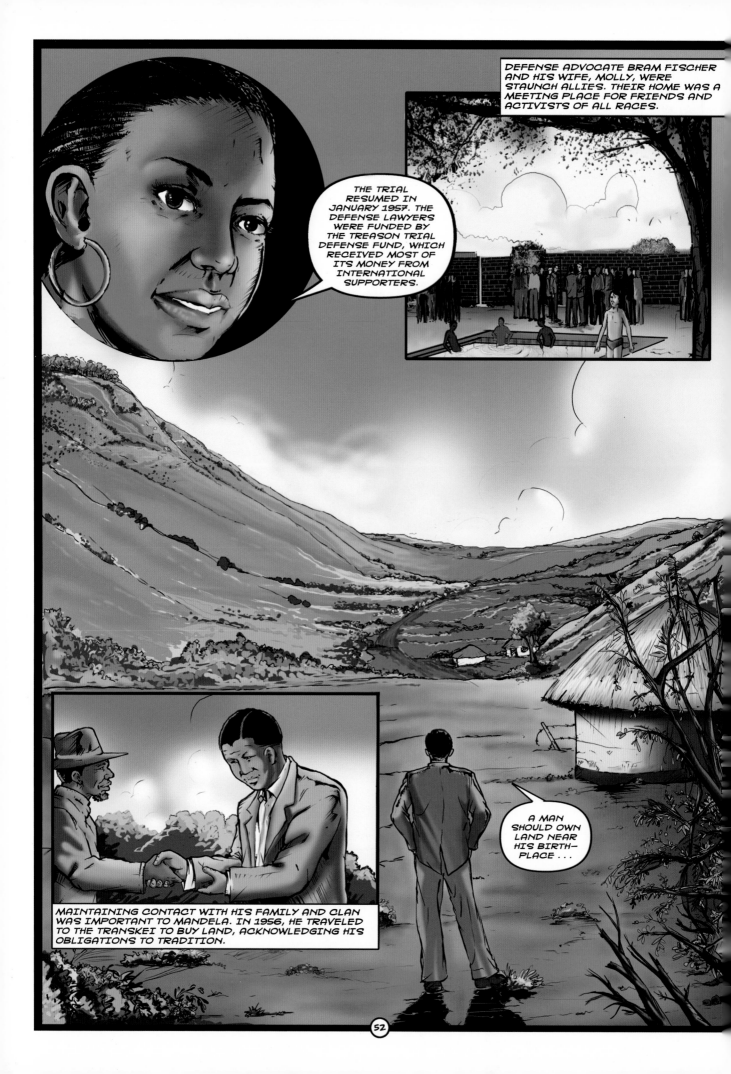

DEFENSE ADVOCATE BRAM FISCHER AND HIS WIFE, MOLLY, WERE STAUNCH ALLIES. THEIR HOME WAS A MEETING PLACE FOR FRIENDS AND ACTIVISTS OF ALL RACES.

THE TRIAL RESUMED IN JANUARY 1957. THE DEFENSE LAWYERS WERE FUNDED BY THE TREASON TRIAL DEFENSE FUND, WHICH RECEIVED MOST OF ITS MONEY FROM INTERNATIONAL SUPPORTERS.

MAINTAINING CONTACT WITH HIS FAMILY AND CLAN WAS IMPORTANT TO MANDELA. IN 1956, HE TRAVELED TO THE TRANSKEI TO BUY LAND, ACKNOWLEDGING HIS OBLIGATIONS TO TRADITION.

A MAN SHOULD OWN LAND NEAR HIS BIRTH-PLACE . . .

BACK IN JOHANNESBURG, MANDELA RACED BETWEEN HIS LAW FIRM AND THE TRIAL, TRYING TO KEEP THE LAW PRACTICE GOING . . .

WHO IS THAT?

A FEW WEEKS LATER, MANDELA WAS SURPRISED TO SEE THE SAME BEAUTIFUL WOMAN IN A DELI SHOP WITH ADELAIDE AND OLIVER TAMBO.

IT'S HER . . .

WE ARE FRIENDS FROM BIZANA.

THIS IS WINNIE MADIKIZELA. WINNIE, THIS IS NELSON MANDELA.

WINNIE WAS THE FIRST AFRICAN SOCIAL WORKER AT BARAGWANATH HOSPITAL IN SOWETO.

SOON AFTERWARD, MANDELA INVITED HER TO LUNCH. THEY DISCUSSED RAISING FUNDS FOR THE ANC . . .

BUT, I ALSO WANTED TO SEE YOU AGAIN.

MANDELA LEARNED THAT WINNIE'S GREAT-GRANDFATHER WAS AN IMPORTANT NINETEENTH-CENTURY CHIEF IN THE MPONDO KINGDOM.

THERE WAS A POWERFUL CONNECTION BETWEEN THEM. LIFE WAS TO TEST IT SEVERELY.

BY DECEMBER 1957, CHARGES AGAINST SIXTY-ONE OF THE ACCUSED HAD BEEN WITHDRAWN. THE REST OF THE ACCUSED HOPED THAT THE ENTIRE CASE WOULD BE DISMISSED, BUT THE MAGISTRATE RULED THAT THERE WAS SUFFICIENT EVIDENCE TO ALLOW THE TRIAL TO GO AHEAD.

WINNIE, I WOULD LIKE YOU TO MEET CHIEF LUTHULI...

I WONDER WHAT HIS INTENTIONS ARE?

MANDELA KNEW WHAT HIS INTENTIONS WERE. HE STARTED WEDDING PLANS, AND GETTING THE BLESSING OF WINNIE'S FATHER AND PAYING LOBOLA. AN ENGAGEMENT NOTICE WAS PLACED IN THE NEWSPAPER.

THE BLESSING FROM WINNIE'S FATHER CAME WITH A WARNING THAT MARRYING "MANDELA FROM THE ANC" WOULD NOT BE EASY.

MANDELA'S BANNING ORDERS WERE RELAXED FOR A FEW DAYS SO THAT HE COULD TRAVEL TO THE TRANSKEI FOR THE WEDDING.

DON'T WORRY, MKHULU, I WILL STAY AWAY FROM HIM!

AT THE BRIDE'S PLACE, MBONGWENI, THEY WERE SEPARATED AS TRADITION REQUIRED.

LATER, THEY CELEBRATED AT THE BIZANA TOWN HALL. WINNIE'S FATHER, COLUMBUS MADIKIZELA, DELIVERED A SPEECH.

...THIS MARRIAGE IS THREATENED FROM ALL SIDES ...BE LIKE YOUR HUSBAND AND HIS PEOPLE...

ON JUNE 14, 1958, THEY WERE MARRIED. THE WEDDING WAS A MIX OF THE MODERN AND THE TRADITIONAL. THERE WAS A CHURCH CEREMONY FOLLOWED BY A CELEBRATION AT THE MADIKIZELA ANCESTRAL HOME.

AFTER FIVE DAYS OF FEASTING, THEY DROVE BACK TO JOHANNESBURG, WITH TWO CHICKENS, GIVEN TO THEM AS GIFTS, ON THE BACKSEAT.

THE CHICKENS ESCAPED WHEN THEY STOPPED FOR LUNCH ALONG THE ROADSIDE.

THE NEWLYWEDS WERE WELCOMED IN ORLANDO WITH ANOTHER CELEBRATION . . .

AND A FEW WEEKS LATER, MEMBERS OF THE MADIBA ARRIVED TO OFFICIALLY WELCOME WINNIE INTO THE CLAN.

YOUR NEW CLAN NAME IS NOBANDLA.

TOMORROW IS YOUR PASS LAW PROTEST . . . EVEN THOUGH YOU ARE PREGNANT THEY WILL ARREST YOU.

I KNOW, BUT I HAVE MADE UP MY MIND.

MORE THAN 1,000 WOMEN WERE ARRESTED IN OCTOBER 1958, AND IMPRISONED FOR TWO WEEKS. WINNIE MANDELA, LILIAN NGOYI, AND ALBERTINA SISULU WERE AMONG THOSE ARRESTED.

OH, ALBERTINA! I HOPE THAT THESE TERRIBLE CONDITIONS WILL NOT HARM MY BABY!

WINNIE, YOU HAVE TO BELIEVE YOUR BABY WILL BE FINE . . .

WE ARE ORGANIZING LEGAL COUNSEL FOR ALL OF YOU . . .

NELSON, THIS PLACE IS OVERCROWDED . . . WE ARE SLEEPING ON MATS AND THE SMELL IS UNBEARABLE . . . BUT WE ARE VERY STRONG.

THE ANC PAID THEIR FINES, BUT WINNIE LOST HER JOB AT THE HOSPITAL. MONEY WORRIES FORCED MANDELA TO SELL HIS LAND IN THE TRANSKEI. BUT A NEW ARRIVAL BROUGHT THEM JOY!

SO, MY DARLING, WHAT HAVE YOU BROUGHT TO THE WORLD? YES, LET US CALL HER ZENANI.*

* "ZENANI" MEANS "WHAT HAVE YOU BROUGHT TO THE WORLD."

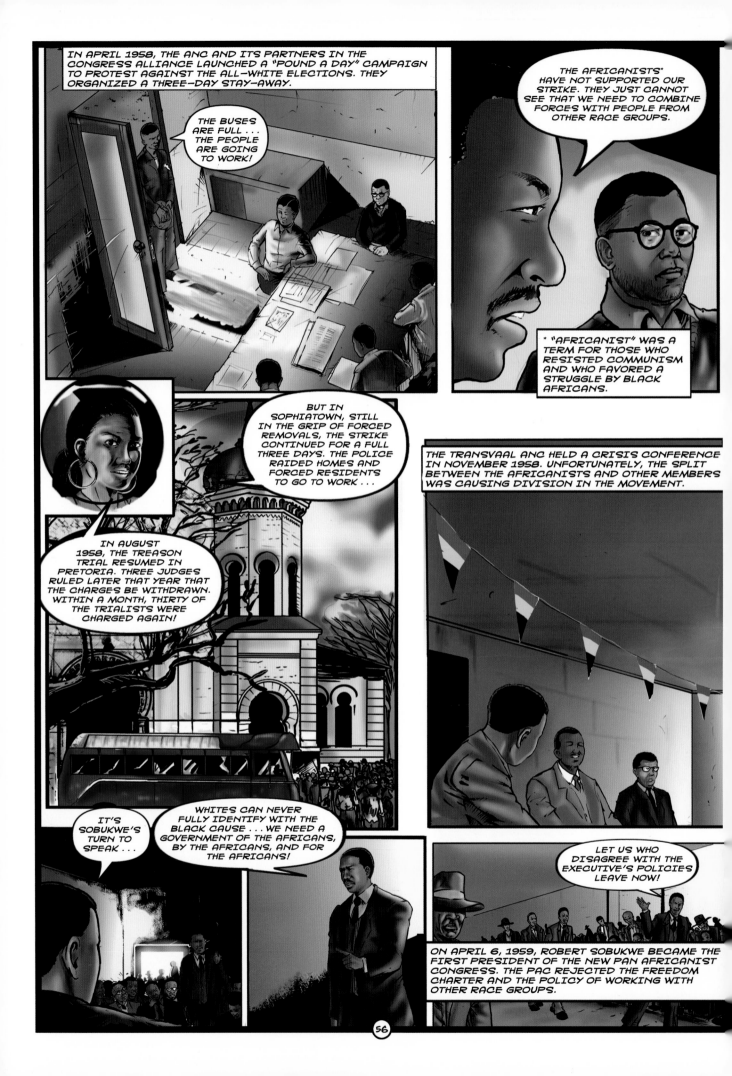

IN 1959, THE GOVERNMENT BEGAN ENFORCING ITS HOMELAND POLICY. THIS MEANT LESS ACCESS TO LAND FOR AFRICANS. PREDICTABLY THERE WERE SEVERAL REVOLTS, ESPECIALLY IN THE PONDOLAND AREA, CLOSE TO MANDELA'S HOME.

BOTH WINNIE AND MANDELA OPPOSED THE HOMELAND LAWS BUT FACED FRAGMENTED LOYALTIES. MANDELA'S NEPHEW, MATANZIMA, WAS A HOMELAND LEADER, AND WINNIE'S FATHER SERVED ON HIS COUNCIL . . .

KINSMEN ARRIVED AT 8115 ORLANDO WEST TO SEEK ADVICE FROM MANDELA.

THE ANC'S POSITION ON THIS IS CLEAR. WE DO NOT SUPPORT THE CHIEFS WHO HAVE CHOSEN TO DO THE GOVERNMENT'S DIRTY WORK!

IT IS WAR . . . WE ARE JAILED, TORTURED, AND MURDERED. WE CANNOT FEED OURSELVES, AS THERE ARE NOT ENOUGH CATTLE OR GRAZING . . .

. . . DURING THE CONFLICT THAT FOLLOWED, WINNIE LOST HER GRANDMOTHER, WHO HAD RAISED HER SINCE HER MOTHER DIED WHEN SHE WAS ONLY TEN YEARS OLD.

DURING 1960, THE ANC CONTINUED TO MOBILIZE AGAINST OPPRESSIVE LAWS.

WE WILL LAUNCH AN ANTI-PASS CAMPAIGN ON MARCH 31. THIS WILL CONTINUE THE WOMEN'S LEAGUE PASS PROTESTS . . .

TWO WEEKS BEFORE THESE PROTESTS WERE DUE TO START, THE PAC LEADERSHIP ANNOUNCED ITS OWN OFFENSIVE AGAINST THE HATED PASS LAWS . . .

. . . TO BE CONCLUDED WITH A BONFIRE OF PASSES ON FREEDOM DAY – JUNE 26 . . .

AFRICA FOR AFRICANS
PAC

IN THREE DAYS' TIME, IN EVERY CITY, TOWN, AND VILLAGE, LEAVE YOUR PASSES AT HOME. SURRENDER YOURSELVES AT POLICE STATIONS FOR ARREST. WE PLEDGE: NO BAIL, NO DEFENSE, NO FINE!

ON MARCH 21, 1960, PAC-ORGANIZED ANTI-PASS MARCHES TOOK PLACE IN SHARPEVILLE, ORLANDO, VANDERBIJL PARK, LANGA, AND NYANGA.

COME, PEOPLE, THIS WAY!

AT SHARPEVILLE POLICE STATION, ABOUT 5,000 PEOPLE GATHERED PEACEFULLY...

BY MID-AFTERNOON, TENSION WAS MOUNTING...

A MINOR INCIDENT CAUSED THE CROWD TO SURGE AGAINST THE FENCE...

THE POLICE STARTED SHOOTING...

...KILLING AT LEAST SIXTY-NINE, AND WOUNDING NEARLY 200 PEOPLE. MOST OF THOSE KILLED WERE SHOT IN THE BACK. IN LANGA, CAPE TOWN, THE PROTESTERS WERE MET BY A BATON CHARGE AND TWO PEOPLE WERE KILLED.

ON MARCH 31, 1960, A STATE OF EMERGENCY WAS DECLARED, GIVING THE GOVERNMENT SWEEPING POWERS TO CRUSH ALL OPPOSITION. THOUSANDS OF PEOPLE WERE DETAINED, INCLUDING ALMOST EVERY KNOWN ACTIVIST IN THE COUNTRY ... THE MANDELA HOUSE WAS RAIDED AFTER MIDNIGHT ...

WHERE ARE YOUR WARRANTS? WHERE ARE YOU TAKING HIM?

MIND YOUR OWN BUSINESS!

MANDELA WAS TAKEN TO NEWLANDS POLICE STATION NEAR SOPHIATOWN ... THE COURTYARD WAS SO CROWDED THAT PRISONERS COULD NOT EVEN SIT DOWN.

BE QUIET OR YOU WILL BE SORRY, BOY!

WE NEED FOOD AND WATER!

THEY WERE GIVEN A THIN MAIZE LIQUID TO EAT AND BLOODSTAINED BLANKETS COVERED IN LICE AND COCKROACHES.

THE NEXT NIGHT THEY WERE RELEASED ...

...FOR A FEW SECONDS, AND THEN FORMALLY ARRESTED UNDER EMERGENCY REGULATIONS.

MANDELA AND SOME OTHERS WERE TRANSFERRED TO PRETORIA LOCAL PRISON.

ON APRIL 8, 1960, THE ANC AND PAC WERE BANNED. SMUGGLED-IN NEWSPAPERS GAVE THE PRISONERS THE NEWS.

WE CANNOT DEFEND YOU FAIRLY UNDER THE EMERGENCY LAWS!

I AGREE WITH YOU, BRAM ...

THE LAWYERS WITHDREW FROM THE CASE ...

MANDELA AND ANOTHER LAWYER, DUMA NOKWE, ADVISED THEIR FELLOW DETAINEES ABOUT THEIR DEFENSE IN THE TREASON TRIAL.

DO NOT WORRY, YOU ARE WELL PREPARED, KATHY* . . .

* KATHY WAS THE NAME THEY USED FOR AHMED KATHRADA.

BY THIS TIME, THE MANDELA AND TAMBO LAW FIRM HAD REACHED THE END OF ITS TEN-YEAR EXISTENCE. MANDELA WAS ESCORTED BY POLICE TO JOHANNESBURG OVER WEEKENDS TO TIE UP THE LAST BUSINESS OF THE FIRM.

AFTER FIVE MONTHS, THOSE ARRESTED WERE RELEASED, AND IN AUGUST THE STATE OF EMERGENCY ENDED.

I'VE MISSED YOU.

WE HAVE DECIDED TO DISSOLVE THE YOUTH AND WOMEN'S LEAGUES AND SET UP A SMALL WORKING COMMITTEE.

THE BANNED ANC NOW HAD TO OPERATE ALONG THE LINES OF THE M-PLAN, RELYING ON A SECRET UNDERGROUND NETWORK OF ACTIVISTS.

YOU KNOW WE WILL HAVE ANOTHER MOUTH TO FEED SOON.

YES, I WILL HAVE TO FIND A PLACE TO WORK FROM FOR US TO SURVIVE. KATHY WILL LET ME USE HIS APARTMENT.

IN DECEMBER 1960, MANDELA RECEIVED NEWS THAT HIS SON MAKGATHO HAD FALLEN ILL IN THE TRANSKEI.

WHAT ABOUT YOUR BANNING ORDER?

LET THEM ARREST ME FOR GOING TO SEE MY SON!

MANDELA DROVE THROUGH THE NIGHT. MAKGATHO WAS BEING CARED FOR BY MATANZIMA'S WIFE. DESPITE THE POLITICAL DIFFERENCES BETWEEN THEM, TIES OF KINSHIP WERE STRONG.

I MUST GET HIM TO A HOSPITAL IN JOHANNES-BURG.

DRIVE CAREFULLY, MADIBA!

HE WILL BE FINE . . . NOW I HAVE TO GO TO WINNIE.

GO NOW.

DURING HIS DASH TO THE TRANSKEI, THEIR SECOND DAUGHTER, ZINDZISWA, MEANING "YOU ARE WELL ESTABLISHED," WAS BORN.

MANDELA'S PROFILE AS AN ANC NATIONAL LEADER MEANT THAT HE WAS ALWAYS TRAVELING. IN JANUARY AND FEBRUARY HE TOURED THE COUNTRY, PREPARING FOR THE ALL-IN-AFRICA CONFERENCE IN MARCH 1961..

WINNIE, THE TRIAL IS ADJOURNED. BUT I WILL SOON BE ATTENDING THE CONFERENCE.

LIFE WITH YOU IS LIKE LIFE WITHOUT YOU . . .

I MUST GO TO EVELYN'S TO SAY GOOD-BYE TO MAKGATHO AND MAKI BEFORE I GO UNDERGROUND. I WON'T BE ABLE TO SEE THEMBI. HE IS IN THE TRANSKEI.

MANDELA LEFT FOR PIETERMARITZBURG, KNOWING THAT HE WOULD GO INTO HIDING AS SOON AS THE TREASON TRIAL ENDED.

SOON AFTER MANDELA WENT UNDERGROUND, ANOTHER WARRANT FOR HIS ARREST WAS ISSUED. BY THIS TIME, HE WAS TRAVELING SECRETLY AROUND THE COUNTRY. IN PORT ELIZABETH, HE MET WITH GOVAN MBEKI AND RAYMOND MHLABA.

SOME ARE UNHAPPY WITH THIS NEW CORE LEADERSHIP. WHAT MUST WE TELL THEM?

WE MUST REMEMBER THAT THE ANC IS NOW ILLEGAL AND WE NEED NEW METHODS OF ORGANIZING.

YES, CREATING SMALL UNDERGROUND CELLS IS WORKING WELL . . .

WE HAVE TO REACH THE WORKERS!

HE MET WITH RELIGIOUS GROUPS IN THE CAPE, RALLYING THEIR SUPPORT.

WE WROTE TO VERWOERD EXPLAINING THE NEED FOR A NONRACIAL CONSTITUTION. HE HAS IGNORED US!

WE ARE CALLING FOR A STAY-AWAY FROM WORK ON REPUBLIC DAY. NO PUBLIC DEMONSTRATIONS. WE DON'T WANT MORE POLICE VIOLENCE.

IN NATAL, HE VISITED SUGAR WORKERS . . .

WE STILL STAND FOR NONVIOLENCE . . .

MANDELA CONTACTED JOURNALISTS AROUND THE COUNTRY, INCLUDING BENJAMIN POGRUND OF THE RAND DAILY MAIL. MANDELA WAS UNDERGROUND, UNTRACEABLE AND MYSTERIOUS, THE BLACK PIMPERNEL . . .

I'LL KEEP YOU INFORMED. THE STAY-AWAY IS GOING AHEAD PEACEFULLY . . .

THE GOVERNMENT SAYS OTHERWISE . . .

THAT IS AN ATTEMPT TO SMEAR OUR CAMPAIGN. WE REMAIN OPPOSED TO VIOLENCE.

IN LONDON, OLIVER TAMBO WARNED THAT IF THE STAY-AWAY WAS CRUSHED, IT WOULD BE THE LAST TIME THE ANC WOULD CAMPAIGN PEACEFULLY.

WHEN ARE YOU COMING HOME?

MANDELA POSED AS A GARDENER ON THE PROPERTY.

...BUT ALSO ATTENDED MEETINGS.

HELLO.

JOE SLOVO AND JACK HODGSON, WHO HAD SERVED IN WORLD WAR II, WERE AMONG THOSE MANDELA MET WITH...

JACK HAS COME TO HELP US WITH SOME IDEAS FOR SABOTAGE.

NOW, IF WE TARGET THESE KEY AREAS, WE CAN DAMAGE THE LINKS BETWEEN MAJOR CENTERS IN THE COUNTRY...

YES, I SEE! MINIMUM MANPOWER, MAXIMUM EFFECT...

BY THE END OF JANUARY, MANDELA ARRIVED IN ADDIS ABABA FOR THE CONFERENCE. EMPEROR HAILE SELASSIE OF ETHIOPIA AND MANY OTHER AFRICAN LEADERS PLEDGED THEIR FULL SUPPORT FOR THE STRUGGLE IN SOUTH AFRICA.

I AM NELSON MANDELA, REPRESENTING THE AFRICAN NATIONAL CONGRESS OF SOUTH AFRICA.

I THANK EMPEROR SELASSIE AND ALL OF THE STATES THAT HAVE GIVEN SUPPORT TO OUR CAUSE...

SOUTH AFRICA IS A LAND RULED BY THE GUN ...ON MARCH 21, 1960, MORE THAN SIXTY AFRICANS WERE SHOT DEAD BY POLICE IN SHARPEVILLE...

...WE NEED A SOLID MOVEMENT IN SOUTH AFRICA THAT CAN SURVIVE ANY ATTACK BY THE GOVERNMENT.

MANDELA HAD TO ANSWER MANY QUESTIONS ON ANC POLICY. HE LATER MET WITH KENNETH KAUNDA, WHO WAS TO BECOME PRESIDENT OF ZAMBIA.

I WILL RETURN TO SOUTH AFRICA AND CONTINUE TO WORK FOR FREEDOM...

PEOPLE ARE UNHAPPY WITH YOUR ALLIANCE WITH WHITE COMMUNISTS. THEY WANT TO SEE AFRICA LED BY AFRICANS...

SOUTH AFRICA NEEDS A NATIONAL CONVENTION OF ALL RACES, AND A CONSTITUTION THAT REPRESENTS ALL OF US...

I AGREE, NELSON. YOU HAVE MY SUPPORT, BUT YOU WILL HAVE TO CONVINCE MANY OTHER PEOPLE...

HE CONTINUED HIS MISSION IN AFRICA, RECEIVING HIS FIRST WEAPONS INSTRUCTION IN OUDJA, MOROCCO.

MANDELA'S DIARY FROM THIS TRIP IS HELD AT THE NATIONAL ARCHIVES IN PRETORIA.

SURROUNDED, MANDELA CONTEMPLATED AN ESCAPE, BUT WAS QUICKLY APPROACHED BY THE POLICE . . .

NAME?

DAVID MOTSAMAYI.

WE KNOW YOU ARE NELSON MANDELA!

THEY ARRESTED MANDELA OUTSIDE HOWICK, KWAZULU-NATAL. THE "BLACK PIMPERNEL" HAD EVADED CAPTURE FOR SEVENTEEN MONTHS . . .

IT'S TOO SOON!

HE WAS TRANSFERRED TO A PRISON IN JOHANNESBURG, WHERE HE WAS ALLOWED TO CONSULT WITH OLD FRIEND JOE SLOVO, A LAWYER. AT THE SAME TIME, SISULU HAD BEEN ARRESTED . . .

I'VE BEEN TOLD THAT THEY HAVE . . .

PLEASE ENSURE MY DIARIES AT LILIESLEAF HAVE BEEN REMOVED.

THE FREE MANDELA COMMITTEE WAS SET UP, WITH KATHRADA AS ITS SECRETARY. PROTEST MEETINGS WERE HELD THROUGHOUT THE COUNTRY.

NO MORE CHAINS

We want to free fra

MAN

FREE MANDELA.

Free M la Prison!

FREE US!

MANDELA IS IN PRISON the PEOPLE ARE IN CHAINS

I WILL CONDUCT MY OWN DEFENSE, BUT I WILL NEED YOU, JOE . . .

79

IN PRISON, MANDELA REGISTERED FOR A LAW DEGREE THROUGH THE UNIVERSITY OF LONDON.

HOW ARE YOU AND THE CHILDREN DOING, WINNIE?

THINGS ARE DIFFICULT, BRAM, BUT WE'RE COPING.

CONDITIONS WERE TOUGH FOR WINNIE, AND BRAM FISCHER ADVISED HER TO LEAVE THE COUNTRY.

BUT WINNIE'S COMMITMENT TO THE STRUGGLE WAS STRONG. SHE WAS INVITED TO SPEAK TO THE INDIAN YOUTH CONGRESS. THIS WAS HER FIRST PUBLIC APPEARANCE.

I SPEAK FOR MY HUSBAND, WHO CANNOT BE HERE . . .

I AM VERY PROUD OF YOU!

YOU HAVE BEEN ELECTED HONORARY PRESIDENT OF THE INDIAN YOUTH CONGRESS!

THE OLD FORT STILL STANDS IN JOHANNESBURG AND HAS BEEN TURNED INTO A MUSEUM.

AFTER THE SPEECH, WINNIE WENT TO THE OLD FORT TO VISIT MANDELA.

SISULU* WAS ALSO ON TRIAL SEPARATELY IN JOHANNESBURG. THEIR TRIALS WERE SPLIT BETWEEN PRETORIA AND JOHANNESBURG TO REDUCE THE NUMBER OF SUPPORTERS. ON OCTOBER 15, 1962, BOTH COURTROOMS WERE PACKED WITH ANC SUPPORTERS.

* HE WAS SENTENCED TO SIX YEARS, BUT JUMPED BAIL AND WENT UNDERGROUND.

THIS IS AN ILLEGAL GATHERING

YOU HAVE 5 MINUTES TO DISPERSE

IT IS OUR RIGHT TO BE HERE

IT IS OUR RIGHT TO BE HERE

IT IS OUR RIGHT TO BE HERE

FREE MANDELA

FREE MANDELA...

FREE MANDELA

LET'S QUIET DOWN. WE DON'T WANT ANYONE HURT . . .

MANDELA WORE A LEOPARD SKIN TO COURT. FOR HIM, IT WAS A POWERFUL SYMBOL OF AFRICAN NATIONALISM.

MANY MEMBERS OF THE MADIBA CLAN WERE IN THE PUBLIC GALLERY. MANDELA REQUESTED A POSTPONEMENT FROM THE MAGISTRATE AND WAS GRANTED A WEEK TO PREPARE THE CASE.

MAYIBUYE!

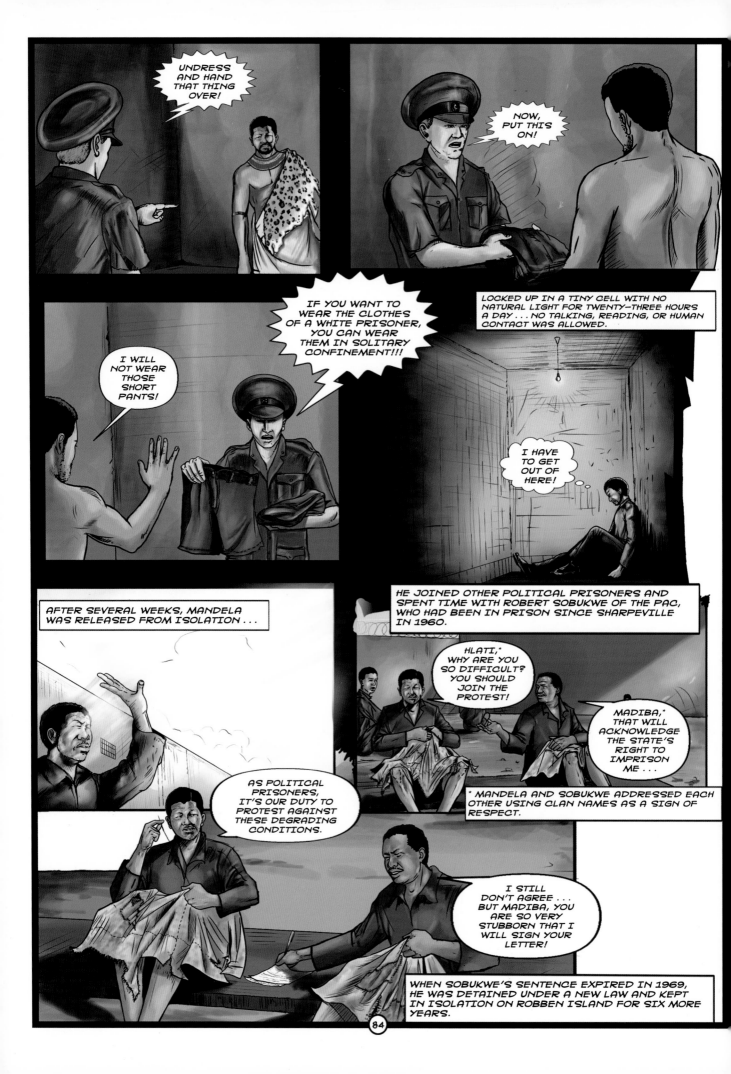

ON MAY 24, WITHOUT WARNING, MANDELA WAS MOVED TO ROBBEN ISLAND. EIGHT MILES OFF THE COAST OF CAPE TOWN, THE ISLAND HAD, AMONG OTHER USES, SERVED AS A PRISON FOR XHOSA CHIEFS IN THE NINETEENTH CENTURY, A LEPER COLONY, A MENTAL ASYLUM, A WORLD WAR II BASE, AND A PRISON. PRISONERS INCLUDED POLITICAL AND RELIGIOUS LEADERS FROM THE EAST INDIES WHO HAD FOUGHT AGAINST DUTCH COLONIAL RULE.

MOVE! MOVE! THIS IS NOT PRETORIA!

PUT TO WORK, MANDELA SAW HIS NEPHEW DIGGING A DITCH.

NQABENI, IS THAT YOU?

MADIBA!

MANDELA'S DISCUSSIONS DURING HIS RECENT AFRICA TRIP HAD STARTED RUMORS . . .

UNCLE, I HEAR YOU HAVE JOINED THE PAC?

NO, THAT'S NOT TRUE.

ON JULY 11, 1963, THE FINAL MEETING WAS HELD AT LILIESLEAF IN RIVONIA . . .

MINUTES AFTER THE MEETING STARTED, THE POLICE SWOOPED IN.

GO! GO!

THEY ARRESTED EVERYONE PRESENT — WALTER SISULU, AHMED KATHRADA, GOVAN MBEKI, RAYMOND MHLABA, BOB HEPPLE, DENIS GOLDBERG, AND RUSTY BERNSTEIN.

DOEF DOEF

MOST OF THE MEN WERE IN DISGUISE. SISULU TRIED TO ESCAPE THROUGH A WINDOW AND KATHRADA ALSO TRIED TO GET AWAY.

WHOOF! WHOOF!

GRR

STOP OR WE SHOOT!

ARTHUR GOLDREICH WAS ALSO ARRESTED AT LILIESLEAF, BUT NOT AT THE SAME TIME AS THE FIRST GROUP. ELIAS MOTSOALEDI, ANDREW MLANGENI, JAMES KANTOR, AND HAROLD WOLPE WERE ARRESTED ELSEWHERE.

MANDELA, UNAWARE OF THE ARRESTS AT LILIESLEAF WAS TRANSFERRED BACK TO PRETORIA. AGAIN, HE WAS ISOLATED IN A SINGLE CELL. HE WAS UNAWARE THAT HIS TRAVEL DIARY AND MANY DOCUMENTS IN HIS HANDWRITING WERE SEIZED AT THE FARM — THE DOCUMENTS HAD NOT BEEN REMOVED AS HE HAD REQUESTED.

THOMAS MASHIFANE!?!

IF THEY GOT THOMAS, THEY MUST HAVE GOTTEN TO LILIESLEAF!

WALTER SISULU

LIONEL BERNSTEIN

DENIS GOLDBERG

ELIAS MOTSOALEDI

GOVAN MBEKI

ANDREW MLANGENI

AHMED KATHRADA

RAYMOND MHLABA

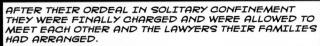

THOSE ARRESTED AT LILIESLEAF WERE DETAINED AT PRETORIA PRISON UNDER THE NINETY-DAY DETENTION LAW ... MOOSA MOOLA, ABDULHAY JASSAT, HAROLD WOLPE, AND ARTHUR GOLDREICH, WHO WERE HELD AT MARSHALL SQUARE POLICE STATION, MANAGED TO ESCAPE ...

AFTER THEIR ORDEAL IN SOLITARY CONFINEMENT THEY WERE FINALLY CHARGED AND WERE ALLOWED TO MEET EACH OTHER AND THE LAWYERS THEIR FAMILIES HAD ARRANGED.

THEY WERE TO BE DEFENDED BY BRAM FISCHER, VERNON BERRANGE, JOEL JOFFE, GEORGE BIZOS, AND ARTHUR CHASKALSON ... BUT JIMMY KANTOR AND BOB HEPPLE'S SITUATIONS WERE NOT SO EASY TO DEAL WITH ...

NELSON! YOU'VE LOST WEIGHT!

IT IS THE COLD PORRIDGE!

THIS IS SERIOUS! THE STATE WILL ASK FOR THE DEATH PENALTY ...

I HAVE TO SEPARATE MY TRIAL FROM THE REST. I AM HERE ONLY BECAUSE MY BROTHER-IN-LAW, WOLPE, ESCAPED!

...AND I HAVE BEEN ASKED TO BE A STATE WITNESS ... I AM STILL CONSIDERING WHAT TO DO ...

PRISONER 466/64

ROBBEN ISLAND, 1964. MANDELA AND NINETEEN OTHERS WERE PLACED IN THE "OLD JAIL" BEFORE THEY WERE MOVED TO B SECTION — A NEWLY BUILT BLOCK FOR POLITICAL PRISONERS . . .

. . . WARDERS WOKE THEM AT 5:30 EACH MORNING TO CLEAN THEIR CELLS, EMPTY THEIR SANITARY BUCKETS, AND EAT A BREAKFAST OF COLD CORNMEAL PORRIDGE. AFTERWARD THEY CRUSHED STONE TO GRAVEL IN THE COURTYARD . . .

REMEMBER: MADIBA SAID, "IT'S ABOUT BALANCE, NOT STRENGTH" . . .

MAKE THAT WHEELBARROW MOVE!

A LIFE SENTENCE IS NOT A DEATH SENTENCE.

THEY LABORED TOGETHER, ATE LUNCH OF CORNCOBS AND BOILED TURNIPS AND YEAST DRINK. THEY WASHED UNDER COLD SHOWERS AND ATE SUPPER IN THE SOLITUDE OF THEIR SINGLE CELLS. THEY WERE TO FIGHT LONG STRUGGLES TO END RACIAL DISCRIMINATION RELATING TO FOOD AND CLOTHING.

"... I AM THE MASTER OF MY FATE; I AM THE CAPTAIN OF MY SOUL."*

466/64

MANDELA WAS PRISONER 466 OF 1964. HE WAS FORTY-SIX YEARS OLD, INCARCERATED IN A CELL OF TWO BY THREE METERS. THE ONLY COMFORT IN A FREEZING WINTER — A SISAL MAT AND THREE THIN BLANKETS . . .

* QUOTE FROM "INVICTUS" BY W. E. HENLEY.

98

WALKING TO AND FROM THE QUARRY, THEY PASSED THE HOUSE WHERE ROBERT SOBUKWE, LEADER OF THE PAC, WAS KEPT IN ISOLATION FOR SIX YEARS . . .

* AN ORGANIZED LEADERSHIP STRUCTURE OF SENIOR ANC MEN WAS SET UP IN 1965. THE FIRST MEMBERS WERE MANDELA, MBEKI, MHLABA, AND SISULU. LATER WILTON MKWAYI, KATHRADA, AND LALOO CHIBA WERE INVITED TO JOIN AS ROTATING MEMBERS. COMMITTEES WERE FORMED IN THE GENERAL SECTION TO ADDRESS DISCIPLINE, EDUCATION, STUDY, AND COMMUNICATION.

1965

CONTACT BETWEEN THE GENERAL PRISONERS IN COMMUNAL CELLS AND B SECTION WAS STRICTLY FORBIDDEN.

BUT THE HIGH ORGAN SET UP A COMMUNICATIONS COMMITTEE TO FIND WAYS OF MAKING CONTACT. APART FROM USING MATCHBOXES WITH FALSE BOTTOMS, THEY ALSO RECEIVED NOTES WRAPPED IN PLASTIC INSIDE FOOD DRUMS THAT MOVED FROM THE KITCHEN TO B SECTION.

IT WAS ESSENTIAL TO KEEP IN TOUCH WITH EACH OTHER AND THE OUTSIDE . . .

IN JULY 1966, A SECRET MESSAGE INFORMED THE PRISONERS OF A HUNGER STRIKE IN THE GENERAL SECTION. B SECTION JOINED IN.

*on hunger strike - general section

A FEW DAYS LATER, THE COMMANDING OFFICER SPOKE TO MANDELA.

WHY STRIKE? YOU DON'T EVEN KNOW WHY THE OTHERS ARE NOT EATING!

WE SEE ANY ACTION OF PROTEST TO ALTER PRISON CONDITIONS AS PART OF THE STRUGGLE AGAINST APARTHEID.

PRISONERS WERE GETTING WEAK FROM LACK OF NOURISHMENT COMBINED WITH HARD LABOR.

MANY MEN FROM THE GENERAL SECTION ENDED UP IN HOSPITAL . . .

COMRADES WILL START DYING SOON!

EVENTUALLY THE AUTHORITIES NEGOTIATED AND THE STRIKE ENDED.

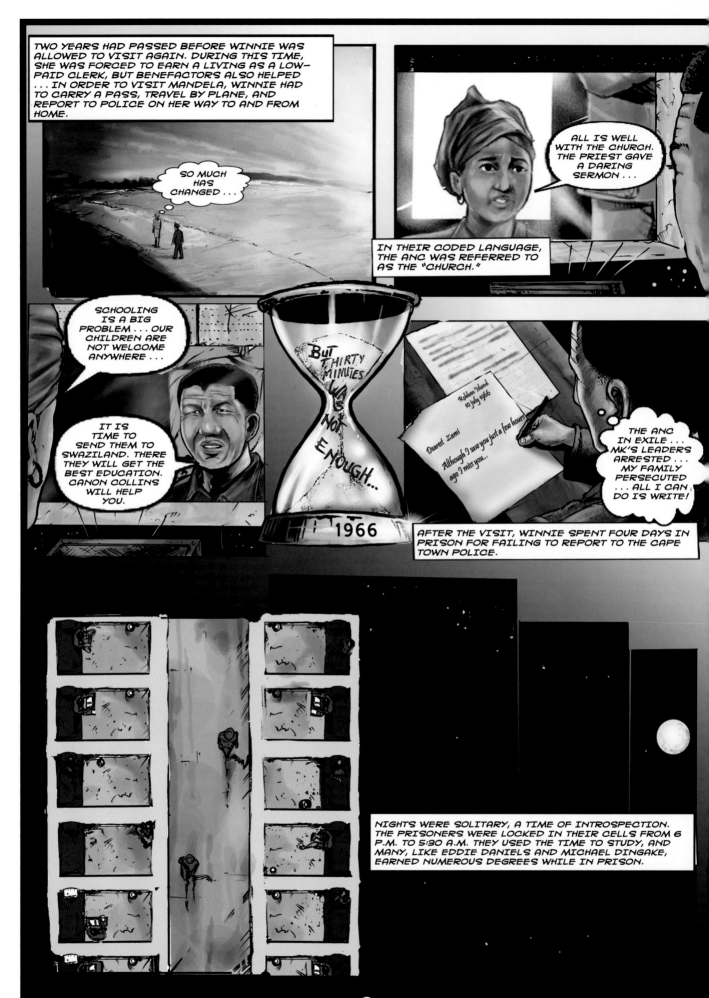

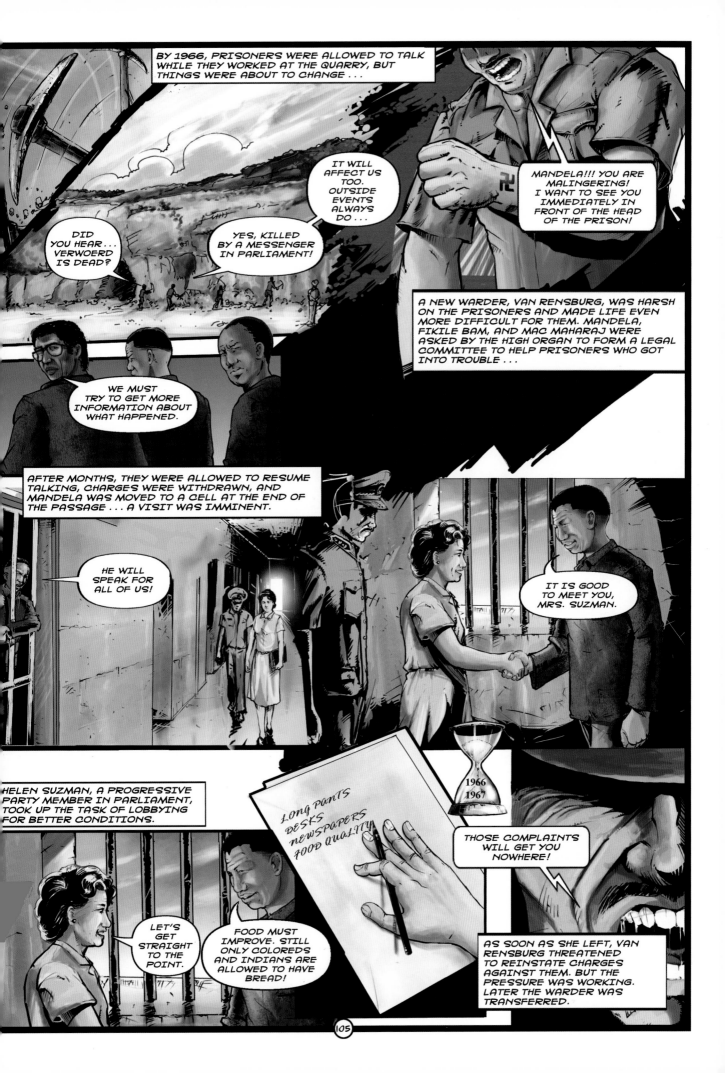

WORSE STILL, MANDELA WAS NOT ABLE TO HELP HIS YOUNG WIFE . . .

WINNIE MANDELA DETAINED

. . . MANDELA'S INABILITY TO PROTECT HIS FAMILY BECAME UNBEARABLE . . .

THEY HAD COME FOR WINNIE IN THE MIDDLE OF THE NIGHT. HER YOUNG DAUGHTERS SAW EVERYTHING.

MOVE! YOU ARE COMING WITH US!

MOM! HELP ME!

JUST LET ME GET THE CHILDREN TO FAMILY . . .

NO! WE WILL SORT THEM OUT!

WINNIE MADIKIZELA-MANDELA WAS SUBJECTED TO INTENSE PSYCHOLOGICAL AND PHYSICAL TORTURE, INCLUDING SEVENTEEN MONTHS IN ISOLATION. AFTER NEARLY 500 DAYS SHE WAS RELEASED, BUT SHE HAD REACHED A TURNING POINT IN HER LIFE . . .

"I AM THE CAPTAIN OF MY SOUL . . ."

THE 1960S WAS A DECADE OF TRIUMPH FOR THE APARTHEID SYSTEM. THE ECONOMY BOOMED, WHITE LIVING STANDARDS SOARED, AND APARTHEID LAWS WERE IMPLEMENTED ON A LARGE SCALE.

AT THE SAME TIME, THE ANC AND OTHER LIBERATION GROUPS WERE WEAK, AS WERE THE TRADE UNIONS, AND THE MASS PROTESTS OF THE 1950S WERE BECOMING A MEMORY . . .

NON-EUROPEANS

EUROPEA

EARLIER IN 1969, MANDELA HAD SENT A PETITION FOR THE RELEASE OF ALL POLITICAL PRISONERS TO THE MINISTER OF JUSTICE.

IN 1970, HE WROTE A LETTER OF COMPLAINT TO THE COMMISSIONER OF PRISONS ABOUT PRISON CONDITIONS.

MANDELA AND HIS FRIENDS WON'T LISTEN! HE STILL ACTS AS THEIR REPRESENTATIVE! YOU MUST RESTORE DISCIPLINE!

...LEAVE IT TO ME. WE WILL BREAK THEM!

A BRUTAL NEW COMMANDING OFFICER ARRIVED. WARDERS WERE REPLACED, STUDY AND RECREATIONAL PERIODS WERE SHORTENED, MANY VISITS WERE CANCELED, CELLS WERE RAIDED, AND FOOD DETERIORATED AND WAS SOMETIMES WITHHELD. BOARD GAMES WERE WITHDRAWN AND CENSORSHIP OF LETTERS INCREASED.

I HAVE BEEN TELLING YOU TO WORK HARDER BUT YOU WON'T LISTEN! SO I AM REDUCING ALL YOUR CLASSIFICATIONS!

ALL PRISONER COMPLAINTS WERE IGNORED AND SOME WHO REQUESTED TO SEE THEIR LAWYERS WERE PLACED IN SOLITARY CONFINEMENT.

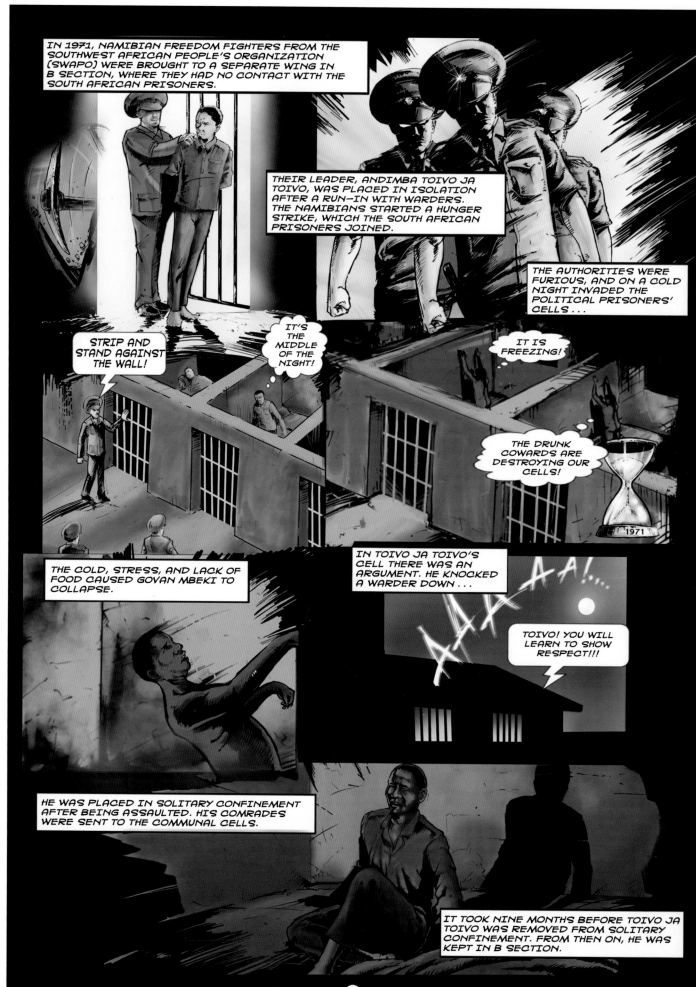

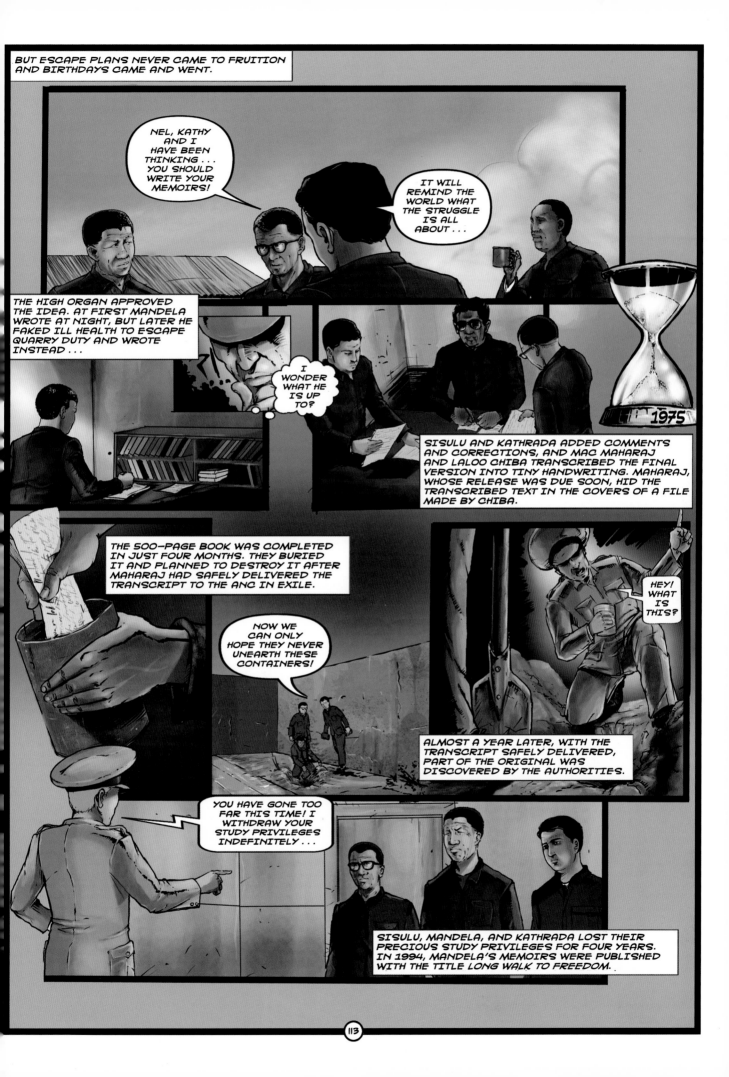

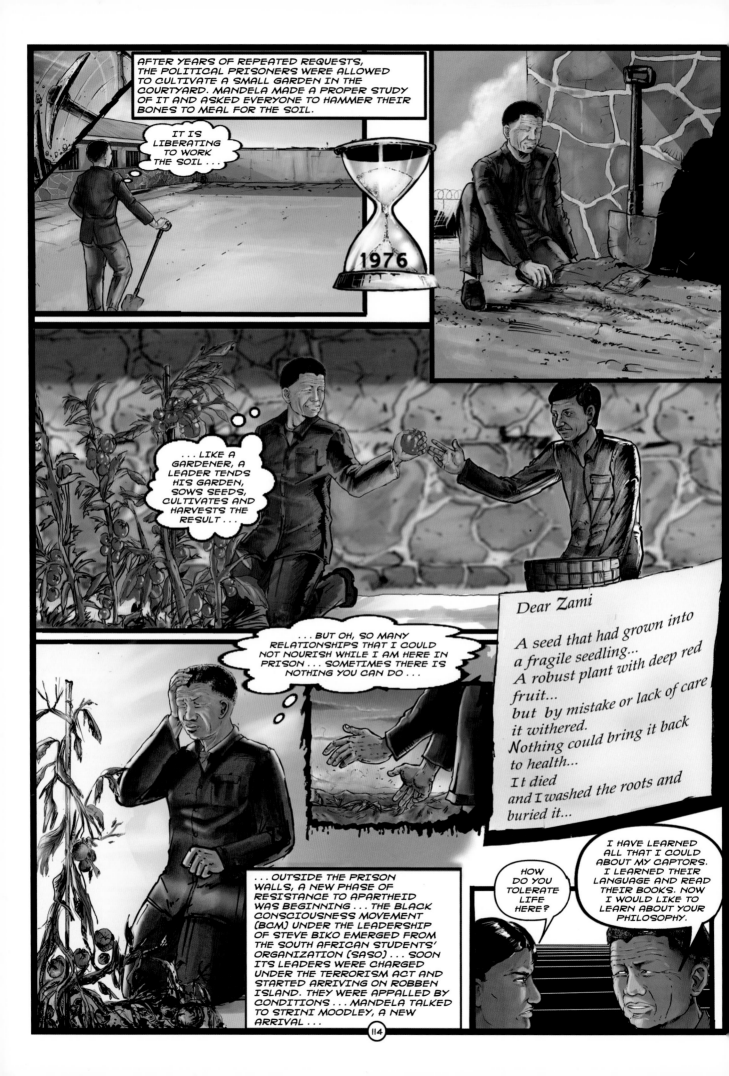

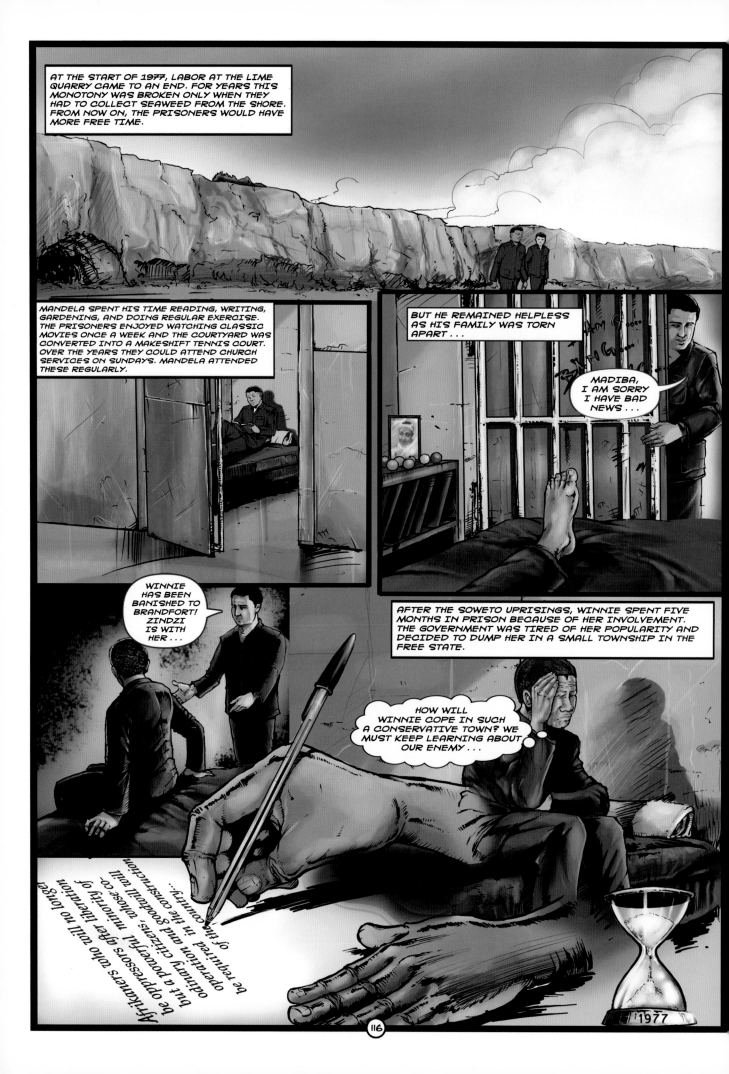

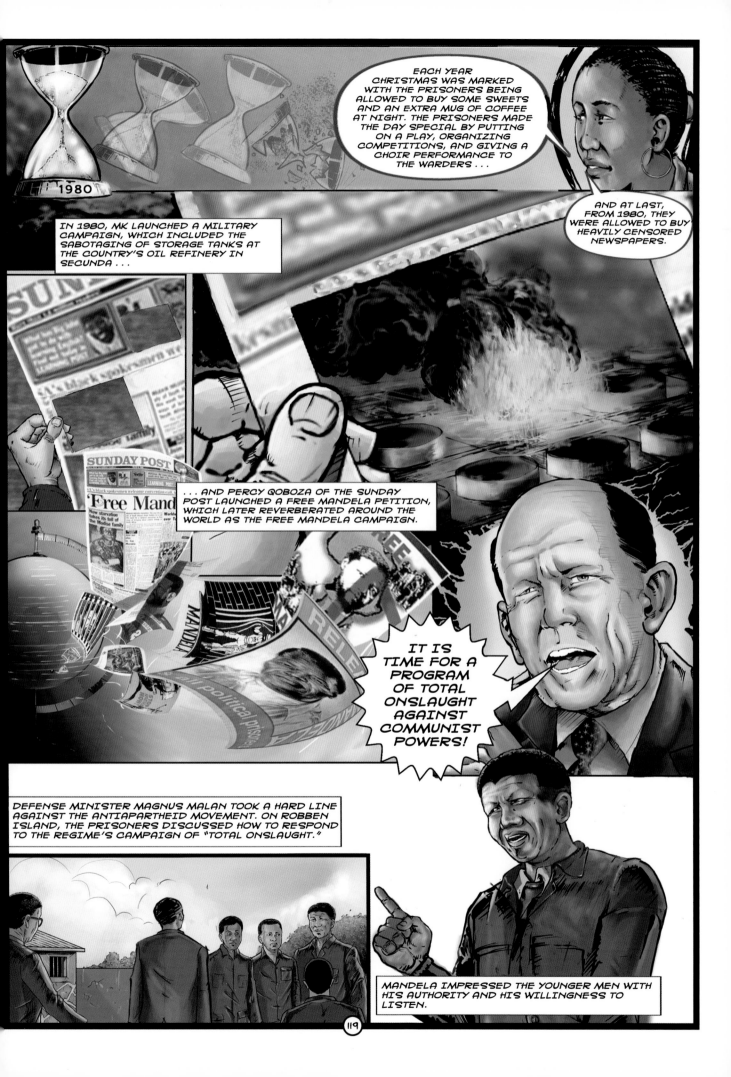

EACH YEAR CHRISTMAS WAS MARKED WITH THE PRISONERS BEING ALLOWED TO BUY SOME SWEETS AND AN EXTRA MUG OF COFFEE AT NIGHT. THE PRISONERS MADE THE DAY SPECIAL BY PUTTING ON A PLAY, ORGANIZING COMPETITIONS, AND GIVING A CHOIR PERFORMANCE TO THE WARDERS . . .

AND AT LAST, FROM 1980, THEY WERE ALLOWED TO BUY HEAVILY CENSORED NEWSPAPERS.

1980

IN 1980, MK LAUNCHED A MILITARY CAMPAIGN, WHICH INCLUDED THE SABOTAGING OF STORAGE TANKS AT THE COUNTRY'S OIL REFINERY IN SECUNDA . . .

. . . AND PERCY QOBOZA OF THE SUNDAY POST LAUNCHED A FREE MANDELA PETITION, WHICH LATER REVERBERATED AROUND THE WORLD AS THE FREE MANDELA CAMPAIGN.

IT IS TIME FOR A PROGRAM OF TOTAL ONSLAUGHT AGAINST COMMUNIST POWERS!

DEFENSE MINISTER MAGNUS MALAN TOOK A HARD LINE AGAINST THE ANTIAPARTHEID MOVEMENT. ON ROBBEN ISLAND, THE PRISONERS DISCUSSED HOW TO RESPOND TO THE REGIME'S CAMPAIGN OF "TOTAL ONSLAUGHT."

MANDELA IMPRESSED THE YOUNGER MEN WITH HIS AUTHORITY AND HIS WILLINGNESS TO LISTEN.

THE GOVERNMENT KEPT A CLOSE EYE ON MANDELA. REGULAR CHARACTER ASSESSMENTS AND PSYCHOLOGICAL ANALYSES WERE UNDERTAKEN.

...IT WOULD SEEM HIS TIME IN PRISON HAS CAUSED HIS PSYCHO-POLITICAL POSTURE TO INCREASE...

...MANDELA COMMANDS ALL THE QUALITIES OF THE NUMBER-ONE BLACK LEADER IN SOUTH AFRICA!

MANDELA IS EXCEPTIONALLY MOTIVATED... NO VISIBLE SIGNS OF BITTERNESS TOWARD WHITES... HE IS A PRACTICAL AND PRAGMATIC THINKER... AND HAS AN UNFLINCHING BELIEF IN HIS CAUSE!

BACK IN PRISON MANDELA RECEIVED BAD NEWS...

YOUR WIFE HAS BEEN IN A CAR ACCIDENT...

HOW IS SHE?

WE DON'T KNOW!

I DEMAND TO KNOW HOW SHE IS!

1982

THEY ARE CLEVER! WITHHOLDING INFORMATION IS A POWERFUL WEAPON!

PACK UP. YOU ARE LEAVING THE ISLAND LATER TODAY!

WHERE ARE YOU TAKING ME?

CAN'T SAY! INSTRUCTIONS FROM PRETORIA...

466/64
N. MANDELA

MANDELA ARRANGED TO SEE DULLAH OMAR, WINNIE'S ATTORNEY, WHO REASSURED HIM THAT WINNIE'S INJURIES WERE MINOR.

AFTER EIGHTEEN YEARS ON ROBBEN ISLAND, WHERE WAS HE BEING TAKEN?

120

6

THE NEGOTIATOR

THIS IS THE ENTRANCE TO THE VICTOR VERSTER PRISON, FROM WHERE THE MOST FAMOUS PRISONER IN THE WORLD WAS RELEASED.

IN OCTOBER THEY WERE JOINED BY THEIR OLD FRIEND AHMED KATHRADA.

IT IS GOOD TO SEE YOU, MADALA! I MISSED YOUR SEVENTIETH BIRTHDAY!

DO YOU KNOW WHY YOU WERE MOVED?

I THINK THEY ARE TRYING TO ISOLATE US. WE HAVE TOO MUCH INFLUENCE OVER OTHER PRISONERS...

THEY WERE JOINED BY PATRICK MAQUBELA, AN ANC MEMBER WHO HAD BEEN MOVED FROM DIEPKLOOF PRISON IN JOHANNESBURG. THEY HAD NO CONTACT WITH ANY OTHER PRISONERS AND HAD TO SPEND ALL THEIR TIME TOGETHER.

THIS CRICKET IS MAKING IT IMPOSSIBLE TO SLEEP!

OFF YOU GO... MAKE NOISE SOMEWHERE ELSE.

TYPICAL! MADIBA WON'T EVEN KILL A CRICKET...

123

MANDELA WROTE TO BISHOP DESMOND TUTU IN OCTOBER 1984, CONGRATULATING HIM ON HIS NOBEL PEACE PRIZE. BUT THE LETTER WAS NEVER DELIVERED. TUTU CALLED FOR EQUAL RIGHTS FOR ALL, THE ABOLITION OF PASS LAWS, ONE EDUCATION SYSTEM, AND THE END OF FORCED REMOVALS TO THE SO-CALLED HOMELANDS . . .

. . . MANDELA WAS OFFENDED THAT HIS COUSIN, MATANZIMA, STILL WANTED HIM RELEASED INTO THE TRANSKEI. HE MADE IT CLEAR THAT HE WOULD NEVER ACCEPT A CONDITIONAL RELEASE . . .

. . . MANDELA REPRESENTED FREEDOM AND DEMOCRACY. PEOPLE AROUND THE WORLD PUSHED FOR HIS RELEASE. IN 1984, THE UNITED NATIONS RECEIVED A 94,000-SIGNATURE PETITION CALLING FOR HIS FREEDOM.

FREE MANDELA

PROTESTS SPREAD. IN JANUARY 1985, ANC PRESIDENT OLIVER TAMBO CALLED ON THE PEOPLE TO MAKE THE COUNTRY "UNGOVERNABLE."

OLIVER IS RIGHT. WE HAVE NO OTHER CHOICE . . .

CONTINUING PROTESTS IS OUR STRONGEST BARGAINING CHIP!

P. W. BOTHA WAS UNDER INCREASING PRESSURE TO RELEASE MANDELA . . .

PLEASE COME WITH ME TO BRIGADIER MUNRO'S OFFICE.

ON JANUARY 31, 1985, BOTHA OFFERED CONDITIONAL RELEASE TO MANDELA, HIS COLLEAGUES, AND OTHER POLITICAL PRISONERS . . .

HERE IS A COPY OF THE ANNOUNCEMENT HE MADE IN PARLIAMENT . . .

WE CAN HAVE OUR FREEDOM PROVIDED WE UNCONDITIONALLY REJECT VIOLENCE AS A POLITICAL INSTRUMENT!

THE PRESIDENT IS OFFERING TO RELEASE YOU . . .

IT'S UNBELIEVABLE THAT BOTHA CAN SAY IT IS NOT THE GOVERNMENT STANDING IN THE WAY OF YOUR FREEDOM, BUT THAT IT IS YOU!

WE TURNED TO ARMED STRUGGLE ONLY AFTER THEY CLOSED THE DOOR TO PEACEFUL PROTEST. IT IS BOTHA WHO SHOULD RENOUNCE VIOLENCE!

BECAUSE YOU WILL NOT RENOUNCE THE ARMED STRUGGLE!

HE HAS MADE A PUBLIC CHALLENGE AND I WILL MAKE A PUBLIC RESPONSE.

MANDELA, SISULU, KATHRADA, MLANGENI, AND MAHLABA ALL REJECTED THE OFFER IN A LETTER TO PRESIDENT BOTHA.

MANDELA PREPARED A STATEMENT TO BE READ BY ZINDZI AT A RALLY AT SOWETO'S JABULANI STADIUM ON FEBRUARY 10. HE GAVE IT TO WINNIE DURING A VISIT.

YOU MUST STOP TALKING ABOUT POLITICS!

THIS IS A MATTER OF NATIONAL IMPORTANCE! IF YOU WANT ME TO STOP, YOU'D BETTER GET DIRECT ORDERS FROM THE PRESIDENT . . .

My father says...
What freedom am I being offered while the organisation of the people remains banned?
What freedom am I being offered when I may be arrested on a pass offence?
What freedom am I being offered to live my life as a family with my dear wife who remains in banishment in Brandfort?
What freedom am I being offered when I must ask for permission to live in an urban area... when my very South African citizenship is not respected?
Only free men can negotiate. Prisoners cannot enter into contracts...
I cannot and will not give any undertaking at a time when I and you, the people, are not free. Your freedom and mine cannot be separated.

I will return!

WE HAVE PAINTED OURSELVES INTO A CORNER . . . A TOTAL DEADLOCK!

BOTHA WAS IN TROUBLE . . .

IT WAS A POWERFUL MESSAGE. THE PEOPLE WERE MOVED . . .

130

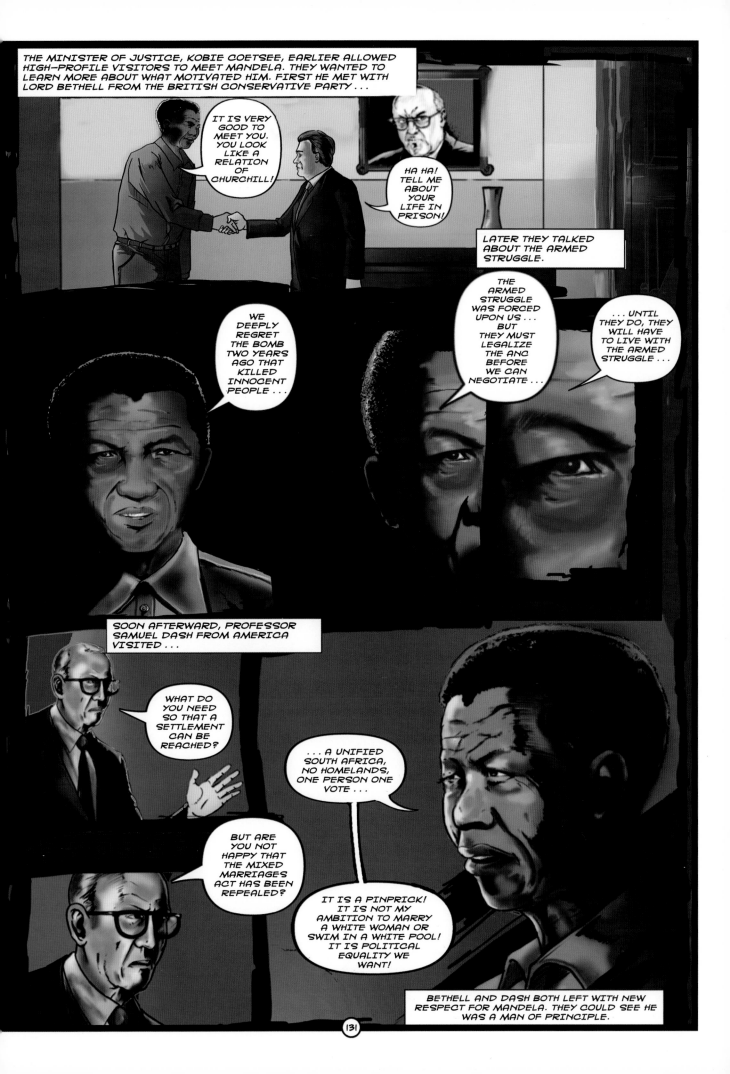

ABOUT TWENTY RADIO NEWS BULLETINS A DAY KEPT THE PRISONERS UP TO DATE WITH WORLD EVENTS . . .

. . . TODAY, ON THE TWENTY-FIFTH ANNIVERSARY OF SHARPEVILLE, NINETEEN PEOPLE DIED IN UITENHAGE DURING A CLASH BETWEEN THE POLICE AND PROTESTORS . . .

AMANDLA!

. . . WINNIE MANDELA WAS ON THE FRONTLINE OF THE STRUGGLE, AND HAD BECOME A LEADER IN HER OWN RIGHT . . .

. . . THE UDF WAS BLAMED FOR THE UNREST. THOUSANDS WERE DETAINED, TORTURED, AND ABDUCTED.

WE BID FAREWELL TO THESE COMRADES . . .

BEYERS NAUDE* SPOKE AT THE FUNERAL OF THE CRADOCK FOUR, WHO HAD BEEN ABDUCTED AND MURDERED BY THE SECURITY POLICE.

* DR. BEYERS NAUDE, AN AFRIKANER PREACHER, REJECTED APARTHEID AND BECAME A LEADING ANTIAPARTHEID ACTIVIST.

SOUTH AFRICA WAS HEADING FOR A "BLACK CHRISTMAS": TOWNSHIP RESIDENTS WERE SET TO BOYCOTT WHITE BUSINESSES. MANDELA WAS ADMITTED TO THE VOLKS HOSPITAL.

WE HAVE TO OPERATE. YOUR PROSTATE GLAND IS ENLARGED.

THE PRESS GATHERED OUT ANXIOUS FOR NEWS ON MA

I WONDER IF IT'S TRUE?

THEY SAY MANDELA WILL BE RELEASED.

IF HE DIES, ALL HELL WILL BREAK LOOSE!

MANDELA WAS RECOVERING WELL. HE HAD WRITTEN EARLIER TO MINISTER COETSEE REQUESTING A MEETING, BUT WAS SURPRISED WHEN HE PAID HIM AN UNSCHEDULED MEETING.

IT IS GOOD TO MEET YOU. YOU MUST HAVE RECEIVED MY LETTER.

YES. BUT TELL ME, HOW ARE YOU DOING?

A FEW WEEKS LATER, RETURNED TO POLLS AND PUT INTO A DIF SECTION, WHERE HE CELLS FOR HIS OWN

AFTER ALL THESE YEARS, THEY ARE ISOLATING ME . . .

THEY DID NOT DISCUSS POLITICS, BUT MANDELA DID ASK COETSEE TO LIFT WINNIE'S BANISHMENT. HE PROMISED TO LOOK INTO IT.

HIS OLD FRIENDS WERE NOT HAPPY . . .

MAYBE I CAN USE THIS ISOLATION . . IT WILL BE EASIER F THE GOVERNMENT TO APPROACH ME ON M OWN . . .

. . . A VIC IMPOS

WE SHOULD PROTEST.

WAIT. I THINK SOMETHING GOOD MIGHT COME OF THIS . . .

THIS REALLY MAKES US ANGRY!

IT IS TIME TO TALK, BUT BOTH SIDES THINK IT IS A SIGN OF WEAKNESS AND BETRAYAL!

MANDELA PUSHED AHEAD AND WROTE TO COETSEE AGAIN. HE REQUESTED "TALKS ABOUT TALKS." LATER, HE ASKED GEORGE BIZOS TO SEND WORD TO OLIVER TAMBO IN LUSAKA.

THE ANC APPROVES THE PRINCIPLE OF PRELIMINARY TALKS . . .

WHY ARE WE ALLOWING THIS COUNTRY TO BE DESTROYED?

MANDELA DECIDED TO LAUNCH A NEW INITIATIVE AND ASKED TO SEE GENERAL WILLEMSE, THE COMMISSIONER OF PRISONS.

GENERAL, I NEED TO MEET WITH MR. COETSEE . . .

ABOUT TALKS BETWEEN THE GOVERNMENT AND THE ANC!

BY NOW, THE ONLY PERMITTED GATHERINGS WERE IN CHURCHES. AFTER THE FAILURE OF THE COMMONWEALTH'S EMINENT PERSONS GROUP MISSION, THATCHER STILL RESISTED IMPOSING SANCTIONS ON SOUTH AFRICA.

INSTEAD SHE SENT BRITISH FOREIGN MINISTER GEOFFREY HOWE TO INTERVENE. BUT IT WAS A FAILURE. BOTH MANDELA AND BISHOP TUTU REFUSED TO MEET WITH HIM . . .

WILLEMSE IMMEDIATELY CALLED COETSEE, WHO TOLD HIM TO SEND MANDELA TO HIS HOUSE. IT WAS A HIGHLY IRREGULAR WAY OF MEETING, AND THEY SPENT THREE HOURS TALKING . . .

SO, MANDELA, WHAT IS THE NEXT STEP?

A MEETING WITH PRESIDENT BOTHA AND THE FOREIGN MINISTER . . .

MANDELA HAD TO PASS THROUGH FIFTEEN GATES, FROM HIS CELL TO THE OUTSIDE, EVERY TIME HE WENT FOR A MEETING . . .

MONTHS PASSED WITH NO WORD FROM COETSEE. MANDELA FELT THE AUTHORITIES MIGHT BE PREPARING HIM FOR RELEASE WHEN, IN DECEMBER, THEY TOOK HIM ON DRIVES AROUND THE CAPE.

THEY ARE GIVING ME LITTLE FREEDOMS . . . BUT STILL I CANNOT HELP BUT THINK OF WHAT I HAVE LOST . . .

THEMBI, MAKGATHO, MAKI, ZINDZI, ZENI, ZAMI . . . MY GRANDCHILDREN . . .

136

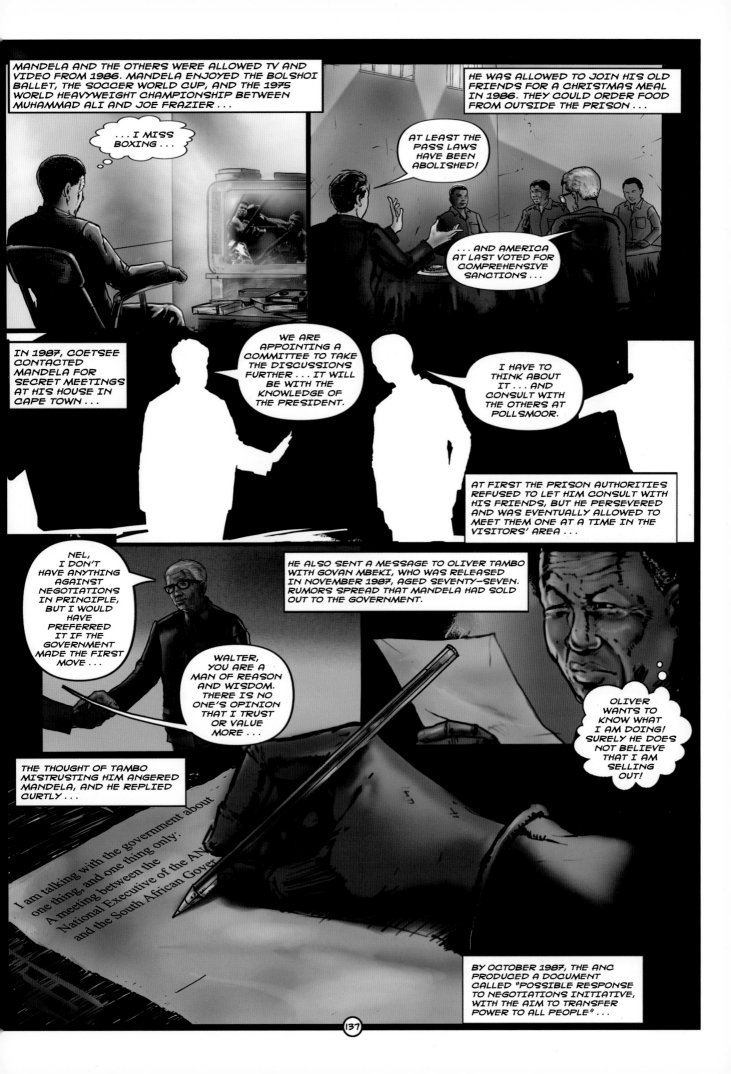

MANDELA AND THE OTHERS WERE ALLOWED TV AND VIDEO FROM 1986. MANDELA ENJOYED THE BOLSHOI BALLET, THE SOCCER WORLD CUP, AND THE 1975 WORLD HEAVYWEIGHT CHAMPIONSHIP BETWEEN MUHAMMAD ALI AND JOE FRAZIER . . .

. . . I MISS BOXING . . .

HE WAS "ALLOWED TO JOIN HIS OLD FRIENDS FOR A CHRISTMAS MEAL IN 1986. THEY COULD ORDER FOOD FROM OUTSIDE THE PRISON . . .

AT LEAST THE PASS LAWS HAVE BEEN ABOLISHED!

. . . AND AMERICA AT LAST VOTED FOR COMPREHENSIVE SANCTIONS . . .

IN 1987, COETSEE CONTACTED MANDELA FOR SECRET MEETINGS AT HIS HOUSE IN CAPE TOWN . . .

WE ARE APPOINTING A COMMITTEE TO TAKE THE DISCUSSIONS FURTHER . . . IT WILL BE WITH THE KNOWLEDGE OF THE PRESIDENT.

I HAVE TO THINK ABOUT IT . . . AND CONSULT WITH THE OTHERS AT POLLSMOOR.

AT FIRST THE PRISON AUTHORITIES REFUSED TO LET HIM CONSULT WITH HIS FRIENDS, BUT HE PERSEVERED AND WAS EVENTUALLY ALLOWED TO MEET THEM ONE AT A TIME IN THE VISITORS' AREA . . .

NEL, I DON'T HAVE ANYTHING AGAINST NEGOTIATIONS IN PRINCIPLE, BUT I WOULD HAVE PREFERRED IT IF THE GOVERNMENT MADE THE FIRST MOVE . . .

WALTER, YOU ARE A MAN OF REASON AND WISDOM. THERE IS NO ONE'S OPINION THAT I TRUST OR VALUE MORE . . .

HE ALSO SENT A MESSAGE TO OLIVER TAMBO WITH GOVAN MBEKI, WHO WAS RELEASED IN NOVEMBER 1987, AGED SEVENTY-SEVEN. RUMORS SPREAD THAT MANDELA HAD SOLD OUT TO THE GOVERNMENT.

OLIVER WANTS TO KNOW WHAT I AM DOING! SURELY HE DOES NOT BELIEVE THAT I AM SELLING OUT!

THE THOUGHT OF TAMBO MISTRUSTING HIM ANGERED MANDELA, AND HE REPLIED CURTLY . . .

I am talking with the government about one thing, and one thing only: A meeting between the National Executive of the ANC and the South African Gover...

BY OCTOBER 1987, THE ANC PRODUCED A DOCUMENT CALLED "POSSIBLE RESPONSE TO NEGOTIATIONS INITIATIVE, WITH THE AIM TO TRANSFER POWER TO ALL PEOPLE" . . .

THE TALKS WITH THE GOVERNMENT TEAM CONTINUED, BUT THEY WERE NOT PROGRESSING . . .

YOU HAVE TO START SEEING ME AS PART OF THE SOLUTION, NOT THE PROBLEM!

WE CANNOT ACCEPT THE CONDITIONS THAT YOU PLACE ON NEGOTIATIONS.

LET ME SPEAK TO PRESIDENT BOTHA . . .

IN JANUARY 1989, MANDELA'S FRIENDS FROM POLLSMOOR WERE ALLOWED TO VISIT HIM.

I DRAFTED A MEMORANDUM TO PRESIDENT BOTHA. I WANT YOU TO GO OVER IT WITH ME.

LET'S SIT WHERE WE CANNOT BE OVERHEARD BY THE GUARDS . . .

PLEASE READ IT, KATHY.

I AM DISTURBED, AS ARE MANY OTHER SOUTH AFRICANS . . . BY THE SPECTER OF SOUTH AFRICA BEING SPLIT INTO TWO HOSTILE CAMPS . . .

BLACKS ON ONE SIDE . . . AND WHITES ON THE OTHER, SLAUGHTERING ONE ANOTHER . . .

THEREFORE, WE NEED TO DEAL WITH THE THREE PRECONDITIONS ON NEGOTIATIONS SET BY THE GOVERNMENT.

WE CANNOT CAST THE SACP ASIDE . . . WE ARE NOT UNDER ITS CONTROL . . .

MAJORITY RULE AND INTERNAL PEACE ARE LIKE THE TWO SIDES OF A SINGLE COIN . . .

. . . THE REFUSAL OF THE ANC TO RENOUNCE VIOLENCE IS NOT THE PROBLEM . . .

THE TRUTH IS THE GOVERNMENT IS NOT YET READY TO SHARE POLITICAL POWER WITH BLACKS.

FROM APRIL 1989, MANDELA AND TAMBO HAD CONTACT THROUGH A SYSTEM INVOLVING CODED MESSAGES SENT VIA A LAPTOP THAT HAD BEEN SMUGGLED INTO THE COUNTRY WITH THE HELP OF MAC MAHARAJ.

. . . AT LEAST NOW WE CAN SPEAK IN CONFIDENCE! BIZOS TOLD ME EVEN THE GARDEN FURNITURE AND FLOWERBEDS AT VICTOR VERSTER ARE BUGGED.

TAMBO DECLARED 1989 THE "YEAR OF MASS ACTION FOR PEOPLE'S POWER." THE COUNTRY WAS IN UPHEAVAL. PRISONERS WENT ON A PROLONGED HUNGER STRIKE. WHILE MANDELA DEMANDED THEIR RELEASE. EVENTUALLY, THE GOVERNMENT WAS FORCED TO RELEASE 900 POLITICAL PRISONERS, INCLUDING UDF LEADERS . . .

THE UDF FORMED AN ALLIANCE WITH TRADE UNIONS LIKE COSATU AND STARTED THE "MASS DEMOCRATIC MOVEMENT," WHICH LAUNCHED A DEFIANCE CAMPAIGN AGAINST APARTHEID INSTITUTIONS SUCH AS HOSPITALS FOR WHITES ONLY . . .

UMKHONTO WE SIZWE INTENSIFIED ATTACKS ON GOVERNMENT PROPERTY. IT USED MORTARS TO DESTROY A MILITARY RADAR STATION . . .

HOSPITAL
whites only

MANDELA AND TAMBO KEPT PUSHING FOR SANCTIONS AGAINST SOUTH AFRICA AS AN ALTERNATIVE TO BLOODSHED.

IN JULY, SIX MONTHS AFTER HE SUFFERED A STROKE, PRESIDENT BOTHA ASKED TO SEE MANDELA . . .

WE NEED THE GOVERNMENT TO RELEASE ALL POLITICAL PRISONERS . . .

I AM SORRY, BUT I CANNOT DO THAT.

I THINK THE AFRIKANERS WERE THE FIRST REAL FREEDOM FIGHTERS IN SOUTH AFRICA.

WELL, I THINK YOU CAN CONTRIBUTE TO A PEACEFUL SOLUTION, AND SO CAN THE AFRIKANERS . . .

SIX WEEKS LATER, BOTHA RESIGNED AS PRESIDENT.

IN AUGUST, THE GOVERNMENT TEAM RESPONDED TO THE MEMORANDUM SENT TO BOTHA. SOME AGREEMENT ABOUT PRE-NEGOTIATIONS WITH THE GOVERNMENT HAD BEEN REACHED . . .

THE OAU ENDORSED TAMBO'S HARARE DECLARATION. IT DID NOT ABANDON THE ARMED STRUGGLE BUT STRESSED THAT THE ANC PREFERRED PEACEFUL METHODS . . .

THABO MBEKI MET NATIONAL INTELLIGENCE AGENT MIKE LOUW IN SWITZERLAND AND SAID THE ANC WAS READY TO NEGOTIATE . . .

F. W. DE KLERK BECAME SOUTH AFRICA'S NEW PRESIDENT. WHEN LOUW TOLD HIM ABOUT THE MBEKI BREAKTHROUGH HE DECIDED TO "TAKE THE BALL AND RUN WITH IT" . . .

... HE ANNOUNCED HIS WILLINGNESS TO TALK TO GROUPS COMMITTED TO PEACE AND STARTED DISMANTLING APARTHEID RESTRICTIONS SUCH AS SEGREGATED BEACHES, PARKS, AND TOILETS, AND THE NATIONAL SECURITY MANAGEMENT SYSTEM THAT CONTROLLED THE TOWNSHIPS.

MANDELA WROTE TO DE KLERK REQUESTING A MEETING. HE ALSO DEMANDED THE RELEASE OF TEN POLITICAL PRISONERS, INCLUDING HIS OLD FRIENDS AT POLLSMOOR. THEY CAME TO VISIT HIM AT VICTOR VERSTER PRISON ...

US! RELEASED? I DON'T BELIEVE IT ...

FRIENDS, THIS IS A GOOD-BYE VISIT.

YOU ARE GOING TO BE RELEASED.

THAT EVENING, AFTER THEY HAD SAID GOOD-BYE TO MANDELA, THE MEN HAD DINNER WITH HIGH-RANKING PRISON OFFICIALS. A TELEVISION WAS BROUGHT IN ...

... EIGHT POLITICAL PRISONERS WILL BE RELEASED ... SISULU, KATHRADA, MHLABA, MKWAYI, MLANGENI, MOTSOALEDI, MASEMOLA, AND MPETHA ...

IT IS TRUE!

!?

FIVE DAYS LATER, ON SUNDAY MORNING, OCTOBER 15, 1989, THE MEN WERE RELEASED ...

MANDELA WAS THE LAST MAJOR OPPOSITION LEADER LEFT IN PRISON. POLITICIANS, FRIENDS, CLERGY, TRADE UNIONISTS, AND YOUTH LEADERS CONVERGED ON VICTOR VERSTER. IN DECEMBER, DE KLERK AND MANDELA MET AT TUYNHUIS.

... I HOPE WE WILL BE ABLE TO WORK TOGETHER ...

IT WAS A TRICKY TIME. MANDELA LOST A VALUABLE LINK TO THE OUTSIDE WHEN TAMBO SUFFERED A STROKE. HE MADE SURE A COPY OF THE MEMORANDUM THAT HE HANDED TO DE KLERK REACHED THE ANC IN LUSAKA.

MANDELA HAD TO TACKLE THE GOVERNMENT'S NEW IDEA OF GROUP RIGHTS, WHERE NO RACIAL GROUP WOULD TAKE PRECEDENCE OVER ANY OTHER ...

THE NP'S IDEA OF GROUP RIGHTS SEEMS LIKE A WAY TO MODERNIZE APARTHEID ...

... THE ANC HAS NOT STRUGGLED AGAINST APARTHEID FOR SEVENTY-FIVE YEARS ONLY TO YIELD TO A DISGUISED FORM OF IT ...

YOU KNOW, WE ARE TRYING TO DEAL WITH WHITE FEARS OF BLACK DOMINATION ... YOU TOLD BOTHA WE HAD TO FIND A WAY TO DEAL WITH IT!

UNFORTUNATELY, MR. DE KLERK, THE IDEA OF GROUP RIGHTS IS DOING MORE TO INCREASE BLACK FEARS THAN TO ALLAY WHITE ONES!

ON FEBRUARY 2, 1990, DE KLERK MADE A DRAMATIC ANNOUNCEMENT IN PARLIAMENT ...

ALL POLITICAL PARTIES WILL BE UNBANNED ... NELSON MANDELA WILL BE RELEASED WITH NO CONDITIONS ...

A WEEK LATER . . . AFTER WORKING THROUGH THE NIGHT ON A SPEECH WITH COLLEAGUES SUCH AS CYRIL RAMAPHOSA AND TREVOR MANUEL, MANDELA PREPARED FOR HIS RELEASE THE NEXT MORNING . . . AFTER MORE THAN 10,000 DAYS IN PRISON.

HIS BAGS PACKED, MANDELA BID FAREWELL TO THE WARDERS AND LEFT TO GREET A WORLD THAT HAD GROWN UP WITHOUT HIM . . . AND ONE THAT HAD LITTLE IDEA OF WHAT WAS GOING TO HAPPEN NEXT . . .

AS HE TOOK HIS FIRST STEPS TO FREEDOM, MANDELA WAS GREETED BY JOURNALISTS FROM ALL OVER THE WORLD AND THOUSANDS OF SUPPORTERS. THEY DANCED, CHEERED, AND CRIED WITH HAPPINESS. THEIR CHANCE FOR A NEW FUTURE HAD COME . . .

7
PRESIDENT-IN-WAITING

THIS IS GROOTE SCHUUR, WHERE THE FIRST BREAKTHROUGH IN NEGOTIATIONS BETWEEN THE ANC AND THE APARTHEID GOVERNMENT TOOK PLACE...

... TO DRIVE TO THE TRANSKEI, VISIT THE PLACES OF MY CHILDHOOD ... MY MOTHER'S GRAVE ... IT WILL HAVE TO WAIT ...

MANDELA WAS WHISKED OFF TO THE HOME OF ARCHBISHOP DESMOND TUTU, IN THE TRADITIONALLY WHITE SUBURB OF BISHOPSCOURT, TO SPEND THE NIGHT.

THE NEXT MORNING HE FACED HUNDREDS OF JOURNALISTS AT HIS FIRST PRESS CONFERENCE.

MR. MANDELA, WHY ARE YOU STILL SUPPORTING THE ARMED STRUGGLE AND SANCTIONS?

THE ABSENCE OF RIGHTS FOR BLACKS IS STILL THE STATUS QUO. I MIGHT BE OUT OF JAIL, BUT I AM NOT YET FREE ...

WHITES ARE FELLOW SOUTH AFRICANS ... ANY MAN OR WOMAN WHO ABANDONS APARTHEID WILL BE EMBRACED IN OUR STRUGGLE FOR A DEMOCRATIC, NON-RACIAL SOUTH AFRICA.

HE TRIED TO ALLEVIATE WHITE FEARS AND SURPRISED THE WORLD WITH HIS COMPLETE LACK OF BITTERNESS ...

THERE WAS NO TIME TO REST AND REFLECT. MANDELA WAS URGED TO RETURN TO JOHANNESBURG, WHERE SUPPORTERS WERE WAITING. HE SPENT HIS SECOND NIGHT OF FREEDOM AT THE HOME OF A SUPPORTER IN JOHANNESBURG.

ON FEBRUARY 13, 1990, A CROWD OF 100,000 CONVERGED AT SOCCER CITY IN SOWETO TO WELCOME MANDELA. HE URGED LEARNERS TO GO TO SCHOOL AND CONDEMNED CRIME. HE LEFT BY HELICOPTER AT THE END OF THE RALLY.

ON FEBRUARY 27, MANDELA AND HIS COLLEAGUES FLEW TO LUSAKA TO REPORT TO THE ANC'S NATIONAL EXECUTIVE COMMITTEE.

THEY WILL WANT TO SEE IF I HAD BEEN BROKEN . . .

MANDELA WAS ELECTED AS DEPUTY PRESIDENT OF THE ANC. ALFRED NZO BECAME ACTING PRESIDENT WHILE OLIVER TAMBO RECUPERATED FROM A STROKE.

WELCOME MANDELA

VIVA! ANC MANDELA

WELL DONE, COMRADE.

MANDELA HAD TO SHOW THAT HE WAS STILL A STRONG LEADER. SOME STILL BELIEVED HE HAD SOLD OUT. HE RECOMMITTED HIMSELF TO THE ARMED STRUGGLE.

WE HAVE NOT YET ACHIEVED THE GOAL FOR WHICH WE HAVE TAKEN UP ARMS . . .

HE WAS APPALLED BY THE VIOLENCE THAT HAD BEEN RAGING IN KWAZULU-NATAL BETWEEN SUPPORTERS OF INKATHA AND THE ANC . . .

HE SPOKE TO 100,000 PEOPLE AT A RALLY IN DURBAN JUST TWO WEEKS AFTER HIS RELEASE:

TAKE YOUR GUNS, YOUR KNIVES, AND YOUR PANGAS, AND THROW THEM INTO THE SEA!

BUT THE KILLINGS CONTINUED . . . VILLAGES WERE SET ALIGHT AND THOUSANDS WERE DISPLACED . . . MANDELA VISITED VIOLENCE-STRICKEN COMMUNITIES.

DE KLERK AND THE GOVERNMENT ARE DOING NOTHING TO STOP THIS! WHY?

WHY IS CHIEF BUTHELEZI NOT TELLING HIS PEOPLE TO STOP?!

MANDELA DID NOT MANAGE TO MEET WITH CHIEF BUTHELEZI AND KING ZWELETHINI, WITH WHOM HE TRIED TO MAINTAIN GOOD RELATIONS.

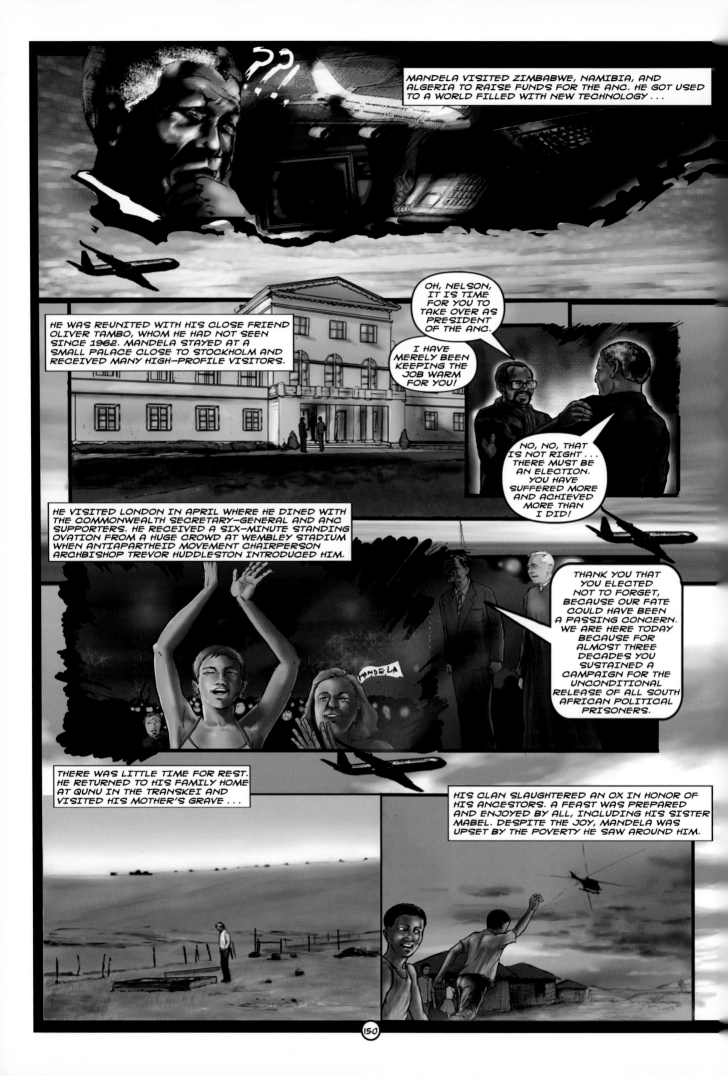

MANDELA VISITED ZIMBABWE, NAMIBIA, AND ALGERIA TO RAISE FUNDS FOR THE ANC. HE GOT USED TO A WORLD FILLED WITH NEW TECHNOLOGY . . .

HE WAS REUNITED WITH HIS CLOSE FRIEND OLIVER TAMBO, WHOM HE HAD NOT SEEN SINCE 1962. MANDELA STAYED AT A SMALL PALACE CLOSE TO STOCKHOLM AND RECEIVED MANY HIGH-PROFILE VISITORS.

OH, NELSON, IT IS TIME FOR YOU TO TAKE OVER AS PRESIDENT OF THE ANC.

I HAVE MERELY BEEN KEEPING THE JOB WARM FOR YOU!

NO, NO, THAT IS NOT RIGHT . . . THERE MUST BE AN ELECTION. YOU HAVE SUFFERED MORE AND ACHIEVED MORE THAN I DID!

HE VISITED LONDON IN APRIL WHERE HE DINED WITH THE COMMONWEALTH SECRETARY-GENERAL AND ANC SUPPORTERS. HE RECEIVED A SIX-MINUTE STANDING OVATION FROM A HUGE CROWD AT WEMBLEY STADIUM WHEN ANTIAPARTHEID MOVEMENT CHAIRPERSON ARCHBISHOP TREVOR HUDDLESTON INTRODUCED HIM.

THANK YOU THAT YOU ELECTED NOT TO FORGET, BECAUSE OUR FATE COULD HAVE BEEN A PASSING CONCERN. WE ARE HERE TODAY BECAUSE FOR ALMOST THREE DECADES YOU SUSTAINED A CAMPAIGN FOR THE UNCONDITIONAL RELEASE OF ALL SOUTH AFRICAN POLITICAL PRISONERS.

MANDELA

THERE WAS LITTLE TIME FOR REST. HE RETURNED TO HIS FAMILY HOME AT QUNU IN THE TRANSKEI AND VISITED HIS MOTHER'S GRAVE . . .

HIS CLAN SLAUGHTERED AN OX IN HONOR OF HIS ANCESTORS. A FEAST WAS PREPARED AND ENJOYED BY ALL, INCLUDING HIS SISTER MABEL. DESPITE THE JOY, MANDELA WAS UPSET BY THE POVERTY HE SAW AROUND HIM.

MANDELA HAD TO HELP LEAD THE ANC TO POLITICAL POWER. BUT FIRST A NEGOTIATED SETTLEMENT HAD TO BE FOUND.

DISASTER STRUCK JUST BEFORE THE ANC AND GOVERNMENT WERE DUE TO SET A DATE FOR "TALKS ABOUT TALKS."

SEVERAL ANC SUPPORTERS WERE KILLED AND HUNDREDS INJURED WHEN THE POLICE FIRED ON DEMONSTRATORS IN SEBOKENG ON MARCH 26, 1990.

EVERY WHITE POLICEMAN IN SOUTH AFRICA REGARDS EVERY BLACK PERSON AS A MILITARY TARGET!

THE ANC IS SUSPENDING TALKS . . . DE KLERK HAS TO UNDERSTAND, YOU CANNOT TALK ABOUT NEGOTIATIONS ON THE ONE HAND AND MURDER OUR PEOPLE ON THE OTHER!

AT LAST, ON MAY 2, 1990, AT GROOTE SCHUUR, THE PRESIDENTIAL RESIDENCE IN CAPE TOWN, THE ANC AND GOVERNMENT MET . . .

MANDELA, SISULU, NZO, THABO MBEKI, KATHRADA, JOE MODISE, RUTH MOMPATI, ARCHIE GUMEDE, BEYERS NAUDE, CHERYL CAROLUS, AND JOE SLOVO REPRESENTED THE ANC IN THE THREE DAYS OF TALKS.

THE TWO PARTIES REACHED AN AGREEMENT CALLED "THE GROOTE SCHUUR MINUTE." IT WAS ABOUT THE RELEASE OF POLITICAL PRISONERS, THE RETURN OF EXILES, AND AMENDING SECURITY LEGISLATION. THE ANC AND THE GOVERNMENT ALSO PROMISED TO CONTINUE PEACEFUL NEGOTIATIONS AND WORK TOWARD LIFTING THE STATE OF EMERGENCY.

WE WENT INTO THESE DISCUSSIONS IN THE SPIRIT THAT THERE SHOULD BE NEITHER WINNERS NOR LOSERS . . .

NOT ONLY ARE WE CLOSER TO ONE ANOTHER, THE ANC, AND THE GOVERNMENT, BUT WE ARE ALL VICTORS. SOUTH AFRICA IS A VICTOR.

ONE OF MANDELA'S CLOSEST FRIENDS, WALTER SISULU, HAD HIS FAMILY BACK TOGETHER FOR THE FIRST TIME IN DECADES.

HIS DAUGHTER LINDIWE RETURNED AFTER 14 YEARS IN EXILE...

HIS SON MAX RETURNED A FEW MONTHS LATER AFTER 24 YEARS IN EXILE...

HIS SON ZWELAKHE, WHO WAS IN DETENTION BETWEEN 1986 AND 1988, WAS WORKING AS MANDELA'S PRESS AIDE...

HIS FREEDOM FIGHTER SON JONGI, WHOM HE HAD LAST SEEN WHEN HE WAS FIVE YEARS OLD, WAS RELEASED FROM PRISON AND WAITED FOR HIS FATHER AT THE AIRPORT...

I DID NOT RECOGNIZE YOU! I JUST DID NOT RECOGNIZE YOU...

TATA, THIS IS JONGI!

IN THE MEANTIME, MANDELA MOVED TO A BIGGER HOUSE IN SOWETO, BUT HIS WORK LEFT HIM LITTLE TIME FOR HIS FAMILY.

BY NOW, WINNIE WAS CAUGHT UP IN THE CONTROVERSY SURROUNDING THE DEATH OF ACTIVIST STOMPIE SEIPEI. MANDELA STUCK BY HER.

YOU KNOW, THE GIRLS WERE SAYING THAT YOU WERE MORE ACCESSIBLE TO THEM WHEN YOU WERE IN PRISON...

IN JUNE, JUST BEFORE MANDELA WENT ON AN INTERNATIONAL TOUR, DE KLERK IMPLORED HIM NOT TO KEEP PUSHING FOR SANCTIONS. BUT MANDELA DID NOT AGREE.

152

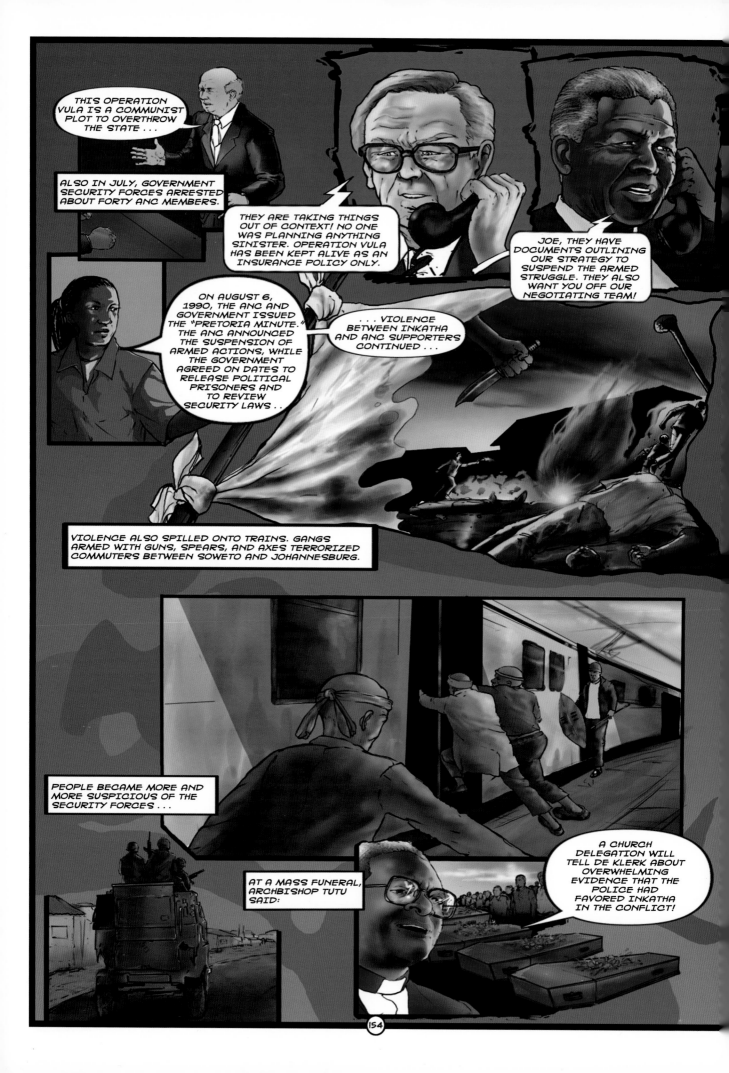

THE ANC SET UP ARMED SELF-DEFENSE UNITS TO PROTECT THE PEOPLE IN THE VIOLENCE-RAVAGED TOWNSHIPS. MANDELA VISITED THE BATTLEFIELDS AND KEPT BEING TOLD THE POLICE SUPPORTED INKATHA . . .

DE KLERK HAD SOUGHT AN ALLIANCE WITH INKATHA BUT IT WAS NOT TO BE. BUTHELEZI WAS ALSO COURTED BY CONSERVATIVES IN THE WEST WHO SAW INKATHA AS AN ANTICOMMUNIST OPPOSITION TO THE ANC.

THE POLICE WERE ON INKATHA'S SIDE . . . I SAW THEM HANDING OUT GUNS!

THERE ARE FORCES CLOSE TO YOU, MR. PRESIDENT, WITH A DOUBLE AGENDA!

I WILL HAVE TO INVESTIGATE THESE ALLEGATIONS!

MANDELA DESPERATELY WANTED THE SENSELESS VIOLENCE TO END. AT LAST, IN JANUARY 1991, HE MET WITH BUTHELEZI. IT WAS THEIR FIRST MEETING IN THIRTY YEARS.

IT IS GOOD TO MEET AFTER SUCH A LONG TIME . . .

THANK YOU FOR ALL YOUR EFFORTS OVER THE YEARS TO SECURE MY RELEASE FROM PRISON . . .

THE MEN AGREED TO PROMOTE PEACE AND TO URGE THEIR PEOPLE TO STOP THE KILLINGS, BUT WORSE WAS TO COME. IN MARCH, FORTY-FIVE PEOPLE WERE KILLED IN ALEXANDRA TOWNSHIP, WHERE MANDELA ONCE LIVED. MORE THAN 400 PEOPLE WERE KILLED IN THE FIRST THREE MONTHS OF THE YEAR. MANDELA MET WITH BUTHELEZI FOR A SECOND TIME.

MANDELA SAID:
"I AM NOW CONVINCED THE GOVERNMENT HAS A HAND IN THIS VIOLENCE"

THE ANC DECLARED IT BELIEVED THE GOVERNMENT WAS BEHIND THE VIOLENCE. IT WROTE AN OPEN LETTER TO THE GOVERNMENT WITH THE BACKING OF THE SACP AND COSATU.

. . . WE CALL FOR THE DISMISSAL OF MINISTERS MALAN AND VLOK BEFORE MAY OR WE WILL SUSPEND ALL TALKS WITH THE GOVERNMENT!

THE GOVERNMENT REFUSED TO COOPERATE, AND THE ANC AGAIN BROKE OFF TALKS. THE PEOPLE THEN EMBARKED ON A CAMPAIGN OF MASS ACTION, TO DEMONSTRATE THEIR STRENGTH.

ON JULY 2, 1991, THE ANC HELD A NATIONAL CONFERENCE IN SOUTH AFRICA FOR THE FIRST TIME IN THIRTY YEARS.

OLIVER TAMBO HAD RETURNED TO THE COUNTRY, BUT STEPPED DOWN AS ANC PRESIDENT. NELSON ROLIHLAHLA MANDELA WAS ELECTED IN HIS PLACE.

THE OLD GUARD WAS STILL STRONG IN THE ANC, BUT YOUNGER LEADERS CAME TO THE FORE. CYRIL RAMAPHOSA WAS ELECTED AS SECRETARY-GENERAL.

MANDELA FACED OPEN CRITICISM FROM MILITANTS IN THE ANC . . .

WE NEED A YOUNGER, MORE MILITANT MAN TO LEAD US IN THE STRUGGLE . . .

AT HOME, HE ALSO FACED CRITICISM WHEN HIS DAUGHTER MAKAZIWE RETURNED FROM AMERICA IN 1990.

MAKI . . .

YOU ARE A FATHER TO ALL OUR PEOPLE, BUT YOU HAVE NEVER HAD THE TIME TO BE A FATHER TO ME . . .

SHE HAS NOT FORGIVEN ME . . .

MANDELA ADORED CHILDREN. HE HAD MISSED THEIR COMPANY FOR TWENTY-SEVEN YEARS.

MADIBA, WHY DID YOU GO TO PRISON FOR SOOOO LONG?

YOU MUST BE VERY STUPID TO STAY THERE SO LONG . . .

HA! I THINK YOU MIGHT BE RIGHT!

WELL, I HAD TO STAY THERE TO FIGHT FOR DEMOCRACY . . .

IN THE MEANTIME, WINNIE WAS CHARGED WITH KIDNAPPING AND ASSAULT IN THE SEIPEI CASE. MANDELA SUPPORTED HER DURING THE FOUR-MONTH TRIAL. HE CALLED ON HIS FRIENDS TO DO THE SAME . . .

I WAS NEVER THERE FOR HER. NOW I WILL STAND BY ZAMI . . .

WINNIE WAS FOUND GUILTY ON FOUR COUNTS OF KIDNAPPING AND AS AN ACCESSORY TO ASSAULT. SHE WAS GRANTED LEAVE TO APPEAL AND HER BAIL WAS EXTENDED.

WINNIE IS INNOCENT

IN JULY, MANDELA'S SUSPICIONS ABOUT THE GOVERNMENT AND INKATHA WERE CONFIRMED.

WEEKLY MAIL

POLICE PAID INKATHA TO BLOCK THE ANC

I KNEW IT! THEY WANTED TO DESTABILIZE THE COUNTRY. THEY HAVE BLOOD ON THEIR HANDS!

IT WAS DIRTY TRICKS! I CANNOT BELIEVE I ONCE CALLED DE KLERK A MAN OF INTEGRITY . . .

AT LEAST NOW THE MINISTERS OF POLICE AND DEFENSE HAVE BEEN REMOVED!

DE KLERK DENIED KNOWLEDGE OF THE COVERT MILITARY OPERATION TO FUND AND TRAIN INKATHA SUPPORTERS. THE GOVERNMENT, ANC, AND INKATHA HELD A PEACE CONFERENCE . . .

WHILE THEY SIGNED A PEACE DEAL, THE CROWDS OUTSIDE CHANTED AGGRESSIVE SLOGANS AND BUTHELEZI REFUSED TO SHAKE HANDS WITH MANDELA AND DE KLERK.

BUT MANDELA'S WISH CAME TRUE. NEGOTIATIONS STARTED ON DECEMBER 20, 1991. THE TALKS WERE CALLED THE CONVENTION FOR DEMOCRATIC CHANGE IN SOUTH AFRICA (CODESA). IN HIS OPENING SPEECH, THE LEADER OF THE NATIONAL PARTY DELEGATION, DAWIE DE VILLIERS, SAID:

IT WAS NOT THE INTENTION TO DEPRIVE OTHER PEOPLE OF THEIR RIGHTS AND TO CONTRIBUTE TO THEIR MISERY . . . BUT EVENTUALLY IT LED TO JUST THAT . . .

. . . THE BRIGHTER DAY IS RISING UPON AFRICA . . . OUR PEOPLE ARE DETERMINED. NO ONE AND NO OBSTACLE WILL STAND BETWEEN THEM AND THEIR SUNSHINE. INDEED, SOUTH AFRICA IS GOING TO BE FREE IN OUR LIFETIME* . . .

*MANDELA QUOTED PIXLEY KA IZAKA SEME, ONE OF THE FOUNDERS OF THE ANC.

MILITANTS WANTED TO EXTEND MASS ACTION TO THE HOMELANDS, TO RALLY SUPPORT FOR THE ANC. IN SEPTEMBER, 70,000 PEOPLE MARCHED TO BHISHO, THE CAPITAL OF THE THEN CISKEI . . .

MANDELA AND DE KLERK BEGGED FOR RESTRAINT, BUT TWENTY-EIGHT PEOPLE LOST THEIR LIVES . . .

MEANWHILE, MANDELA SET THREE CONDITIONS FOR THE RESUMPTION OF NEGOTIATIONS . . .

IN APRIL, MULTIPARTY TALKS RESUMED.

RELEASE POLITICAL PRISONERS, FENCE OFF HOSTELS, AND BAN TRADITIONAL WEAPONS AT MEETINGS!

TALKS RESUMED, AND THE ANC AGREED TO SUNSET CLAUSES, WHICH SAFEGUARDED THE JOBS OF WHITE CIVIL SERVANTS AND ALLOWED FOR A COALITION GOVERNMENT.

THIS IS WHAT OUR PEOPLE WANT, THIS IS WHAT OUR ECONOMY NEEDS, THIS IS WHAT OUR COUNTRY YEARNS FOR!

MANDELA WENT TO QUNU, WHERE HE HAD BUILT A HOUSE IN THE SAME DESIGN AS THE ONE HE HAD BEEN IN AT VICTOR VERSTER PRISON.

CHRIS HANI WAS THE FORMER CHIEF OF STAFF OF MK, AND THE SECRETARY-GENERAL OF THE SA COMMUNIST PARTY. THE VILLAGE WHERE HIS FATHER STILL LIVED HAD NO RUNNING WATER OR ELECTRICITY.

I HAVE BAD NEWS MADIBA. CHRIS HANI WAS SHOT BY RIGHT-WING EXTREMISTS.

I AM ON MY WAY BACK . . . BUT FIRST I MUST SEE CHRIS'S DAD IN COMFIMVABA.

I AM SO SORRY FOR YOUR LOSS. YOUR SON WAS ONE OF THE MOST POPULAR LEADERS IN THE COUNTRY.

MANDELA WAS THE ONLY PERSON WHO COULD CALM THE PEOPLE. HE WAS ASKED TO APPEAR ON TELEVISION TO ADDRESS A NATION IN CRISIS.

TONIGHT I AM REACHING OUT TO EVERY SINGLE SOUTH AFRICAN, BLACK AND WHITE, FROM THE DEPTHS OF MY BEING . . .

RALLIES WERE HELD TO GIVE PEOPLE AN OUTLET FOR THEIR GRIEF AND FRUSTRATION. TWO WEEKS LATER, OLIVER TAMBO SUFFERED ANOTHER STROKE AND DIED.

MANDELA FELT LIKE THE LONELIEST MAN IN THE WORLD. HE HONORED HIS FRIEND WITH A TWENTY-ONE-GUN SALUTE AT HIS FUNERAL.

ON JUNE 2, 1999, THE APPEALS COURT UPHELD WINNIE'S CONVICTION FOR KIDNAPPING IN THE STOMPIE SEIPEI CASE, BUT RULED SHE HAD NOT BEEN AN ACCESSORY TO ASSAULT. SHE RECEIVED A TWO-YEAR SUSPENDED SENTENCE AND WAS FINED R15,000.

AMANDLA!!!

THE COUNTDOWN TO THE DEMOCRATIC TRANSFER OF POWER TO THE PEOPLE HAS BEGUN.

JUST A DAY LATER, MANDELA TASTED VICTORY WHEN AGREEMENT WAS REACHED ON AN ELECTION DATE.

FIRST DEMOCRATIC ELECTIONS DATE 27 APRIL 1994

THE URGENCY TO NEGOTIATE A NEW CONSTITUTION BEFORE THE ELECTIONS INTENSIFIED, AND A CAMARADERIE DEVELOPED BETWEEN NEGOTIATORS.

BUT THERE WERE OTHERS WHO WOULD DO ANYTHING TO DISRUPT THE DEMOCRATIC PROCESS. ON JUNE 25, 1999, 3,000 THUGS FROM THE AWB, A SMALL RIGHT-WING MILITANT GROUP, DESCENDED ON THE WORLD TRADE CENTER.

THEY CRASHED THROUGH THE GLASS DOORS, URINATED ON CARPETS, AND HELD A BARBEQUE.

THE AZANIAN PEOPLE'S LIBERATION ARMY (APLA) ATTACKED WORSHIPERS AT ST. JAMES' CHURCH IN CAPE TOWN, KILLING ELEVEN PEOPLE AND INJURING FIFTY-FIVE MORE.

BUT IN SEPTEMBER 1993, DE KLERK AGREED TO A TRANSITIONAL EXECUTIVE COUNCIL TO PREPARE FOR ELECTIONS. MANDELA FLEW TO THE UN IN NEW YORK TO ARGUE THAT THE TIME FOR ENDING SANCTIONS HAD COME.

THE ANC'S AND NP'S CHIEF NEGOTIATORS, RAMAPHOSA AND MEYER, SOMETIMES STRUGGLED TO CONVINCE THEIR PARTIES TO ACCEPT THEIR PROPOSALS. A BIG BREAKTHROUGH CAME ON NOVEMBER 18, WHEN AN INTERIM CONSTITUTION WAS AGREED TO.

I WILL NOT BUDGE! MAJORITY RULE WILL APPLY.

MINORITIES MUST BE SAFE-GUARDED!

WE DID IT! THEY ACCEPTED OUR COMPROMISE BETWEEN POWER-SHARING AND MAJORITY RULE!

YES! IT WAS TOUGH CONVINCING THEM, BUT THE NP NOW AGREES TO MAJORITY RULE . . .

AS SOON AS THE DEAL WAS STRUCK, THE CELEBRATIONS STARTED.

NOT EVERYONE WAS HAPPY. INKATHA AND THE CONSERVATIVE PARTY DID NOT RECOGNIZE THE AGREEMENT, AND MANY AFRIKANERS FELT THAT DE KLERK HAD SOLD THEM OUT.

IN DECEMBER, MANDELA AND DE KLERK JOINTLY RECEIVED THE NOBEL PEACE PRIZE. MANDELA WAS NOW IN THE COMPANY OF LEADERS LIKE CHIEF LUTHULI AND ARCHBISHOP TUTU WHO HAD ALSO RECEIVED THE AWARD . . . SOME PEOPLE WERE OFFENDED THAT HE HAD TO SHARE THE PRIZE WITH DE KLERK.

AT THE NOBEL CEREMONY IN OSLO, MANDELA SAID:

. . . LET IT NEVER BE SAID BY FUTURE GENERATIONS THAT INDIFFERENCE, CYNICISM, OR SELFISHNESS . . .

. . . MADE US FAIL TO LIVE UP TO THE IDEALS OF HUMANISM, WHICH THE NOBEL PEACE PRIZE ENCAPSULATES . . .

A CROWD OF 50,000 PEOPLE GAVE MANDELA A HERO'S WELCOME AT BOPHUTHATSWANA'S INDEPENDENCE STADIUM. HE DESCRIBED AS "A PEOPLE'S UPRISING" THE REVOLT THAT LED TO THE FALL OF LUCAS MANGOPE'S GOVERNMENT.

MANDELA FOR PRESIDENT

THE PEOPLE'S CHOICE

BUT BUTHELEZI STILL REFUSED TO PARTICIPATE IN THE ELECTION, AND DID NOT REGISTER BY THE MARCH 11 DEADLINE.

THE MEDIA ARE NOT VERY OPTIMISTIC ABOUT BUTHELEZI... THEY ARE PREDICTING THE CONFLICT BETWEEN THE ANC AND IFP CAN ONLY END WITH A FIGHT RIGHT TO THE FINISH!

DE KLERK AND I WILL NOT ALLOW THE ELECTION DATE TO BE MOVED BECAUSE OF THEM.

TO MAKE THINGS WORSE, THE GOLDSTONE COMMISSION IMPLICATED THREE SOUTH AFRICAN POLICE GENERALS IN SUPPLYING WEAPONS TO INKATHA.

ON APRIL 8, 1994: MANDELA, DE KLERK, BUTHELEZI, AND KING GOODWILL MET IN THE KRUGER PARK BUT COULD NOT RESOLVE THEIR DIFFERENCES. AN INTERNATIONAL MEDIATOR LATER SUCCEEDED IN PERSUADING BUTHELEZI TO RECONSIDER...

AT LAST INKATHA AGREED TO PARTICIPATE IN THE ELECTIONS AND THE PARTY'S NAME HAD TO BE STUCK ONTO THE BALLOT SHEETS. BUT THE SUCCESS OF THE ELECTIONS WAS THROWN INTO DOUBT AFTER A SERIES OF BOMBS SHOOK THE COUNTRY.

THE FIRST DEMOCRATICALLY ELECTED PARLIAMENT GATHERED IN CAPE TOWN ON MAY 9, 1994, TO GREAT EXCITEMENT.

MA ALBERTINA SISULU STOOD TO SPEAK.

I NOMINATE NELSON ROLIHLAHLA MANDELA AS PRESIDENT!

AN IMBONGI SANG THE PRAISES OF MANDELA . . .

TODAY AFRICA HAS RETURNED!!

IN A SHOW OF RECONCILIATION, MANDELA HUGGED BUTHELEZI.

EVERYONE CHEERED AS CHIEF JUSTICE MICHAEL CORBETT DECLARED MANDELA SOUTH AFRICA'S PRESIDENT—ELECT, WHILE FRENE GINWALA WAS NOMINATED AS SPEAKER OF PARLIAMENT.

THE AFRICAN NATIONAL CONGRESS HAD WON 252 SEATS, THE NATIONAL PARTY EIGHTY-TWO, THE INKATHA FREEDOM PARTY FORTY-THREE, WHILE THE REMAINING SEATS WERE SHARED BY THE FREEDOM FRONT, DEMOCRATIC PARTY, PAN AFRICANIST CONGRESS, AND THE AFRICAN CHRISTIAN DEMOCRATIC PARTY. SEVENTY OF THE 400 MEMBERS OF PARLIAMENT (MP'S) WERE WOMEN.

WALTER SISULU LATER SAID:

IT IS THE BIGGEST DAY OF ALL!

MANDELA AND HIS DEPUTIES, MBEKI AND DE KLERK, NOW HAD TO MOVE FORWARD IN THE GOVERNMENT OF NATIONAL UNITY.

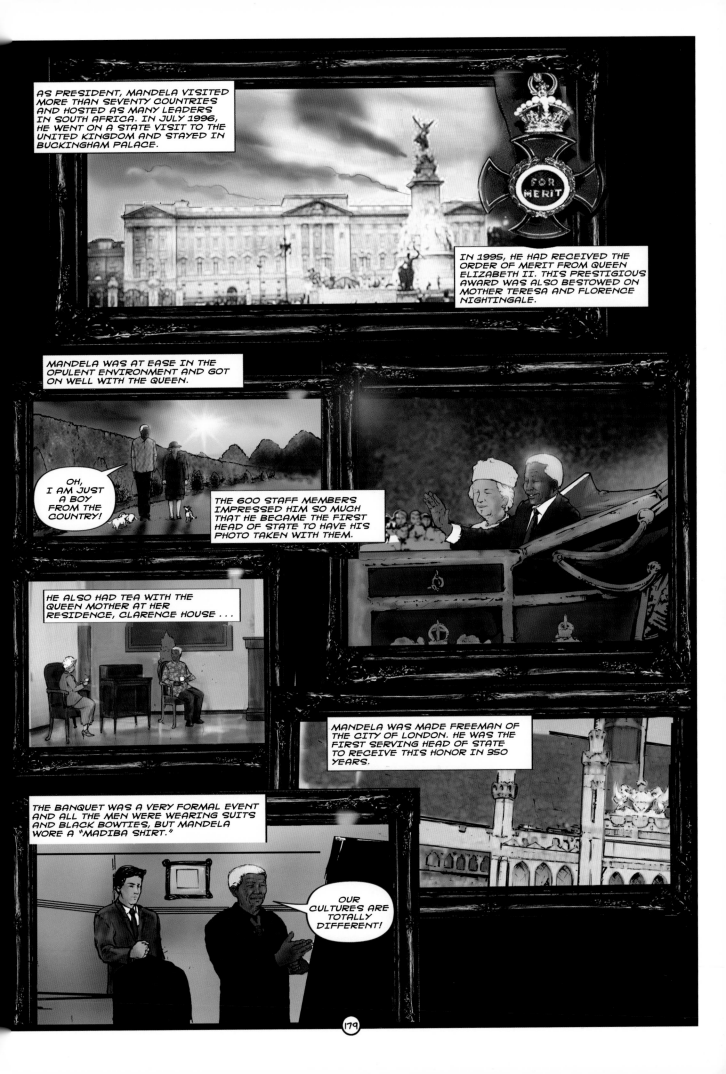

AT NEETHLINGSHOF WINE FARM, HE ADDRESSED A MOSTLY WHITE AUDIENCE OF BUSINESS LEADERS ABOUT ECONOMIC RECONSTRUCTION.

MY WARDER AT VICTOR VERSTER TOLD ME THE BEST WINES WERE DRY. BUT I ALWAYS THOUGHT ALL WINE WAS WET!

AFTER A FULL DAY OF MEETINGS, INCLUDING THE SWEARING-IN OF A NEW DEPUTY MINISTER TO REPLACE HIS ESTRANGED WIFE, MANDELA BOARDED A PLANE TO CAPE TOWN.

HE RETURNED TO JOHANNESBURG THE SAME NIGHT. IT WAS CLOSE TO MIDNIGHT WHEN HE FINALLY WENT TO BED IN HIS HOUGHTON HOME.

HE PREFERRED TO STAY THERE AND MOSTLY USED HIS OFFICIAL RESIDENCE, LIBERTAS, IN PRETORIA, DURING THE DAY FOR OFFICIAL MEETINGS OR LUNCH.

IN 1995, HE CHANGED THE NAME OF LIBERTAS TO MAHLAMBA NOLOPFU. IT COMES FROM A SHANGAAN EXPRESSION MEANING "NEW DAWN."

ALTHOUGH MANDELA MADE MANY NEW RICH AND FAMOUS FRIENDS, HE KEPT CLOSE TO HIS OLD COMRADES LIKE AHMED KATHRADA. IN 1994, KATHY HAD BEEN APPOINTED MANDELA'S PARLIAMENTARY COUNSELOR.

AHHH! LUNCH IS HERE! AND ON TIME!

OH, MADIBA – IT IS SAMP AND BEANS! JAIL FOOD IS STILL YOUR FAVORITE!

YES! DO YOU REMEMBER HOW AFRICANS WERE NOT ALLOWED TO EAT BREAD FOR TEN YEARS?

MANDELA OFTEN SET HIS OWN MENU. IT WAS SIMPLE AND HEALTHY, AND SOMETIMES INCLUDED INDIAN CURRIES.

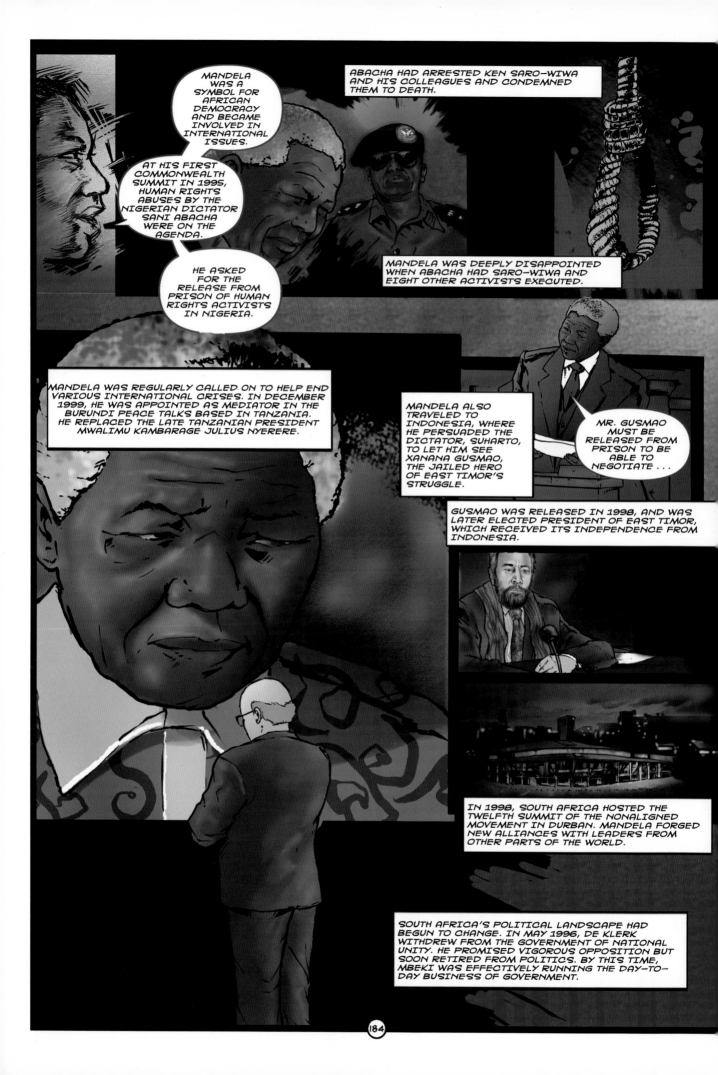

MANDELA WAS A SYMBOL FOR AFRICAN DEMOCRACY AND BECAME INVOLVED IN INTERNATIONAL ISSUES.

AT HIS FIRST COMMONWEALTH SUMMIT IN 1995, HUMAN RIGHTS ABUSES BY THE NIGERIAN DICTATOR SANI ABACHA WERE ON THE AGENDA.

HE ASKED FOR THE RELEASE FROM PRISON OF HUMAN RIGHTS ACTIVISTS IN NIGERIA.

ABACHA HAD ARRESTED KEN SARO-WIWA AND HIS COLLEAGUES AND CONDEMNED THEM TO DEATH.

MANDELA WAS DEEPLY DISAPPOINTED WHEN ABACHA HAD SARO-WIWA AND EIGHT OTHER ACTIVISTS EXECUTED.

MANDELA WAS REGULARLY CALLED ON TO HELP END VARIOUS INTERNATIONAL CRISES. IN DECEMBER 1999, HE WAS APPOINTED AS MEDIATOR IN THE BURUNDI PEACE TALKS BASED IN TANZANIA. HE REPLACED THE LATE TANZANIAN PRESIDENT MWALIMU KAMBARAGE JULIUS NYERERE.

MANDELA ALSO TRAVELED TO INDONESIA, WHERE HE PERSUADED THE DICTATOR, SUHARTO, TO LET HIM SEE XANANA GUSMAO, THE JAILED HERO OF EAST TIMOR'S STRUGGLE.

MR. GUSMAO MUST BE RELEASED FROM PRISON TO BE ABLE TO NEGOTIATE . . .

GUSMAO WAS RELEASED IN 1998, AND WAS LATER ELECTED PRESIDENT OF EAST TIMOR, WHICH RECEIVED ITS INDEPENDENCE FROM INDONESIA.

IN 1998, SOUTH AFRICA HOSTED THE TWELFTH SUMMIT OF THE NONALIGNED MOVEMENT IN DURBAN. MANDELA FORGED NEW ALLIANCES WITH LEADERS FROM OTHER PARTS OF THE WORLD.

SOUTH AFRICA'S POLITICAL LANDSCAPE HAD BEGUN TO CHANGE. IN MAY 1996, DE KLERK WITHDREW FROM THE GOVERNMENT OF NATIONAL UNITY. HE PROMISED VIGOROUS OPPOSITION BUT SOON RETIRED FROM POLITICS. BY THIS TIME, MBEKI WAS EFFECTIVELY RUNNING THE DAY-TO-DAY BUSINESS OF GOVERNMENT.

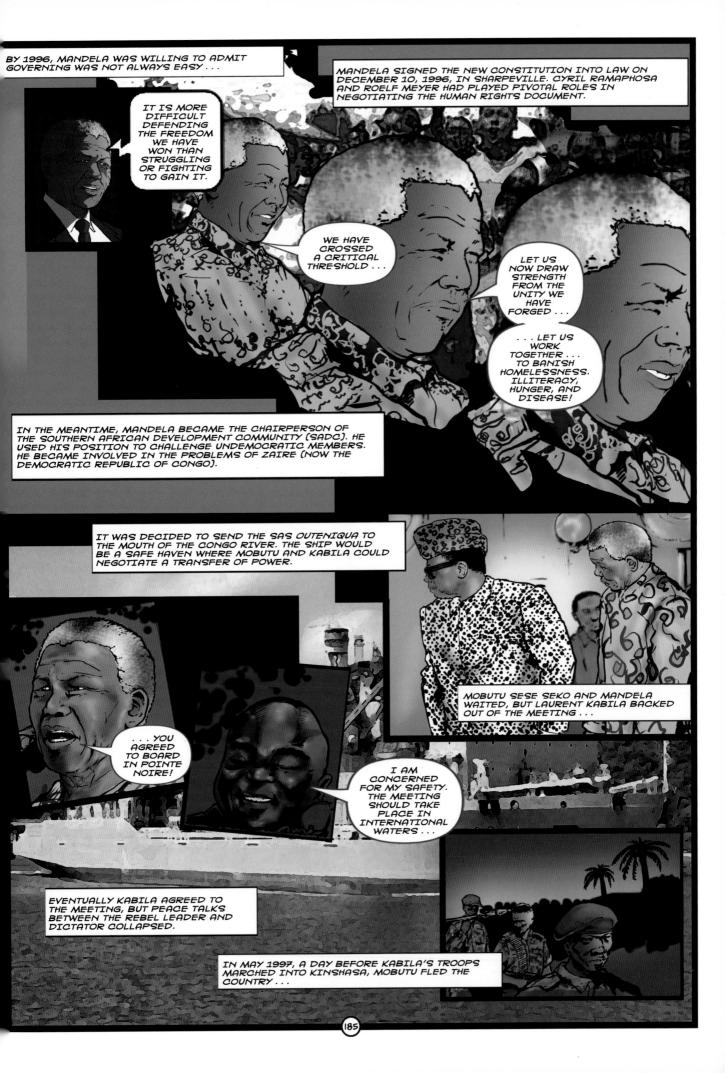

APARTHEID ERA ATROCITIES WERE STILL HAUNTING THE NATION . . .

THE TRUTH AND RECONCILIATION COMMISSION (TRC) WAS CREATED IN 1995 TO DEAL WITH THE APARTHEID PAST AND PROMOTE RECONCILIATION. PERPETRATORS OF HUMAN RIGHTS VIOLATIONS COULD GET AMNESTY.

ARCHBISHOP DESMOND TUTU WAS CHAIR AND ALEX BORAINE HIS DEPUTY.

THE NP WANTED A GENERAL AMNESTY FOR ALL PERPETRATORS. MANDELA REFUSED.

THE TRC WAS DEDICATED IN ST. GEORGE'S CATHEDRAL IN CAPE TOWN. NOT EVERYONE WAS PLEASED. SOME WANTED VENGEANCE AND SOME WERE FEARFUL.

OVER THE NEXT EIGHT YEARS, A RANGE OF HORRORS WERE DESCRIBED. ORDINARY APARTHEID SECURITY PERSONNEL CLAIMED THEY WERE JUST FOLLOWING ORDERS.

All South Africans face the challenge of coming to terms with the past in ways which will enable us to face the future as a united nation at peace with itself.
To you has been entrusted the particular task of dealing with gross violations of human rights in a manner that ensures that the painful truth is laid bare and that justice is done to the victims within the capacity of our society and within the framework of the constitution and the law.
By doing so and by means of amnesty, your goal is to ensure lasting reconciliation.

I AM TRULY SORRY FOR WHAT I HAVE DONE . . .

I CAN NEVER HAVE PEACE.

NOT EVERYONE WAS SATISFIED WITH THE OUTCOME. SOME VICTIMS WHO TESTIFIED FELT LET DOWN. THEY DID NOT GET THE REPARATIONS THEY HAD HOPED FOR . .

. . . STRATEGIES NEVER INCLUDED THE AUTHORIZATION OF ASSASSINATION, MURDER, TORTURE, RAPE, ASSAULT, OR THE LIKE . . .

P. W. BOTHA REFUSED TO PARTICIPATE AND DENOUNCED THE TRC AS A CIRCUS. MANDELA EVEN ASKED BOTHA'S CHILDREN TO TRY AND MAKE HIM CHANGE HIS MIND. THE TRC FOUND THAT HE HAD CONTRIBUTED TO A CLIMATE IN WHICH GROSS VIOLATIONS OF HUMAN RIGHTS OCCURRED.

F. W. DE KLERK LATER SUCCESSFULLY APPEALED TO COURT TO SUPPRESS THE TRC'S FINDINGS ON HIM.

BY THE TIME THE WORK OF THE TRC WAS COMPLETE, IT HAD BECOME CLEAR THAT THE WOUNDS OF THE PAST WOULD TAKE TIME TO HEAL.

MANDELA HAD BEEN BECOMING INCREASINGLY LONELY, BUT . . .

IS IT TRUE? ARE YOU DATING?

WELL, THERE IS A SPECIAL PERSON . . .

. . . BUT, I AM NOT READY TO TALK ABOUT IT.

YEARS AFTER HIS RELEASE, MANDELA FELL FOR GRAÇA MACHEL, THE FORMER FIRST LADY OF MOZAMBIQUE, BUT HE KEPT IT A SECRET . . .

HER HUSBAND HAD DIED IN A SUSPICIOUS PLANE CRASH IN 1986. AT THE TIME, MANDELA WROTE HER A LETTER OF CONDOLENCE FROM PRISON.

EVENTUALLY, MANDELA WON HER OVER AND GRAÇA STARTED TO SPEND TWO WEEKS A MONTH IN JOHANNESBURG. THEY WERE IN LOVE, AND WERE SNAPPED WALKING IN THE STREETS OF HOUGHTON . . .

GRAÇA BECAME HIS OFFICIAL CONSORT AND JOINED HIM ON A TRIP TO SOUTHEAST ASIA.

ARE YOU GOING TO GET MARRIED SOON?

I WILL ALWAYS BELONG TO MOZAMBIQUE.

HE FOBBED OFF JOURNALISTS WITH A STANDARD REPLY:

MY CULTURAL BACKGROUND DOES NOT PERMIT ME TO ANSWER QUESTIONS FROM SOMEONE YOUNGER THAN MY GRANDCHILDREN.

HIS OLD FRIEND, DESMOND TUTU, MADE IT CLEAR THEY SHOULD MARRY. THEY TIED THE KNOT ON MANDELA'S EIGHTIETH BIRTHDAY UNDER A CLOAK OF SECRECY.

THE CEREMONY TOOK PLACE AT HIS HOME AND ONLY A FEW FRIENDS AND FAMILY MEMBERS WERE THERE . . .

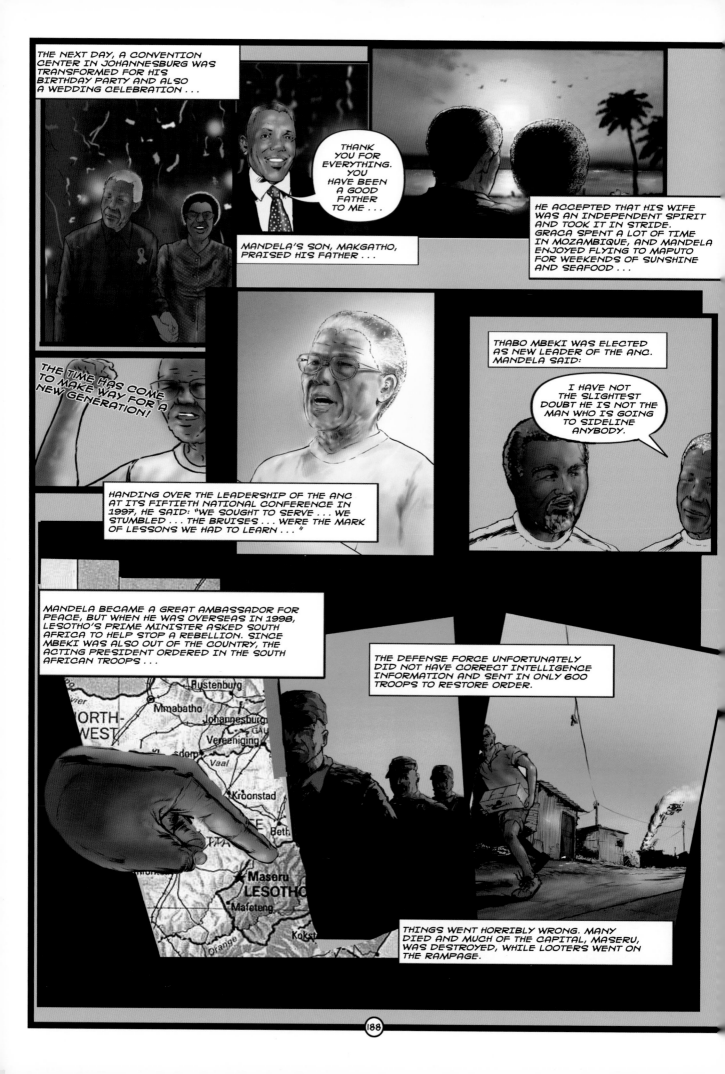

THE NEXT DAY, A CONVENTION CENTER IN JOHANNESBURG WAS TRANSFORMED FOR HIS BIRTHDAY PARTY AND ALSO A WEDDING CELEBRATION...

THANK YOU FOR EVERYTHING. YOU HAVE BEEN A GOOD FATHER TO ME...

MANDELA'S SON, MAKGATHO, PRAISED HIS FATHER...

HE ACCEPTED THAT HIS WIFE WAS AN INDEPENDENT SPIRIT AND TOOK IT IN STRIDE. GRACA SPENT A LOT OF TIME IN MOZAMBIQUE, AND MANDELA ENJOYED FLYING TO MAPUTO FOR WEEKENDS OF SUNSHINE AND SEAFOOD...

THE TIME HAS COME TO MAKE WAY FOR A NEW GENERATION!

HANDING OVER THE LEADERSHIP OF THE ANC AT ITS FIFTIETH NATIONAL CONFERENCE IN 1997, HE SAID: "WE SOUGHT TO SERVE... WE STUMBLED... THE BRUISES... WERE THE MARK OF LESSONS WE HAD TO LEARN..."

THABO MBEKI WAS ELECTED AS NEW LEADER OF THE ANC. MANDELA SAID:

I HAVE NOT THE SLIGHTEST DOUBT HE IS NOT THE MAN WHO IS GOING TO SIDELINE ANYBODY.

MANDELA BECAME A GREAT AMBASSADOR FOR PEACE, BUT WHEN HE WAS OVERSEAS IN 1998, LESOTHO'S PRIME MINISTER ASKED SOUTH AFRICA TO HELP STOP A REBELLION. SINCE MBEKI WAS ALSO OUT OF THE COUNTRY, THE ACTING PRESIDENT ORDERED IN THE SOUTH AFRICAN TROOPS...

THE DEFENSE FORCE UNFORTUNATELY DID NOT HAVE CORRECT INTELLIGENCE INFORMATION AND SENT IN ONLY 600 TROOPS TO RESTORE ORDER.

THINGS WENT HORRIBLY WRONG. MANY DIED AND MUCH OF THE CAPITAL, MASERU, WAS DESTROYED, WHILE LOOTERS WENT ON THE RAMPAGE.

SOME OF MANDELA'S FRIENDS WERE CONTROVERSIAL, INCLUDING U.S. PRESIDENT BILL CLINTON WHO WAS AT THE CENTER OF A SCANDAL IN HIS OWN COUNTRY OVER HIS RELATIONSHIP WITH A WHITE HOUSE INTERN . . .

AT A JOINT PRESS CONFERENCE WHEN CLINTON WAS ON A STATE VISIT TO SOUTH AFRICA, MANDELA DEFENDED HIS SUPPORT OF LIBYA, CUBA, AND THE PALESTINE LIBERATION ORGANIZATION.

WE SHOULD NOT ABANDON THOSE WHO HELPED US IN OUR DARKEST HOUR . . .

THOSE WHO BERATE ME FOR BEING LOYAL TO OUR FRIENDS, LITERALLY THEY CAN GO AND THROW THEMSELVES INTO A POOL . . .

THE TWO MEN ALSO VISITED MANDELA'S CELL ON ROBBEN ISLAND . . .

HOW DID YOU MANAGE TO FORGIVE YOUR OPPRESSORS?

THEY TOOK THE BEST YEARS OF MY LIFE . . .

THEY COULD TAKE EVERYTHING . . . EXCEPT MY MIND AND HEART . . .

BUT I WOULD NOT LET THEM . . . NEITHER SHOULD YOU.

YEARS LATER CLINTON RECALLED HOW MUCH MANDELA'S SUPPORT HELPED HIM THROUGH "DIFFICULT TIMES" . . .

189

MANDELA DID NOT WANT TO STAY ON FOR LONGER THAN ONE TERM AS PRESIDENT. ON FEBRUARY 10, 1999, HE DELIVERED HIS LAST STATE OF THE NATION ADDRESS.

FIVE YEARS AGO, THE SENSE OF COMMON BELONGING, OUR SHARED DESTINY, FOCUSED THE MIND . . .

WE WERE ABLE TO FIND SOLUTIONS TO PROBLEMS THAT SEEMED DEFIANT OF RESOLUTION . . .

THIS IS SOUTH AFRICA'S ACHIEVEMENT . . . OF NATION-BUILDING AND RECONCILIATION.

HE TOOK TIME TO GREET STAFF WHO HAD BEEN WITH HIM FOR FIVE YEARS . . .

YOUR EXAMPLE HAS CHANGED MY LIFE. THANK YOU, TATA.

AT THE END OF MANDELA'S TENURE AS PRESIDENT, THE NELSON MANDELA FOUNDATION WAS ESTABLISHED TO PROMOTE HIS LEGACY.

MANDELA CAMPAIGNED FOR PEACE, CHILDREN'S RIGHTS, AND THE FIGHT AGAINST HIV/AIDS.

IN 2002, THE MANDELA RHODES FOUNDATION WAS ANNOUNCED.

MANDELA LAUNCHED THE 46664 CAMPAIGN TO RAISE AWARENESS ABOUT AIDS. THE NAME COMES FROM HIS PRISON NUMBER, 466/64, INDICATING HE WAS THE 466TH PRISONER IN 1964.

THE AIM OF THE FOUNDATION IS TO BUILD EXCEPTIONAL LEADERSHIP CAPACITY IN AFRICA.

AIDS TODAY IN AFRICA IS CLAIMING MORE LIVES THAN THE SUM TOTAL OF ALL WARS, FAMINES, FLOODS, AND DISEASES SUCH AS MALARIA . . .

WE MUST ACT NOW FOR THE SAKE OF THE WORLD . . . AIDS IS NO LONGER A DISEASE, IT IS A HUMAN RIGHTS ISSUE!

MORE THAN TWO BILLION PEOPLE IN 166 COUNTRIES SAW THE FIRST CONCERT. EVERY YEAR, 46664 CONCERTS WERE STAGED, RAISING MONEY FOR HIV/AIDS PROJECTS IN SOUTH AFRICA AND OTHER AFRICAN COUNTRIES.

IN 2003, MANDELA EXPERIENCED THE DEVASTATING LOSS OF HIS GREAT FRIEND WALTER SISULU . . .

FROM THE MOMENT WE FIRST MET, HE HAS BEEN MY FRIEND, MY BROTHER, MY KEEPER, MY COMRADE.

. . . AND TWO YEARS LATER, HE SUFFERED THE TRAGIC DEATH OF HIS FIFTY-FOUR-YEAR-OLD SON MAKGATHO.

MY SON DIED OF AIDS. WE WILL HAVE TO TELL THE WORLD, TO TAKE AWAY THE STIGMA ATTACHED TO THIS DISEASE.

MANDELA'S STAFF HAD TO GUARD AGAINST PEOPLE WHO WANTED TO EXPLOIT HIS NAME FOR THEIR PERSONAL OR COMMERCIAL GAIN.

I MET MANDELA!
DISGRACED POLITICIAN BOASTS OF MANDELA'S SUPPORT

Accuris...

REQUESTS FLOODED IN FROM PEOPLE ASKING HIM TO ENDORSE THEIR PROJECTS.

SOME PEOPLE WOULD USE THEIR MEETINGS WITH MANDELA TO INCREASE THEIR STANDING IN THEIR OWN COUNTRIES OR COMMUNITIES.

MANDELA CONTINUED TO ENJOY RAISING AWARENESS THROUGHOUT THE WORLD ABOUT ISSUES THAT WERE CLOSE TO HIS HEART.

191

BY 2004, MANDELA FOUND THAT HE WAS STILL HIGHLY IN DEMAND, BUT HE WANTED TO SLOW DOWN. HE FAMOUSLY ANNOUNCED HIS RETIREMENT . . .

IN HIS POST-PRESIDENTIAL YEARS, MANDELA RELIED HEAVILY ON HIS EXECUTIVE PERSONAL ASSISTANT AND SPOKESPERSON, ZELDA LA GRANGE. SHE WAS NEVER FAR FROM HIS SIDE.

I AM CONFIDENT THAT NO ONE HERE WILL ACCUSE ME OF SELFISHNESS IF I ASK TO SPEND MORE TIME . . . WITH FAMILY, FRIENDS, AND MYSELF . . .

MY APPEAL THEREFORE IS: DON'T CALL ME, I WILL CALL YOU!

NELSON MANDELA
FOUNDATION
Living the Legacy

Nelson Mandela
CHILDREN'S FUND
CHANGING THE WAY SOCIETY TREATS ITS CHILDREN AND YOUTH

THE NELSON MANDELA CHILDREN'S FUND FOCUSES ON IMPROVING SOCIETY'S TREATMENT OF ITS CHILDREN AND YOUTH.

THE MANDELA RHODES FOUNDATION AIMS TO GIVE EXPRESSION TO THE LEGACIES OF LEADERSHIP, EDUCATION, RECONCILIATION, AND ENTREPRENEURSHIP.

THE MANDELA RHODES
FOUNDATION

HE HANDED OVER THE BULK OF HIS "LEGACY WORK" TO HIS THREE INDEPENDENT BUT INTERLINKED CHARITABLE ORGANIZATIONS. HE WANTED THE FOCUS TO BE ON THEM AND NOT HIM AS AN INDIVIDUAL.

FROM 2004, THE NELSON MANDELA FOUNDATION WAS RESTRUCTURED AROUND ITS CENTRE OF MEMORY AND DIALOGUE, DEDICATED TO COMMEMORATING THE LIFE AND TIMES OF NELSON MANDELA AND CONVENING DIALOG AROUND CRITICAL SOCIAL ISSUES.

MANDELA STARTED SPENDING MORE TIME AT HIS HOME IN QUNU . . .

IN 2007, HE ATTENDED THE INSTALLATION OF HIS GRANDSON, MANDLA, AS CHIEF OF THE MVEZO TRADITIONAL COUNCIL.

HE STILL GAVE MANY HOURS OF HIS TIME TO DOCUMENTING HIS MEMORIES.

NELSON MANDELA'S LEGACY IS IN ALL OUR HANDS . . .

INDEX

A

"A Pound a Day" Campaign 56
Abacha, Sani 184
Action Committee 65
African Christian Democratic Party 170
African National Congress see ANC
Afrikaner Volksfront 163, 165
Alexandra 28
Alexandra bus strike 30
All-in-Africa Conference 62, 63
ANC 32, 37, 39, 41, 45, 56, 60, 62, 63, 65,
        66, 72, 74, 104, 107, 108, 125, 134,
        135, 138, 142, 149, 159, 170, 186, 188
    High Organ 102, 103, 108, 113
    National High Command 89
    Women's League 61
    Youth League 32, 33, 35, 37, 61
Anti-Pass Campaign 57, 58
Apartheid 36, 43, 107, 186
AWB 161, 165
Azanian People's Liberation Army
        (APLA) 161

B

Bam, Fikile 105
Bantu Education 43, 46
Barnard, Niel 138
Bernstein, Lionel "Rusty" 87, 88, 94
Berrange, Vernon 50, 88
Bethell, Lord 131
Biko, Steve 114
Bizos, George 31, 44, 50, 88, 134, 140
Black Consciousness Movement 114
Boesak, Allan 126
Boipatong 159
Bophuthatswana 165, 166
Boraine, Alex 186
Botha, P. W. 126, 127, 129, 130, 133, 135,
        142, 163, 183, 186
Brand, Christo 118
Buthelezi, Mangosuthu 149, 155, 157,
        163, 166, 170

C

Cachalia, Amina 183
Cachalia, Yusuf 40
Carolus, Cheryl 151
Chaskalson, Arthur 50
Chiba, Laloo 102
Clarkebury 14, 15
Clinton, Bill 189

CODESA, see Convention for
        Democratic Change in South
        Africa

Coetsee, Kobie 131, 134, 135, 137, 138, 139
Collins, Canon John 76
Colored People's Organization 45
Commonwealth Eminent Persons
        Group 135, 136
Communist Party 37, 43, 68
Congress Alliance 45, 48, 56
Congress of Democrats 45
Conservative Party 162
Constitution 159, 160, 161, 162, 185
Convention for Democratic Change in
        South Africa (CODESA) 157, 158,
        159, 160, 161, 162
Corbett, Michael 170
COSATU 142
Cradock Four 132
Criminal Law Amendment Act 42

D

Dadoo, Yusuf 40, 76
Dalibhunga, see Mandela, Nelson
        Rolihlahla
Dalindyebo, Justice 10, 19, 20, 21, 22, 23,
        24, 29, 40
Daliwonga, see Matanzima, Kaiser
Dash, Samuel 131
De Klerk, F. W. 142, 143, 149, 152, 153, 154,
        155, 157, 159, 162, 166, 168, 170, 173,
        184, 186
De Klerk, Marike 173
De Villiers, Dawie 157
De Wet, Quartus 89
Defend Free Speech Convention 36
Defiance Campaign 40, 41, 42
Democratic Party 170
Diederichs, Marga 183
Dlamini, Zaziwe 118
Duarte, Jesse 164, 172
Dube, John 167

E

Elections, 1994 163, 164, 166, 167

F

Federation of South African Women 47
First, Ruth 31, 65, 125
Fischer, Bram 31, 50, 52, 60, 80, 88, 89,
        91, 96, 112

Fischer, Molly 52, 96
Forced removals 43
Fort Hare University 17, 18, 31, 34
Franks, Maurice 50
Free Mandela Campaign 119
Free Mandela Committee 79
Freedom Charter 44, 45
Freedom Front 165

G

Gandhi, M. K. 40
Gerwel, Jakes 174
Ginwala, Frene 172
Goldberg, Denis 87, 88, 94
Goldreich, Arthur 87, 88
Goldstone Commission 166
Groote Schuur Minute 151
Growth Employment and
        Redistribution strategy (GEAR)
        181
Gumede, Archie 151
Gusmao, Xanana 184

H

Haile Selassie 75
Hani, Chris 160
Harare Declaration 143
Harris, Reverend 15
Healdtown 16
Hepple, Bob 87, 88
Hlati, see Sobukwe, Robert
Hodgson, Jack 69, 70
Howe, Geoffrey 136
Huddleston, Father Trevor 43, 150

I

Indian Congress 45
Indian Youth Congress 80
Inkatha Freedom Party 149, 154, 155,
        157, 162, 165, 166, 170

J

Jassat, Abdulhay 68
Joffe, Joel 88, 96
Jongintaba, Chief 8, 9, 20, 21, 29
Jordan, Pallo 125
Joseph, Helen 47

K

Kabila, Laurent 184
Kantor, James 87, 88

Kathrada, Ahmed "Kathy" 37, 61, 78, 79, 87, 88, 93, 102, 113, 115, 123, 140, 143, 151, 182, 190
Kaunda, Kenneth 75
Kerr, Dr. Alexander 18
King, Martin Luther 163
Kodesh, Wolfie 66, 67, 70
Kruger, Jimmy 117

L

La Grange, Zelda 192
Lembede, Anton 32, 33, 34
Liliesleaf Farm 68, 77, 78, 86, 87
Lusaka 149
Luthuli, Chief Albert 41, 44, 54, 70, 71, 72, 78, 106

M

Machel, Graca 187, 188
Machel, Samora 187
Madiba clan 81
Madikizela, Columbus 54
Madikizela-Mandela, Winnie 53, 54, 55, 57, 62, 68, 70, 77, 80, 86, 90, 100, 104, 107, 108, 112, 116, 124, 127, 132, 152, 157, 158, 161
Maharaj, Mac 105, 113, 140
Maisels, Israel 50
Majombozi, Lionel 32
Makgatho, Sefako Mapogo 39
Malan, D. F. 40
Malan, Magnus 119, 135, 155
Mandela & Tambo Law Firm 42, 53, 61
Mandela Football Club 138, 140
Mandela Rhodes Foundation 190
Mandela, Andile 172
Mandela, Evelyn, see Mase, Evelyn
Mandela, Madiba Thembekile 33, 106
Mandela, Makaziwe 34, 45, 105, 156
Mandela, Makgatho Lewanika 39, 62, 105, 172, 188, 191
Mandela, Mandla 172, 193
Mandela, Mbuso 172
Mandela, Mphakanyiswa 3, 4, 8
Mandela, Ndaba 172
Mandela, Nelson Rolihlahla
  also see ANC
  46664 campaign 190
  ambassador for peace 188
  ANC deputy president 149
  ANC president 156
  arrest 79
  banned 42, 43, 46
  birth 2
  Black Pimpernel 49, 64, 79
  church membership 10
  conditional release offer 129, 130
  "David Motsamayi" 68, 79

Defiance Campaign 40, 41
  health 134, 139
  initiation 12, 13
  law studies 28
  memoirs 113
  military training 75, 77
  MK commander-in-chief 66
  M-Plan 43
  negotiations 157–162
  Nobel Peace Prize 162
  political prisoner 84
  Pollsmoor Prison 122
  President 170, 172–190
  release 144, 146
  retirement 192
  Rivonia Trial 90–94
  Robben Island 85, 95, 98–122, 175
  schooling 7, 14, 15, 16
  statement from the dock 92
  talks about talks 134, 151
  Treason Trial 48, 50, 52, 54, 61, 63
  trial 1962 81–83
  underground 64
  university 17, 18
  Youth League 32, 33, 35, 37, 61
Mandela, Nosekeni 3, 5, 8, 31, 106
Mandela, Winnie, see Madikizela-Mandela, Winnie
Mandela, Zenani 55, 118, 127, 133
Mandela, Zindziswa 62, 112, 116, 130, 158
Mangope, Lucas 165, 166
Manuel, Trevor 144
Maqubela, Patrick 123
Marais, Major 139
Marks, J. B. 40
Mase, Evelyn 30, 33, 34, 39, 46, 62
Masekela, Barbara 164, 172
Mashifane, Thomas 88, 90
Mass Action Campaign 155, 159, 160
Mass Democratic Movement 142
Matanzima, Kaiser 17, 18, 31, 46, 57, 117, 129
Matshikiza, Todd and Esme 76
Matthews, Z. K. 40, 44
May Day strike 37, 38
Mbekeni, Garlick 27
Mbeki, Govan 46, 64, 87, 88, 94, 102, 110, 137
Mbeki, Thabo 142, 151, 170, 184, 188
Mbongweni 54
Mda, A. P. 32, 34, 35
Meer, Ismail 31, 40
Meyer, Roelf 158, 162, 185
Mhlaba, Raymond 41, 64, 68, 87, 88, 94, 102, 122, 130, 143
MK, see Umkhonto we Sizwe
Mkwayi, Wilton 102, 143
Mlangeni, Andrew 87, 88, 94, 122, 130, 143

Mobuto Sese Seko 185
Modise, Joe 150
Mogoba, Stanley 140
Mompati, Ruth 44, 65, 151
Moodley, Strini 114
Moola, Moosa 88
Moose, Rahima 47
Moroka, Dr. 35
Motsoaledi, Elias 87, 88, 94, 143
Mpetha, Oscar 143
M-Plan 43, 61, 70
Mpondombini, Chief 22
Mqhekezweni 9
Mtirara, Rochelle 178
Mtolo, Bruno 90
Mvezo 2, 3, 4
Mxadana, Mary 177

N

Naicker, Dr. 41
Naidoo, Jay 155, 181
Natal Indian Congress 41
National Party 35, 125, 127, 128, 135, 142, 143, 151, 154, 155, 157, 159, 162, 170, 186
Native Resettlement Bill 43
Naude, Beyers 132, 151
Nelson Mandela Centre of Memory and Dialogue 192
Nelson Mandela Children's Fund 176, 192
Nelson Mandela Foundation 190, 192
Netshitenzhe, Joel 164
Ngoyi, Lilian 47, 55
Niehaus, Carl 164
Nkomo, William 32
No-England 31
Nokwe, Duma 61
Nonaligned Movement 184
Nqabeni 85
Nyerere, Julius 74
Nzima, Petrus and Jabu 126
Nzo, Alfred 149, 151

O

OAU 142
Operation Mayibuye 86, 91
Operation Vula 153, 154

P

Pan Africanist Congress (PAC) 56, 57, 58, 60, 65, 74, 170
Pan-African Freedom Movement for East, Central and Southern Africa Conference 72, 74
Pass laws 36
Pass-burning Campaign 59
Pienaar, Francois 177

Piliso 26
Pogrund, Benjamin 64
Pollsmoor Prison 122
Pretoria Minute 154
Public Safety Amendment Act 42

Q
Qoboza, Percy 119
Queen Elizabeth II 179
Queen Mother 179
Qunu 4, 5, 150, 178, 180, 193

R
Radebe, Gaur 28, 29
Ramaphosa, Cyril 144, 156, 158, 162, 172, 185
Reconstruction and Development Program (RDP) 181
Rivonia Trial 90–95
Robben Island 84, 85, 95, 97, 98, 99, 111, 175
   B Section 98, 103, 110
Rosenberg, Norman 50

S
Sabata 8, 117
Sabotage 71
Sanctions 133, 137, 142, 152
Saro-Wiwa, Ken 184
Sebokeng 151
Seipei, Stompie 152
Seme, Pixley ka Izaka 157
Senghor, Leopold 76
Sharpeville 58, 128
Sidelsky, Lazar 27
Singh, J. N. 31, 40
Sisulu, Albertina 55, 100, 126, 128, 170
Sisulu, Jongi 152

Sisulu, Lindiwe 152
Sisulu, Max 152
Sisulu, Walter 27, 30, 32, 33, 35, 38, 39, 40, 41, 43, 81, 87, 88, 93, 102, 113, 122, 130, 137, 143, 151, 152, 170, 181, 191
Sisulu, Zwelakhe 126, 152
Sita, Nana 41
Slabbert, Frederik van Zyl 138
Slovo, Joe 39, 59, 68, 69, 79, 151, 154
Sobukwe, Robert 56, 74, 84, 102
Sophiatown 36, 43, 56
South African Students Organization 114
South West African People's Organization (SWAPO) 110
Southern African Development Community (SADCC) 185
Soweto 1976 uprising 115
Strijdom, J. G. 47
Suharto 184
Suppression of Communism Act 36, 39, 42, 43
Suzman, Helen 105
SWAPO, see South West African People's Organization
Swart, Jack 140

T
Tambo, Adelaide 53
Tambo, Oliver 17, 32, 33, 35, 42, 44, 53, 59, 64, 74, 75, 76, 108, 126, 129, 133, 135, 137, 140, 142, 143, 149, 150, 156, 160
Thatcher, Margaret 133, 136, 153
Thumbumuzi, Prince 118
Toivo ja Toivo, Andimba 110
Transvaal Indian Youth Congress 37
Treason Trial 48, 50, 52, 54, 56, 61, 63

Tricameral parliament 126, 127, 128
Truth and Reconciliation Commission (TRC) 186
Tutu, Archbishop Desmond 129, 136, 147, 154, 186, 187

U
Umkhonto we Sizwe 66, 68, 74, 86, 119, 125, 142
United Democratic Front (UDF) 126, 127, 128, 132, 138, 142
University of London 80

V
Vance, Cyrus 158
Verwoerd, H. F. 46, 63, 82, 105
Victor Verster Prison 163, 165
Viljoen, Constand 163, 165
Vlok, Adriaan 155

W
Willemse, General 136
Williams, Cecil 78
Williams, Sophia 47
Witkin, Sidelsky and Eidelman 28
Wits University 31
Wolpe, Harold 87, 88
Women's March against Pass Laws 47

X
Xuma, Dr. 32, 33, 35

Y
Young Lions 115
Yutar, Percy 89, 90, 93, 183

Z
Zwelithini, King Goodwill 166

ACKNOWLEDGMENTS

This book began as a series of eight comics distributed free by the Nelson Mandela Foundation in partnership with comic publisher Umlando Wezithombe between 2005 and 2007. The series was a project of the Foundation's Centre of Memory and Dialogue, and was aimed at reaching young South Africans with the story of the life and times of Nelson Mandela, in accessible form. The series drew on a wide range of published work, but also made use of previously unused archival material as well as formal and informal interviews with individuals who appear as characters in the story. We are particularly grateful to Ahmed Kathrada, who acted as special advisor to the series and also assisted with the preparation of this book. His contribution has been immeasurable. The series was made possible financially by a number of generous donors and sponsors—Anglo American, BHP Billiton, the Ford Foundation, GTZ, Independent Newspapers, the Nelson Mandela Legacy Trust (UK), E Oppenheimer and Son, Sasol, and Staedtler.

The Centre of Memory and Dialogue team has relied heavily on the research expertise of Sahm Venter for both the series and this book. Others who have contributed are Anthea Josias, Shadrack Katuu, Boniswa Qabaka, and Razia Saleh. Luli Callinicos acted as a consultant for the first five comics in the series.

The Umlando Wezithombe team has been marshaled by Nic Buchanan, and has comprised:
Scriptwriting and research: Santa Buchanan and Andrew Smith
Storyboarding: Santa Buchanan and Pitshou Mampa
Illustrating: Pitshou Mampa, Pascal "Freehand" Nzoni, and Sivuyile Matwa
Inking and Coloring: Richie Orphan, Pascal Nzoni, Sivuyile Matwa, Jose "King" Jungo, Pitshou Mampa, and Sean Abbood

The Foundation and Umlando have been supported by an exceptional Jonathan Ball Publishers' team: Francine Blum, Jeremy Boraine, and Frances Perryer.

Key reference works utilized by our researchers are as follows:
The World that Made Mandela, *Beyond the Engeli Mountains*, and *Gold and Workers* by Luli Callinicos, *Drum Magazine*, *Winnie Mandela—A Life* by Anne Marie du Preez Bezdrob, *Walter Sisulu: I Will Go Singing* by George Houser and Herbert Shore, *The Rivonia Story* by Joel Joffe, *Memoirs* by Ahmed Kathrada, *Mandela* by Tom Lodge, *Long Walk to Freedom* by Nelson Mandela, *Higher than Hope* by Fatima Meer, *A Fortunate Life* by Ismail Meer, *Mandela* by Anthony Sampson, *In Our Lifetime* by Elinor Sisulu, *A Step Behind Mandela* by Rory Steyn, and *Portrait of a People* by Eli Weinberg.

Archival holdings of the following institutions were consulted:
Baileys Historical Archives, Brenthurst Library, Historical Papers (University of the Witwatersrand), the National Archives, the Nelson Mandela Centre of Memory and Dialogue, Robben Island Museum, and the University of Fort Hare Library.

Inspiration for this project, of course, came primarily from Nelson Mandela himself. This is his story constellated by numerous other stories. In a profound way the constellation is the story of the country, South Africa, for which Tata Nelson Mandela sacrificed so much. More than this, Tata gave his blessing to the project, launched it with a rousing speech, and shared his memories. The book is a gift to him in his ninetieth year.

Verne Harris
Project Manager
Nelson Mandela Foundation